HMH Florida Science

Grade 4

This Write-In Book belongs to

_____

Teacher/Room

_____

The American alligator is symbolic of the large number of swamps found in Florida.

Houghton Mifflin Harcourt.

Consulting Authors

Michael A. DiSpezio
Global Educator
North Falmouth, Massachusetts

Marjorie Frank
Science Writer and Content-Area Reading
* Specialist*
Brooklyn, New York

Michael R. Heithaus, Ph.D.
Dean, College of Arts, Sciences & Education
Professor, Department of Biological Sciences
Florida International University
Miami, Florida

Houghton Mifflin Harcourt

Cover: ©Kristian Bell/RooM the Agency/Alamy

Contents

THE NATURE OF SCIENCE

UNIT 1 — STUDYING SCIENCE 1

BIG IDEA 1: **THE PRACTICE OF SCIENCE**

BIG IDEA 2: **THE CHARACTERISTICS OF SCIENTIFIC KNOWLEDGE**

BIG IDEA 3: **THE ROLE OF THEORIES, LAWS, HYPOTHESES, AND MODELS**

LESSON 1   **What Do Scientists Do?** 3

LESSON 2   **What Skills Do Scientists Use?** 17

LESSON 3   **How Do Scientists Collect and Use Data?** 27

LESSON 4   **Why Do Scientists Compare Results?** 41

PEOPLE **IN SCIENCE**—John Diebold/Martin Culpepper 45

LESSON 5   **What Kinds of Models Do Scientists Use?** 47

LESSON 6   **How Can You Model a School?** 57

  Unit 1 Benchmark Review 61

UNIT 2 — THE ENGINEERING PROCESS 65

BIG IDEA 1: **THE PRACTICE OF SCIENCE**

LESSON 1   **What Is an Engineering Design Process?** 67

LESSON 2   **How Can You Design a Solution to a Problem?** 81

LESSON 3   **What Is Technology?** 85

LESSON 4   **How Do We Use Technology?** 99

PEOPLE **IN SCIENCE**—Ayanna Howard 103

  Unit 2 Benchmark Review 105

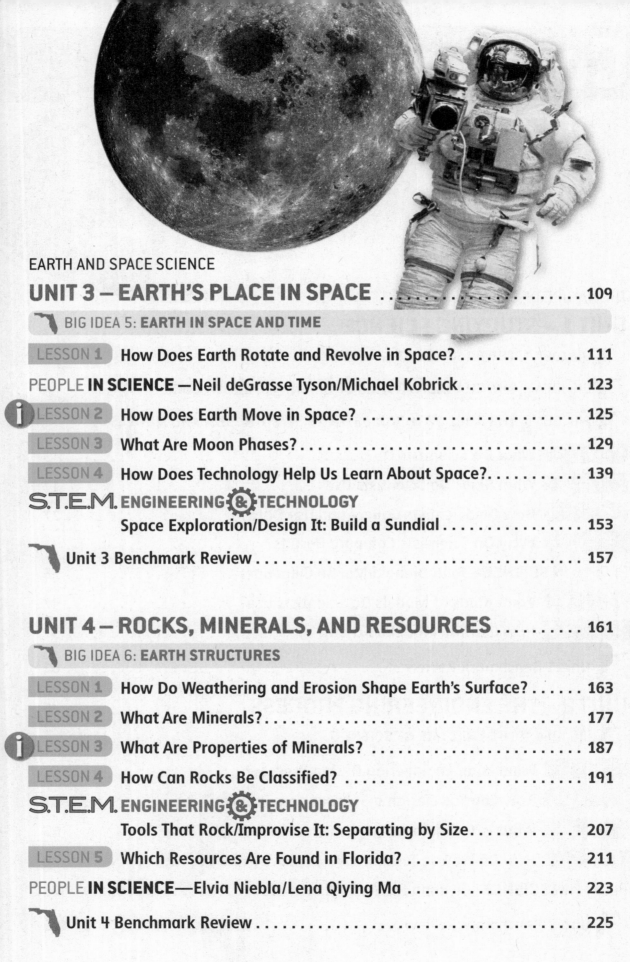

EARTH AND SPACE SCIENCE

UNIT 3 — EARTH'S PLACE IN SPACE 109

BIG IDEA 5: **EARTH IN SPACE AND TIME**

LESSON 1 **How Does Earth Rotate and Revolve in Space?** 111

PEOPLE **IN SCIENCE** —Neil deGrasse Tyson/Michael Kobrick 123

LESSON 2 **How Does Earth Move in Space?** 125

LESSON 3 **What Are Moon Phases?** 129

LESSON 4 **How Does Technology Help Us Learn About Space?** 139

S.T.E.M. ENGINEERING & TECHNOLOGY
Space Exploration/Design It: Build a Sundial 153

Unit 3 Benchmark Review 157

UNIT 4 — ROCKS, MINERALS, AND RESOURCES 161

BIG IDEA 6: **EARTH STRUCTURES**

LESSON 1 **How Do Weathering and Erosion Shape Earth's Surface?** 163

LESSON 2 **What Are Minerals?** 177

LESSON 3 **What Are Properties of Minerals?** 187

LESSON 4 **How Can Rocks Be Classified?** 191

S.T.E.M. ENGINEERING & TECHNOLOGY
Tools That Rock/Improvise It: Separating by Size 207

LESSON 5 **Which Resources Are Found in Florida?** 211

PEOPLE **IN SCIENCE**—Elvia Niebla/Lena Qiying Ma 223

Unit 4 Benchmark Review 225

PHYSICAL SCIENCE

UNIT 5 — MATTER AND ITS PROPERTIES 229

BIG IDEA 8: **PROPERTIES OF MATTER**

LESSON 1 **What Are Physical Properties of Matter?** 231

LESSON 2 **How Are Physical Properties Observed?** 247

CAREERS **IN SCIENCE**—Medical Chemist 251

LESSON 3 **What Is Conservation of Mass?** 253

LESSON 4 **What Are the States of Water?** 257

S.T.E.M. ENGINEERING & TECHNOLOGY
**Baby, It's Cold Inside: Refrigeration/
Improvise It: Build a Rubber Band Scale** 267

LESSON 5 **What Are Magnets?** 271

LESSON 6 **How Do Magnets Attract Objects?** 285

Unit 5 Benchmark Review 289

UNIT 6 — MATTER AND ITS CHANGES 293

BIG IDEA 9: **CHANGES IN MATTER**

LESSON 1 **What Are Physical and Chemical Changes?** 295

LESSON 2 **How Can You Tell When a New Substance Forms?** 311

PEOPLE **IN SCIENCE**—Héctor Abruña/Ruth Rogan Benerito 315

S.T.E.M. ENGINEERING & TECHNOLOGY
**What's It Made Of? Body Armor/
Build in Some Science: Making Carbon Dioxide** 317

Unit 6 Benchmark Review 321

PHYSICAL SCIENCE

UNIT 7 — ENERGY AND ITS USES 323

BIG IDEA 10: FORMS OF ENERGY

LESSON 1 What Are Some Forms of Energy? 325

S.T.E.M. ENGINEERING & TECHNOLOGY
How It Works: Piezoelectricity/
Design It: Solar Water Heater 341

LESSON 2 Where Does Energy Come From? 345

CAREERS **IN SCIENCE** —Civil Engineers 349

LESSON 3 What Is Sound? 351

LESSON 4 How Do We Use Wind and Water for Energy? 355

Unit 7 Benchmark Review 367

UNIT 8 — HEAT 371

BIG IDEA 11: ENERGY TRANSFER AND TRANSFORMATIONS

LESSON 1 What Is Heat? 373

LESSON 2 How Is Heat Produced? 385

LESSON 3 What Are Conductors and Insulators? 389

LESSON 4 Which Materials Are Conductors? 399

PEOPLE **IN SCIENCE** —Halimaton Hamdan 403

Unit 8 Benchmark Review 405

UNIT 9 — FORCES AND MOTION 407

BIG IDEA 12: MOTION OF OBJECTS

LESSON 1 What Is Motion? 409

LESSON 2 What Is Speed? 425

CAREERS **IN SCIENCE** —Biomechanists 429

S.T.E.M. ENGINEERING & TECHNOLOGY
How It Works: Gyroscopes/
Improvise It: A Game Of Skill and Motion 431

Unit 9 Benchmark Review 435

LIFE SCIENCE

UNIT 10 — LIFE CYCLES AND GROWTH 439

BIG IDEA 16: HEREDITY AND REPRODUCTION

LESSON 1 How Do Plants Reproduce? 441

LESSON 2 What Factors Affect Germination Rate? 457

S.T.E.M. ENGINEERING & TECHNOLOGY
How It Works: Water Irrigation System/
Make a Process: Planting and Caring for a Garden 461

LESSON 3 How Do Animals Reproduce? 465

LESSON 4 What Are Heredity, Instincts, and Learned Behaviors? 479

CAREERS IN SCIENCE —Animal Behaviorist 493

Unit 10 Benchmark Review 495

UNIT 11 — ORGANISMS AND THEIR ENVIRONMENT 499

BIG IDEA 17: INTERDEPENDENCE

LESSON 1 How Do Organisms Change with the Seasons? 501

LESSON 2 How Do Organisms Obtain and Use Food? 515

LESSON 3 What Are Food Chains? 527

LESSON 4 How Do Organisms Affect Their Environment? 543

LESSON 5 How Do People Affect Their Environment? 555

PEOPLE IN SCIENCE —Wangari Maathai/Willie Smits 559

S.T.E.M. ENGINEERING & TECHNOLOGY
Underwater Exploration/Solve It: Getting Around a Dam 561

Unit 11 Benchmark Review 565

21ST CENTURY SKILLS: TECHNOLOGY AND CODING 569

Interactive Glossary R1

Index R16

Safety in Science

Doing investigations in science can be fun, but you need to be sure you do them safely. Here are some rules to follow.

 1. Think ahead.
Study the steps of the investigation so you know what to expect. If you have any questions, ask your teacher. Be sure you understand any caution statements or safety reminders.

 2. Be neat.
Keep your work area clean. If you have long hair, pull it back so it doesn't get in the way. Roll or push up long sleeves to keep them away from your experiment.

 3. Oops!
If you spill or break something, or if you get cut, tell your teacher right away.

 4. Watch your eyes.
Wear safety goggles anytime you are directed to do so. If you get anything in your eyes, tell your teacher right away.

 5. Yuck!
Never eat or drink anything during a science activity.

 6. Don't get shocked.
Be especially careful if an electric appliance is used. Be sure that electrical cords are in a safe place where you can't trip over them. Never pull a plug out of an outlet by pulling on the cord.

 7. Keep it clean.
Always clean up when you have finished. Put everything away and wipe your work area. Wash your hands.

Studying Science

© Jonathan Blair/Corbis Documentary/Getty Images

FLORIDA **BIG IDEA 1**

The Practice of Science

FLORIDA **BIG IDEA 2**

The Characteristics of Scientific Knowledge

FLORIDA **BIG IDEA 3**

The Role of Theories, Laws, Hypotheses, and Models

A scientist works with a turtle.

I Wonder Why

Why is the work of a conservation biologist like the work of a scientist who mixes chemicals in a lab? *Turn the page to find out.*

Here's Why

All scientists ask questions, answer them with investigations, and communicate their results to other scientists.

Essential Questions and Florida Benchmarks

LESSON 1
What Do Scientists Do?.............................3
SC.4.N.1.1 Raise questions . . . and generate appropriate explanations. . . .
SC.4.N.1.3 Explain that science does not always follow a rigidly defined method. . . .
SC.4.N.1.7, SC.4.N.1.8, SC.4.N.2.1

LESSON 2
What Skills Do Scientists Use?.............................17
SC.4.N.1.1, SC.4.N.1.3, SC.4.N.1.6

LESSON 3
How Do Scientists Collect and Use Data?.............................27
SC.4.N.1.2 Compare the observations made by different groups. . . .
SC.4.N.1.4 Attempt reasonable answers to scientific questions. . . .
SC.4.N.1.1, SC.4.N.1.6, SC.4.N.1.7

(i) LESSON 4
Why Do Scientists Compare Results?.............................41
SC.4.N.1.5 Compare the methods and results . . . done by other classmates.
SC.4.N.1.2

PEOPLE **IN SCIENCE**
John Diebold/Martin Culpepper.............................45
SC.4.N.2.1 Explain that science focuses solely on the natural world.
SC.4.E.6.5 Explain how technology and tools help ... humans. . . .

LESSON 5
What Kinds of Models Do Scientists Use?.............................47
SC.4.N.3.1 Explain that models can be three dimensional, two dimensional . . .

(i) LESSON 6
How Can You Model a School?.............................57
SC.4.N.1.4, SC.4.N.1.5, SC.4.N.1.6, SC.4.N.3.1

Unit 1 Benchmark Review.............................61

📖 Science Notebook

Before you begin each lesson, write your thoughts about the Essential Question.

SC.4.N.1.1 Raise questions… and generate appropriate explanations… SC.4.N.1.3 … science does not always follow a rigidly defined method… SC.4.N.1.7 … scientists base their explanations on evidence. SC.4.N.1.8 Recognize that science involves creativity in designing experiments. SC.4.N.2.1 Explain that science focuses solely on the natural world.

ESSENTIAL **QUESTION**

What Do Scientists Do?

 Engage Your Brain

Find the answer to the following question in this lesson and record it here.

Biologists make observations about living things. What are some observations you can make about lizards?

_____

_____

_____

_____

_____

ACTIVE READING

Lesson Vocabulary
List the terms. As you learn about each one, make notes in the Interactive Glossary.

_____   _____

_____   _____

_____

Main Ideas
In this lesson, you'll read about how scientists do their work. Active readers look for main ideas before they read to give their reading a purpose. Often, the headings in a lesson state its main ideas. Preview the headings in this lesson to give your reading a purpose.

The Role of Scientists

It's career day for Mr. Green's fourth-grade class! Mr. Green invited a scientist named Dr. Sims to talk to the class. The students are ready, and they have many questions to ask.

ACTIVE READING As you read these two pages, turn the heading into a question in your mind. Then underline the sentence that answers the question.

What do scientists do?

▶ Write a question you would ask a scientist.

_____

_____

_____

_____

"Thank you for inviting me to your school! My name is Dr. Sims, and I am a scientist. A **scientist** asks questions about the natural world. There are many kinds of scientists and many questions to ask!

Science is the study of the natural world. Earth scientists study things like rocks, weather, and the planets. Physical scientists study matter and energy. Life scientists, like me, study living things. I am a wildlife biologist, which means I study animals in the wild.

Scientists work alone and in teams. Sometimes, I travel alone on long hikes to watch animals. At other times, I ask other biologists to go with me. I share ideas with other scientists every day.

Science is hard work but fun, too. I like being outdoors. Discovering something new is exciting. The best part, for me, is helping animals. The best way to explain what a scientist does is to show you."

▶ For each area of science, write a question a scientist might ask.
Earth Science

_____

_____

Life Science

_____

_____

Physical Science

_____

_____

_____

Do you work all by yourself?

Is it fun to be a scientist?

Making Observations and
Asking Questions

Dr. Sims looks around the classroom. She observes everything for a few moments. Then she asks questions about what she sees.

How does that plant produce offspring?

Does the lizard's skin ever change colors?

Dr. Sims

Does the goldfish spend more time near the top of the tank or the bottom of the tank?

▶ Ask your own question about the classroom in the photo.

_____

_____

_____

▶ Name five things you observe in this classroom.

_____

_____

_____

Scientists make observations about the world around them. An **observation** is information collected by using the five senses.

Scientists ask questions about their observations. Notice that Dr. Sims' questions are about the living things in the classroom. That's because she is a wildlife biologist. Your questions might be different if you observed different things than she did.

Dr. Sims asks, "How would you find an answer to my question about the goldfish?" She and the students talk about watching the fish. Someone suggests writing observations in a notebook. Someone else says a stopwatch can help.

Dr. Sims says, "I could do all these things in an investigation." Scientists conduct an **investigation** to answer questions. The steps of an investigation may include asking questions, making observations, reading or talking to experts, drawing conclusions, and sharing what you learn.

Experiments

Dr. Sims seems very excited to talk about investigations. She says, "Describing what you see is one kind of investigation. Other investigations include doing an experiment."

ACTIVE **READING** As you read these two pages, circle the lesson vocabulary word each time it is used.

A Fair Test

An *experiment* is a fair test. It can show that one thing causes another thing to happen. In each test, you change only one factor, or *variable*. To be fair and accurate, you conduct the experiment multiple times.

To test something else, you must start a new experiment. Being creative and working in teams can help scientists conduct experiments.

Carlos is conducting an experiment. He gives the lizard fruit and crickets to see which will be eaten. The food is the only variable that is changed. Each day, the lizard gets two different types of food at the same time and in the same amounts.

Scientific Methods

Scientific investigations use scientific methods. Scientific methods may include the following activities:

- make observations

- ask a question

- form a hypothesis

- plan and conduct an experiment

- record and analyze results

- draw conclusions

- communicate results

Sometimes, these steps are done in this order. At other times, they're not.

A **hypothesis** is an idea or explanation that can be tested with an investigation. Dr. Sims gives the students an example from their classroom. She says, "I hypothesize that this lizard eats more insects than fruit."

▶ Talk with other students in your class. Then write a hypothesis to explain what makes the lizard in the photo change color.

_____

_____

_____

_____

_____

_____

Other Kinds of Investigations

Dr. Sims smiles. She says, "I hope this doesn't confuse anyone, but doing an experiment isn't always possible."

ACTIVE **READING** As you read these two pages, circle the clue words or phrases that signal a detail such as an example or an added fact.

Many science questions cannot be answered by doing an experiment. Here's one question: What kind of lizard have I found? This question can be answered by using an identification guide. Here's another question: What causes the sun to seem to rise and set? This question can be answered by making and using a model of Earth and the sun. Here's another: At what time of year does a state get the most rain? This question can be answered by looking for patterns through many years of rainfall records. Here's another: How did people who lived 100 years ago describe Mars? This question can be answered with research. Research includes reading what others have written and asking experts.

What is the surface of Mars like? This question is hard to answer with an experiment. NASA scientists sent robot spacecraft to Mars. Cameras on these spacecraft take pictures of the planet for scientists to observe.

(inset) ©NASA Jet Propulsion Laboratory; (bkgd) ©Getty Images/PhotoDisc

Use an Identification Guide

Draw lines to match the lizard with its description.

Texas Horned Lizard

- **Colors:** brownish
- **Body:** wider and flatter than other lizards
- **Tail:** straight and shorter than the body
- **Spines:** several short horns on head, spiny scales on sides of body

Common Chameleon

- **Colors:** green, yellow, gray, or brown
- **Eyes:** big and bulge out from side of head
- **Body:** tall and flat, a ridge of scales along the backbone
- **Tail:** curls for grasping branches

Common Iguana

- **Colors:** green, gray, brown, blue, lavender, or black
- **Spines:** along center of back and tail
- **Body:** Large flap of skin under the chin

Scientists Share Their Results as Evidence

Dr. Sims says, "Tell me something you know." You tell her that it is going to be stormy tomorrow. She says, "*How* do you know?"

ACTIVE **READING** As you read these two pages, draw two lines under the main idea.

When scientists explain how things work, they must give evidence. *Evidence* is data gathered during an investigation. Evidence might support your hypothesis, or it might not. For example, think about the class with their lizard. The students tell Dr. Sims a hypothesis: Lizards eat more insects than fruit. They carry out an experiment, putting tiny crickets and fruit in the lizard's tank. After two hours, they observe how much food is left, and then repeat the experiment each day for a week.

The students tell Dr. Sims that their lizard ate more crickets than fruit. She says, "What is your evidence?" The students share their recorded results. They report that the lizard ate 13 crickets and no fruit.

Science Notebook

A *claim* is a statement that is supported by evidence. Write claims that are supported by the evidence given below.

Evidence

We used thermometers and found that when the air temperature changed by 5 degrees, a chameleon's skin color changed.

Claim

_____

_____

_____

_____

Evidence

We measured the temperature at the same time each morning and afternoon for one month. Each day, the air temperature was higher in the afternoon than in the morning.

Claim

_____

_____

_____

_____

_____

Evidence

Paper Airplane Wingspan (cm)	Time in the Air (sec)
5	7
10	12
15	21
20	28

Claim

_____

_____

_____

_____

Sum It Up »

Fill in the missing words to tell what scientists do.

Mr. Brown's fourth-grade class wants a pet in their classroom. Their teacher says they have to think like a (1) _____ to care for animals. The students know that means (2) _____ about the natural world. The class wonders what kinds of animals make good classroom pets. They decide to do an (3) _____ to find out. They go to the library and use books and websites to (4) _____ pets.

The class claims that guinea pigs are the best pets for their classroom. Mr. Brown asks them what (5) _____ they have to support their claim. The students explain that guinea pigs are quiet and gentle. They are also active in the daytime and sleep at night.

Once the guinea pigs are in the classroom, the students watch and listen. They keep a science journal and list all their (6) _____. Then, students ask (7) _____ based on what they observe. One is: What does it mean when the guinea pigs make squeaking sounds? Two students have a (8) _____ : guinea pigs make that noise when they want to be fed.

Mr. Brown suggests that the students record the time when they hear the sound and write down what they are doing at the same time. After a few days, the students see that their guinea pigs make that noise just as the zippered bag that holds the fresh vegetables is opened. So, what do you think the sound means? (9) _____•_____

_____

Name _____

Vocabulary Review

1 Draw a line from each term to its definition or description.

1. experiment*

2. hypothesis*

3. communicate

4. investigation*

5. scientist*

6. claim

7. question

A. an explanation based on evidence

B. Scientists do one of these to answer questions.

C. an idea or explanation that can be tested with an investigation

D. to share the results of investigations

E. a person who asks questions about the natural world

F. You ask this.

G. A kind of investigation that is a fair test

* Key Lesson Vocabulary

Apply Concepts

2 Choose an object to observe. List some observations. Then ask some questions related to your observations.

Name of Object: _____   Questions: _____

Observations: _____   _____

_____   _____

_____   _____

_____   _____

3 Your family uses steel wool soap pads for cleaning pots and pans. Often they get rusty after use. What could you do to stop the pads from rusting? Write a hypothesis you could test. _____

_____

_____

4 The graph shows the results of a national online poll in which students were asked to name their favorite lunch food. What claim can you make? _____

_____

_____

_____

_____

_____

Pita pockets

Grilled cheese

Pizza

Lasagna

Hamburgers

Take It Home!

See *ScienceSaurus*® for more information about scientific investigations.

SC.4.N.1.1 Raise questions… use appropriate reference materials… conduct both individual and team investigations… and generate appropriate explanations… SC.4.N.1.3 Explain that science does not always follow a rigidly defined method… SC.4.N.1.6 Keep records that describe observations made…

LESSON 2

ESSENTIAL **QUESTION**

What Skills Do Scientists Use?

 Engage Your Brain

Find the answer to the following question in the lesson and record it here.

Splash it. Pour it. Freeze it. Make bubbles in it. What skills might a scientist use to test how water behaves?

_____

_____

_____

_____

ACTIVE **READING**

Lesson Vocabulary
List the terms. As you learn about each one, make notes in the interactive Glossary.

_____

_____

_____

Visual Aids
In this lesson, you'll see large graphics with labels. The labels call attention to important details. Active readers preview a lesson's graphics and decide how the information in them provides details about the main idea.

Everyday Science Skills

Do you ask questions about the world around you? If so, you use these science skills all day, every day—just like a scientist!

ACTIVE READING As you read the next four pages, circle the names of nine science skills.

As you read about scientists, think **"Hey, I can do this, too!"**

Infer

Observe

Scientists may *observe* many things, such as changes in color, temperature, and bubbling.

Scientists *infer* how things work by thinking about their observations. A biologist may infer that the color patterns of fish enable them to blend in and avoid predators.

Scientists use inquiry skills every day—and so do you. When you observe, you use your five senses to get information. Let's say you smell cheese, bread, and spicy odors. You *infer* "I think we are having pizza for lunch today!" An **inference** is a statement that explains an observation.

When you think about how things are the same and different, you *compare* them. For example, your family wants to adopt a new kitten. You compare different kittens, looking for one that is playful and friendly. When you decide which kitten is the best, you *communicate* that decision to your family. You can communicate by speaking, writing, and by using pictures or models.

Compare

Scientists *compare* objects and things that happen.

▶ Practice the skill of *comparing*. List ways these two fish are similar and different.

Powder–Blue Tang   Porcupinefish

Similarities	Differences

Communicate

▶ Scientists *communicate,* or share, their results and inferences with other scientists. What did you communicate today?

_____

_____

_____

Think Like a Scientist

Scientists use these skills every day in their investigations. Find out what they are and when you might use them.

Predict

Scientists use their observations and existing research to make predictions about what will happen in the future. For example, a meteorologist uses weather patterns to determine whether it will rain over the weekend.

Some science skills are part of doing science investigations, including experiments. They may sound unfamiliar to you. But when you read about these skills, you might realize that you already use them.

Use Variables

When scientists plan experiments, they think, "What is the one thing I will change?" That one thing is a variable. Let's say you want to find out how cold a freezer has to be to make fruit pops. The variable that you will change is the temperature inside the freezer.

Plan and Conduct Investigations

Scientists plan and conduct investigations that will answer science questions. Say you want to know how salty water must be to make an egg float. First, you think about the steps you'll take to find the answer. Next, you gather the materials you'll use. Then, you test the amount of salt.

▶ You are a marine biologist. You study living things in the ocean. What is one investigation you might plan?

_____

_____

_____

Predict what a marine biologist might look for on a dive.

_____

_____

_____

Hypothesize

Scientists hypothesize when they think of a testable statement that tries to explain an observation. Suppose you notice that water seems to evaporate at different rates from containers with different shapes. What would you hypothesize is a cause?

Draw Conclusions

Scientists draw conclusions when they use evidence to evaluate a hypothesis. If you investigate how the size of a sail affects how quickly a toy boat moves, you might conclude that boats with larger sails move faster because larger sails collect more wind.

Math and Science Skills

Using rulers and balances. Putting things in order. Measuring the speed of a car. Making tables and graphs. Sounds like math, but it's science, too!

ACTIVE READING As you read this page, turn the heading into a question in your mind. Then underline the parts of the text that answer the question.

Every scientist uses math. Let's say you are a marine biologist who studies whales. You *classify* whales by how much they weigh or how long they are from head to tail. You put them in *order* when you arrange them by length from smallest to largest. You *use numbers* to tell how many are alive today. You *use time and space relationships* to investigate when and where they migrate each year. You *measure* how long they are and how much food they eat. You *record and display* the results of your investigations in writing and in tables, graphs, and maps.

Classify and Order

You classify things when you put them into groups. To put things in order, you may make a list in which position matters, such as ordering bird species by how fast they fly or move.

Measure

In science and math, you measure by using tools to find length, width, height, mass, weight, volume, and elapsed time.

Use Numbers

You use numbers when you observe by counting or measuring. You also use numbers to compare and order. And, you use numbers to describe speed and force.

⊞ DO THE **MATH**

Compare Numbers

Some of the world's biggest mammals live under the oceans' waves. The table gives the names of several kinds of whales and the number that scientists estimate are alive today.

Kind of Whale	Population
Beluga whale	200,000
Blue whale	14,000
Fin whale	55,000
Humpback whale	40,000
Minke whale	1,000,000
Pilot whale	1,200,000
Sei whale	54,000
Sperm whale	

1. Which two kinds of whales have the closest number alive?

   _____

2. How many more Pilot whales are there than Minke whales?

   _____

3. Scientists estimate there are about three hundred and sixty thousand sperm whales alive today. Write that number, using numerals, in the table.

Use Time and Space Relationships

You use stopwatches and clocks to tell the time. You can predict when it will be high tide or low tide. You can also determine how the planets move in space.

Record and Display Data

You record observations on clipboards, in notebooks, and on computers. You display, or show, data so that it's easy to understand by making tables, graphs, or diagrams.

Sum It Up »

Fill in the missing skills in the column where they belong.

Scientists Use Skills

Everyday Science Skills	Science Investigation Skills	Math and Science Skills
1. _____ _____	5. _____ _____	10. _____ _____
2. _____ _____	6. _____	11. _____ _____
3. _____ _____	7. _____ _____	12. _____ _____
4. _____ _____	8. _____ 9. _____ _____	13. _____ _____ 14. _____ _____

Name _____

Vocabulary Review

1 It's easy to get tongue-tied describing what scientists do. Look at the statements below. Switch the red words around until each statement about inquiry skills makes sense.

In order to sort his beakers and other tools, Dr. Mallory hypothesizes each object by size and shape. _____

Gabriella measures that her dog will want his favorite food for dinner, because she has observed him eat it quickly many times before. _____

Kim predicts when planning an experiment with her older brother. She keeps everything the same during their procedure, except for the one factor being tested. _____

After completing an experiment and summarizing her findings, Dr. Garcia classifies what she has learned with other scientists. _____

Dr. Jefferson studies the age of rocks and fossils. She uses variables to tell how old each specimen is. _____

Before conducting his experiment for the science fair, Derrick uses time and space relationships about which sample of fertilizer will make his tomato plant grow the fastest. _____

To find out how long it takes Deshawn to ride his bike 100 m, Jessica communicates the time with a stopwatch. _____

Apply Concepts

2 Write how you would use numbers to investigate each object.

_____   _____   _____

_____   _____   _____

_____   _____   _____

_____   _____   _____

3 For each one, what kinds of observations could you record on a calendar?

_____   _____   _____

_____   _____   _____

_____   _____   _____

_____   _____   _____

Take It Home!

There are many books in the library about scientists and how they think about the world around them. Pick a book with a family member. Find examples of the skills you learned about and make a list.

SC.4.N.1.1 ... use appropriate reference materials... **SC.4.N.1.2** Compare the observations made by different groups using multiple tools... **SC.4.N.1.4** Attempt reasonable answers to scientific questions... **SC.4.N.1.6** Keep records that describe observations made... **SC.4.N.1.7** Recognize and explain that scientists base their explanations on evidence.

ESSENTIAL QUESTION

How Do Scientists Collect and Use Data?

 Engage Your Brain

Find the answer to the following question in this lesson and record it here.

Are the ladybugs on this tree identical to each other? How would you investigate this question?

_____

_____

_____

_____

 ACTIVE **READING**

Lesson Vocabulary

List the terms. As you learn about each one, make notes in the Interactive Glossary.

_____   _____

_____   _____

_____

Main Idea and Details

Details give information about a topic. The information may be examples, features, or characteristics. Active readers stay focused on the topic when they ask, What facts or information do these details add to the topic?

Research Is the Key

Tiny insects fly and flash on a summer night. Are you curious about them? Do you wonder how to find out what they are and how they light up? Do some research!

ACTIVE **READING** As you read the next page, check the research sources you have used.

INSECTS
FIREFLIES
Bugs
INSECTS
BUGS
Entomology

INSECTS

Dr. Dwален
407-555-1234
+ bug scientist

Journal of Insect Science

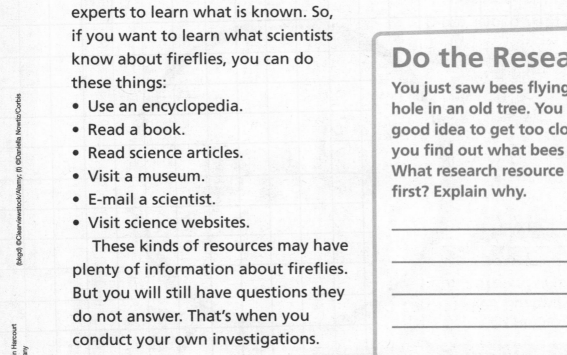

Natural history museums have insect collections as well as scientists who can answer questions about them.

Often scientists ask themselves, "What do other scientists know about this?" To find out, they do *research*. When you research, you use reference materials and talk to experts to learn what is known. So, if you want to learn what scientists know about fireflies, you can do these things:

- Use an encyclopedia.
- Read a book.
- Read science articles.
- Visit a museum.
- E-mail a scientist.
- Visit science websites.

These kinds of resources may have plenty of information about fireflies. But you will still have questions they do not answer. That's when you conduct your own investigations.

Do the Research!

You just saw bees flying in and out of a hole in an old tree. You know it's not a good idea to get too close. So, how can you find out what bees do inside a tree? What research resource would you go to first? Explain why.

_____

_____

_____

_____

Science Tools

What comes to mind when you hear the word *tools*? Hammers, saws, and screwdrivers? How about computers and calculators? All of these are science tools.

ACTIVE READING As you read these two pages, circle the lesson vocabulary each time it is used.

Scientists use all kinds of tools. Many turn the five senses into "super-senses." Tools enable scientists to see things that are far away, to smell faint odors, to hear quiet sounds, and to feel vibrations their bodies can't.

Let's say you want to observe craters on the moon. A telescope, which makes faraway objects look closer, will turn your sense of sight into "super-vision."

An ant looks larger in a magnifying box or with a hand lens.

What if you're interested in studying tiny critters, such as leaf cutter ants? Take along a hand lens. Hand lenses make small objects look bigger. Is the ant crawling away too fast to see it with the hand lens? Try gently placing the ant in a magnifying box. The top of the box has a lens in it.

Wondering what the ant's bite marks look like? Place a tiny piece of a cut leaf under a microscope. A **microscope** is a tool for looking at objects that cannot be seen with the eye alone.

▶ **Predict how the ant would look using a microscope. Make a drawing and add labels.**

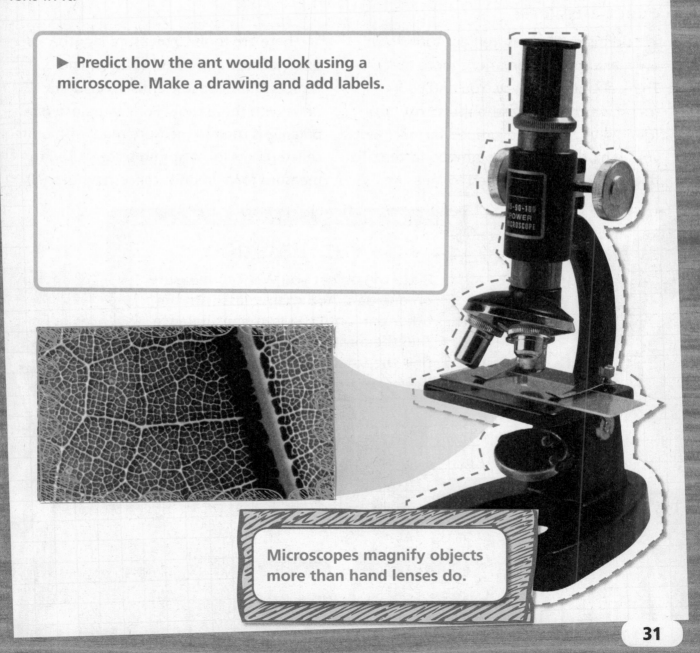

Microscopes magnify objects more than hand lenses do.

Measurement Tools

What's the biggest bug in the world?
How far can a grasshopper hop? How long
can a butterfly fly? How do scientists find
exact answers?

Scientists use measurement tools to make their observations more exact. Think about it this way. You and your friend watch two grasshoppers hop. Your friend says, "This one jumped farther." But you think the other one jumped farther. To find out for sure, you need to measure.

There are tools to measure length or distance, mass, force, volume, and temperature. Most scientists use metric units with these tools. For example, a **pan balance** is used to measure mass with units called grams (g). A **spring scale** is used to measure force in units called newtons (N).

Pan Balance

Place the object you want to measure on one pan. Add gram masses to the other pan until the two pans balance. Add the masses together to find the total in grams (g).

Tape Measure

This tool is used to measure length in millimeters (mm), centimeters (cm), and meters (m).

Spring Scale

Hang an object from the hook. As the spring stretches, the marker will show the size of the force in newtons (N). What could you measure with a spring scale?

_____

_____

Thermometer

Used to measure temperature, this tool has two sets of units: degrees Celsius (°C) and degrees Fahrenheit (°F).

⊞ DO THE MATH

Make Measurements

You've found a stick insect! Use the ruler to find the length of its body. Write the number and units.

_____

_____

_____

Find an object in your classroom to measure with a spring scale. Write the name of the object and number of units.

_____

_____

_____

Look at the thermometer on this page. Write the temperature in degrees Celsius (°C) and degrees Fahrenheit (°F).

_____

_____

_____

Recording and Displaying Data

You're crawling through a tropical jungle.
A butterfly flutters by. Then another appears.
How will you keep track of how many you see?

ACTIVE READING As you read these two pages, turn
each heading into a question that will point you to the main
idea. Underline the answers to your questions in the text.

A poster is one way to display data.

head

antenna

eye

elytra

pronotum

leg

wing

abdomen

Recording Data

The bits of information you observe are called **data**. Some data are in the form of numbers. For example, the number of butterflies you see in an hour is a piece of data. Other data are in the form of descriptions. Examples include written notes, diagrams, audio recordings, and photographs.

Only observations are data. So when you think, "There are more butterflies here than in Canada," that's a guess, not data.

Displaying Data

The data you record as you investigate may be correct, but not easy to understand. Later, you can decide how to display the data. For example, you might use your scribbled notes from the jungle to draw a map showing where you saw each butterfly. You might compare the number of each kind of butterfly you found in a circle graph. You might use a bar graph to show the number of butterflies you saw each hour.

Data Two Ways

The table on the left lists six butterflies and the number of wing flaps each one made as it passed by an observer. The bar graph on the right can display the same data. Use the data in the table to complete the graph.

Individual Butterfly	Number of Wing Flaps in a Row
A	3
B	9
C	4
D	3
E	3
F	10

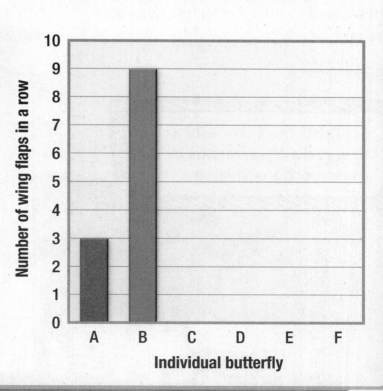

Using Data

You see on the news that the number of honeybees in the United States is decreasing. What is happening to them? How do scientists use data to solve problems and share information?

Drawing Conclusions

You've recorded your data. You've displayed it in a way that is easy to understand. Your next step is to analyze, or look for patterns in, the data. You might identify a trend, or a direction in the data over time. For example, you might conclude that the number of honeybees in your hometown has decreased by 30% in the last five years. What's next?

Communicating

Scientists communicate in many ways. They may work together to collect data. They compare their data with other scientists doing similar investigations. They report their results and conclusions by giving talks and writing reports. Conclusions often lead to new questions to investigate. Scientists are still studying why the number of honeybees is decreasing.

Scientists can share data as they make observations by using electronic devices.

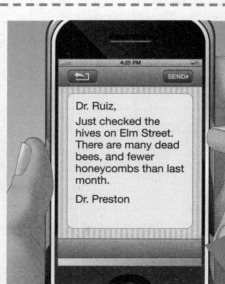

4:25 PM

SEND▶

Dr. Ruiz,
Just checked the hives on Elm Street. There are many dead bees, and fewer honeycombs than last month.

Dr. Preston

Scientists may work alone or in teams to analyze data and draw conclusions.

▶ A database is a collection of information or objects. Databases are organized so they are easy to search—like a search website. How would you search a database of insect facts to see what others have learned about the decrease in the number of honeybees?

_____

_____

_____

_____

Museums often have large collections of specimens, so scientists can compare what they have found to what's in a museum.

Sum It Up »

Change the part of the summary in blue to make it correct.

I. Research Is the Key
- A. Scientists do research to find out what others know.
- B. Reference sources you can use:
    1. encyclopedias
    2. _____
    3. _____
    4. _____
    5. _____
    6. _____

II. Science Tools
- A. Scientists use tools to make the senses more powerful.
- B. Tools that aid the sense of sight:
    1. telescope
    2. _____
    3. _____
    4. _____

III. _____
- A. pan balance
- B. spring scale
- C. tape measure/ruler
- D. _____

IV. Recording and Displaying Data
- A. Data are the bits of information you observe.
- B. Ways to display data:
    1. tables
    2. _____
    3. _____

Name _____

Vocabulary Review

1 Put the mixed-up letters in order to spell a science term from the box.

tada

eama supteer

crasheer

priclg harce

croopsmice

gripes clans

montumceica

axingbynim fog

metermother

lap cannaeb

| circle graph | communicate | data* | magnifying box | microscope* |
| pan balance* | research | spring scale* | tape measure | thermometer |

* Key Lesson Vocabulary

Apply Concepts

2 Someone gives you an object. You think it's a rock, but you aren't sure. Write how you could use each resource to do research.

encyclopedia   websites   books

_____   _____   _____

_____   _____   _____

_____   _____   _____

contact a scientist   museum

_____

_____

_____

_____

3 Draw lines to match the tool to its use.

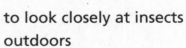
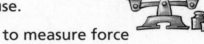
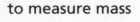
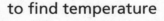
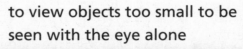

pan balance   to measure force

spring scale   to look closely at insects outdoors

thermometer   to measure mass

microscope   to find temperature

hand lens   to view objects too small to be seen with the eye alone

SC.4.N.1.2 Compare the observations made by different groups using multiple tools and seek reasons to explain the differences... SC.4.N.1.5 Compare the methods and results... done by other classmates.

INQUIRY
LESSON 4

Name _____

ESSENTIAL QUESTION

Why Do Scientists Compare Results?

EXPLORE

Does everyone use tools the same way? In this activity, you and your team will explore tools for measuring.

Materials

classroom object
pan balance
spring scale
ruler

Before You Begin—Preview the Steps

(1) Find the mass of the object. Discuss with your team what units to use.

(2) Use the ruler to measure the object. Discuss with your team what units to use.

(3) Decide which way to hold the spring scale to measure force. Measure how much force it takes to make the object move.

(4) Make up your own units and use them to measure the object in another way. Try it!

(5) Compare your team's measurements with those of other teams.

Set a Purpose

What will you learn from this investigation?

_____

_____

_____

Think About the Procedure

Which tool will you use to measure mass?

_____

_____

_____

Which units of length will your group use? Explain your choice.

_____

_____

_____

Name _____

Record Your Data

In the space below, make a table in which you record your measurements.

Draw Conclusions

Of the three measurement tools you used, which did you find the easiest to use? Which was the hardest? Explain.

_____

_____

_____

_____

Claims • Evidence • Reasoning

1. Why is it helpful to compare results with others? What should you do if you find out that your measurements are very different than those of other teams?

_____

_____

2. What other characteristics of the object can you measure?

_____

_____

3. The picture shows two more measurement tools. What could you measure with each one?

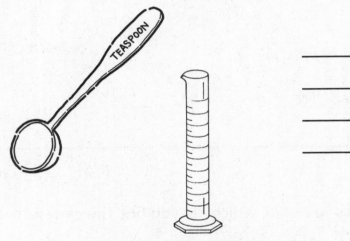

_____

_____

_____

_____

Graduated cylinder

4. A student is collecting evidence to support the claim that Container A contains more liquid than Container B. How could the student use one of the tools in the picture to support the claim?

_____

_____

_____

SC.4.E.6.5 Explain how technology and tools help ... humans....
SC.4.N.2.1 Explain that science focuses solely on the natural world..

⬡ PEOPLE IN SCIENCE

John Diebold

Dr. John Diebold spent much of his life studying Earth's oceans. He worked in the lab and in the field. He studied volcanoes, ancient ice sheets, and faults that cause earthquakes under water. Dr. Diebold improved the design of the *air gun*, a tool used to make underwater sound waves. Then he used these sound waves to make 3-D pictures of the ocean floor.

Much of Earth's oceans are too deep to study directly. John Diebold used many tools like this air gun to help people study the ocean floor from the surface.

Meet the Inventors

These gears are many times smaller than a millimeter! Dr. Culpepper's tools can be used to assemble objects this small.

Martin Culpepper

Dr. Martin Culpepper is a mechanical engineer. He invents tools that work with machines so small you cannot see them with a regular light microscope. These machines are many times smaller than the thickness of a human hair! One day these tiny machines could be used to find cancer cells. Unlike Dr. Diebold, Dr. Culpepper does most of his research in a lab. His lab has to be dust-free; a tiny bit of dust could ruin the results of his investigations.

Field Versus Lab

In the Field Scientists often work in the field, or the world outside of labs. What did Dr. Diebold learn from his studies in the field?

_____
_____
_____
_____

Research done by Dr. Diebold and others in the field led to the development of maps like this one. The map shows rock and sediment layers beneath the ocean floor.

This tool is a tiny lifter! It moves and sets into position the incredibly small parts of tiny machines.

In the Lab Why do you think Dr. Culpepper builds machines in a lab? Why would he not build them in the field?

_____
_____
_____
_____

Think About It!

How might a scientist's work be both in the field and in a lab? Think of an example.

_____
_____
_____

SC.4.N.3.1 Explain that models can be three dimensional, two dimensional, an explanation in your mind, or a computer model.

LESSON **5**

ESSENTIAL QUESTION

What Kinds of Models Do Scientists Use?

🧠 Engage Your Brain

Find the answer to the following question in this lesson and record it here.

This is a scale model of the moon. What can scientists learn by studying it?

_____

_____

_____

_____

📖 ACTIVE **READING**

Lesson Vocabulary

List the terms. As you learn about each one, make notes in the Interactive Glossary.

_____

_____

_____

_____

Cause and Effect

Signal phrases show connections between ideas. Words that signal comparisons, or similarities, include *like*, *better than*, *also*, *alike*, as *close as*, and *stands for*. Active readers remember what they read because they are alert to signal phrases that identify comparisons.

47

Two-dimensional model
of the solar system

Models and Science

Native Americans had mental models for the sun, moon, and planets. Several tribes in North America tell stories of the beginning of time, when Earth did not exist. All of the animals applied mud to the shell of a turtle. Earth was born when the mud became thick and large on the turtle's back.

Make a Two-dimensional Model!

Good models are as close to the real thing as possible. Draw a floor plan of a room in your home. Show the doorways and windows. Show the objects that sit on the floor. Add labels. Be as accurate as you can!

A toy car. A doll's house. A person who shows off clothes on a runway. These are all models. But what is a model in science?

ACTIVE READING As you read these two pages, draw a star next to what you think is the most important sentence. Be ready to explain why.

Scientists make models to investigate questions and explain conclusions. In science, a **model** represents something real that is too big, too small, or has too many parts to investigate directly. For example, our solar system is too big to see all the parts at once. So, scientists make models of the solar system. They use models to investigate the motion and positions of planets and moons. They can use the models to predict when a comet or asteroid will pass close to Earth.

Models can take many forms. A *mental model* is a picture you create in your mind. One good thing about this kind of model is that you always have it with you! A **two-dimensional model** has length and width. It can be a drawing, a diagram, or a map.

Other Models Scientists Use

 DO THE **MATH**

Use Fractions

You plan to make a model of the solar system. You make the tiniest ball of clay you can for Mercury. The ball is 4 mm across. If Mercury were that size, the chart shows how big all the other objects in your model would be.

Object	Diameter (mm)
Sun	1,100
Mercury	4
Venus	9
Earth	10
Mars	5
Jupiter	110
Saturn	92
Uranus	37
Neptune	36

1. What fraction tells how the size of Mars compares to Earth?

_____

2. Which object is about ¼ the diameter of Neptune?

_____

3. Which object is about ⅑ the diameter of Saturn?

_____

© Houghton Mifflin Harcourt Publishing Company

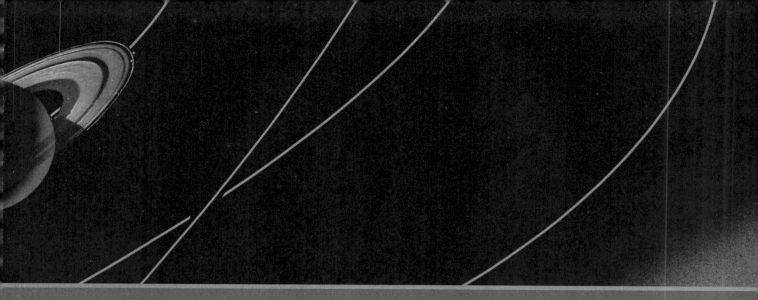

You see thousands of stars in the night sky. You point to a very bright star. Suddenly, you are zooming through space. As you get closer, the star gets bigger and brighter. Your trip isn't real, but it feels like it is. It's another kind of model!

Three-Dimensional Models

The more a model is like the real thing, the better it is. If the object you want to model has length, width, and height, a **three-dimensional model** is useful. Such a model can show the positions of planets, moons, and the sun better than a two-dimensional model can.

If you want to compare sizes and distances in a model, then you make a *scale model*. The scale tells how much smaller or bigger the model is than the real thing. For example, a model railroad may have a scale of 1 to 48. This means each one inch on the model stands for 48 inches on the real train.

Computer Models

What if you want to understand how asteroids move through the solar system? You'd use a computer model. A **computer model** is a computer program that models an event or object. Some computer models make you feel like you are moving through the solar system!

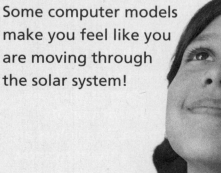

Weather Models Save Lives

Dangerous weather can happen suddenly. Hurricanes, tornadoes, floods, and winter storms can harm people, pets, and homes. How can models save lives?

FLORIDA

Data from Space

Satellites circle Earth 24 hours each day. Images and other weather data are beamed back to Earth. It's called *real-time* data because scientists see the pictures almost as soon as they are taken. In this image, a hurricane sits along the coast of Florida. The colors are not real. Scientists choose them to show differences in wind speeds, heights of clouds, and other factors.

Using Models

Meteorologists use satellite data to make computer models of weather. They model hurricanes, tornadoes, and thunderstorms. The models are used to predict how and where storms will get started.

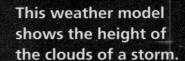

This weather model shows the height of the clouds of a storm.

Getting the Word Out

Weather reporters also use models. They make two-dimensional maps for TV and Internet viewers to see. The maps can change to show how fast and where bad weather will be.

What Can We Do?

You can use models to help your family be prepared for dangerous weather. Draw a diagram of your home in your Science Notebook. Label the exits. Does your family have a safe place to meet in an emergency? Where is it?

_____

_____

_____

_____

_____

How can your model help you in an emergency?

_____

_____

_____

_____

Sum It Up »

Use information from the summary to complete the graphic organizer in your own words.

For scientists, a model represents something real that is too big, too small, or has too many parts to investigate directly. Scientists use models to investigate and understand the real thing. Several kinds of models are used in science. Two-dimensional models, such as drawings, diagrams, and maps, have length and width. Three-dimensional models have length, width, and height. Computer models are computer programs that behave like the real thing. Some models, such as models of storms, can be used to save lives.

Main Idea: Models in science are like real things and are used to understand real things.

Detail: Two-dimensional models are flat, like a map or a diagram.

Detail:
_____
_____
_____
_____

Detail:
_____
_____
_____

Name _____

Vocabulary Review

1 Use the clues to fill in the missing letters of the words.

1. m _ _ _ _ l _ _ d _ _   a type of model that is in your head

2. _ _ _ _ l   something that represents the real thing

3. w _ _ _ h e _   these kinds of models can save lives

4. _ _ o - _ _ _ e _ s _ _ _ _ _ _   a type of model that has length and width
   m _ _ _ _

5. _ a _ _ _ l _ _ _   a device that sends weather images back
   to Earth

6. _ _ _ p u _ _ _ _ _ _ e _   a type of model made with a computer
   program

7. _ h _ _ e - d _ _ _ _ _ _ _ _ n _ _   a type of model that has length,
   _ o _ _ _   width, and height

8. _ c _ _ _ _ _ _ _ l   In this type of model, a measurement on
   the model stands for a measurement on
   the real thing

9. r _ _ _ t _ _ _   data that scientists can see as soon as it is
   collected

Apply Concepts

2 Tell how making or using each model below could help people.

A model to show where lightning is likely to strike

_____

_____

_____

_____

3 A model to show where water flows during a storm

_____

_____

_____

_____

4 A model to show how traffic moves in a city

_____

_____

5 A model to show equipment for a new playground

_____

_____

Take It Home! Many kids' toys are models of real things. Challenge your family to find such toys at home, in ads, or where you shop. Ask yourself: How is this toy like the real thing? How is it different?

SC.4.N.1.4 Attempt reasonable answers to scientific questions and cite evidence in support. SC.4.N.1.5 Compare the methods and results... done by other classmates. SC.4.N.1.6 Keep records that describe observations made... SC.4.N.3.1 Explain that models can be three dimensional, two dimensional....

INQUIRY
LESSON 6

Name _____

ESSENTIAL QUESTION

How Can You Model a School?

EXPLORE

There are many types of models: mental models, two-dimensional, three-dimensional, and computer models. In this activity, you'll model a part of your school in two ways.

Materials

drawing paper
graph paper
tape measure
cardboard boxes
computer drawing
or modeling
program

Before You Begin—Preview the Steps

1 With a team, choose a part of your school to model. It may be a single room, a floor, or a whole building.

2 Next, choose two types of models to make. Get permission from your teacher to carry out your plans.

3 With your team, choose the materials you will use. Make any measurements you need, and record them carefully.

4 Make the two models, and compare them to those of another team.

Set a Purpose

What inquiry skills will you practice in this investigation?

_____

_____

_____

Think About the Procedure

How will you decide what part of your school to model?

_____

_____

_____

How will you choose the two types of models?

_____

_____

_____

Name _____

Record Your Data

Identify the part of your school you modeled.

_____

_____

_____

_____

Identify the two types of models you made and describe them.

_____

_____

_____

_____

_____

_____

Draw Conclusions

What was something you learned about your school from making the models?

_____

_____

_____

Claims • Evidence • Reasoning

1. Write a claim about the benefit of comparing models. Cite evidence that supports your claim and explain why it supports the claim.

_____

_____

_____

_____

_____

2. What was the hardest part of making the models? Explain your reasoning.

_____

_____

3. Why is it important to be accurate when making your measurements? Explain your reasoning.

_____

_____

_____

4. Why is it important for engineers to make and try out models before making a real building or bridge? Explain your reasoning.

_____

_____

_____

5. What other things or places would you like to learn about by making a model?

_____

_____

Name _____

Vocabulary Review

Use the terms in the box to complete the sentences.

inference
investigation
observation
pan balance
spring scale

1. When people collect information by using their five senses, they make a(n) _____.

2. A tool used to measure the mass of an object is a(n) _____.

3. When people ask questions, make observations, and use other methods to gather data to answer a question, they are doing a(n) _____.

4. Someone who makes a statement that explains an observation is making a(n) _____.

5. If you want to measure the pull of a force, such as the force of gravity, you would use a tool called a(n) _____.

Science Concepts

Fill in the letter of the choice that best answers the question.

6. Amira wants to compare close-up views of different bird feathers. Which tool should he use?

   (A) microscope   (C) pan balance
   (B) meterstick   (D) measuring cup

7. Mia wants to know how fast a ball rolls down a ramp. Which action would **best** help her find this out?

   (F) construct a hypothesis
   (G) measure the ball's speed
   (H) observe the ball rolling on the floor
   (I) explain why the ball rolls so fast

8. Junichi looks at this 2-D model on a computer that uses perspective to make it appear like a 3-D model.

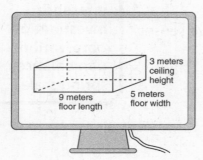

He wants to know if the classroom is longer than it is tall. How can he use evidence from this model to answer the question?

Ⓐ He can look at the length of the floor.

Ⓑ He can look at the height of the ceiling.

Ⓒ He can compare the length and the width.

Ⓓ He can compare the length and the ceiling height.

9. Camilla is studying minerals in different types of rocks. Which of the following would not help Camilla obtain data about the rock?

Ⓕ measure the volume of the rock

Ⓖ infer that the rock is millions of years old

Ⓗ test the effect of dripping vinegar onto the rock

Ⓘ make observations of the rock's minerals

10. A scientist has spent a year conducting an experiment. He concludes that evidence from his experiment does not support his hypothesis. What should the scientist do next?

Ⓐ forget this experiment and choose a new problem

Ⓑ try to make up evidence that supports his hypothesis

Ⓒ look at the evidence and see if he can make a new hypothesis

Ⓓ look at the information and find a different way to organize his results

11. Diego has been observing how well a type of plant grows in different locations. He concludes that a location with bright sunlight is best for the plant. Which of the following could be evidence for his conclusion?

Ⓕ Plants that he kept in shade grew better than plants that he kept in sunlight.

Ⓖ His friend told him that all plants need bright sunlight to grow.

Ⓗ Plants that he kept in shade did not grow as well as plants that he kept in sunlight.

Ⓘ He thinks that the plants he kept in sunlight would have grown better with more water.

Name _____

12. Gia hypothesizes that hot water will cause a sugar cube to dissolve faster than cold water will. She investigates by filling three cups: one with hot water, one with cold water, and one with ice water. She drops a sugar cube in each cup. Which evidence will help Gia decide whether her hypothesis is correct?

(A) which cup the sugar cube dissolves in first

(B) the time it takes for two sugar cubes to dissolve

(C) changes in water temperature from start to finish

(D) changes in the size of the sugar cube in cold water

13. Francisco uses a model to investigate volcanoes. Francisco mixes baking soda and vinegar to make his volcano erupt. How is the model like a real volcano?

(F) It looks just like a real volcano.

(G) It erupts like some volcanoes.

(H) It sparks fire like a real volcano.

(I) It shoots out material that is hot and then cools.

14. Raina looks at two models that show how the moon orbits Earth. One model is a computer animation. One model is a diagram. What can Raina do with the computer animation that she cannot do with the diagram?

(A) She can compare the sizes of the moon and Earth.

(B) She can study features of both the moon and Earth.

(C) She can watch the moon in motion as it orbits Earth.

(D) She can get information about the distance between the moon and Earth.

15. During gym class, Julia had an ice pack on one arm. You think she hurt her arm. What scientific skill did you use?

(F) communicating   (H) inferring

(G) comparing   (I) measuring

16. Scientists state a hypothesis for each experiment. What is one way that scientists can test a hypothesis?

(A) ask questions

(B) draw conclusions

(C) gather materials

(D) conduct an experiment

Apply Inquiry and Review the Big Idea

Write the answers to these questions.

17. Luis fed his cat in the kitchen. These pictures show what Luis saw as he left the kitchen and then what he saw when he returned.

Luis figured out that the cat jumped on the table and knocked the mitt onto the floor. Make a claim about which inquiry skill Luis used. Explain your claim with reasoning.

_____

_____

_____

18. Write three observations about this leaf.

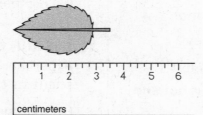

My observations

a. _____

b. _____

c. _____

19. Rachel wonders if a heavy ball rolls down a ramp faster than a light ball. Describe an investigation she could do to find out.

_____

_____

_____

The Engineering Process

FLORIDA *BIG IDEA 1*

The Practice of Science

A diver finds a tool made of bone.

I Wonder Why

Ancient people used bone tools. Today, scientists study these tools to learn how ancient people lived. I wonder how scientists know why ancient people made these tools? *Turn the page to find out.*

Here's Why

Throughout history, people have designed and built tools to help meet their needs. Whether a tool is a simple stone or bone or a high-tech electronic device, it can help solve a problem. By figuring out how an ancient tool was used, scientists can draw conclusions about the needs of the person who made it.

Essential Questions

LESSON 1

What Is an Engineering Design Process? 68
SC.4.N.1.1 Raise questions ... conduct both individual and team investigations ... and generate appropriate explanations.
SC.4.N.1.8 Recognize that science includes creativity in designing experiments.

LESSON 2

How Can You Design a Solution to a Problem? 81
SC.4.N.1.6 Keep records that describe observations made.
SC.4.N.1.7 Recognize ... that scientists base their explanations on evidence.
SC.4.N.1.1, SC.4.N.1.8

LESSON 3

What Is Technology? 85
SC.4.N.3.1 Explain that models can be three dimensional, two dimensional, an explanation in your mind, or a computer model.
SC.4.N.1.1, SC.4.N.1.6

LESSON 4

How Do We Use Technology? 99
SC.4.N.1.1, SC.4.N.1.6, SC.4.N.3.1

PEOPLE IN SCIENCE
Ayanna Howard 103
SC.4.E.6.5 Explain how technology and tools help ... humans....
SC.4.N.2.1 Explain that science focuses solely on the natural world.

Unit 2 Benchmark Review 105

Science Notebook

Before you begin each lesson, write your thoughts about the Essential Question.

SC.4.N.1.1 Raise questions about the natural world, use appropriate reference materials that support understanding to obtain information (identifyingnthe source), conduct both individual and team investigations through free exploration and systematic investigations, and generate appropriate explanations based on those explorations. **SC.4.N.1.8** Recognize that science involves creativity in designing experiments.

LESSON **1**

ESSENTIAL QUESTION

What Is an Engineering Design Process?

 Engage Your Brain

Find the answer to the following question in this lesson and record it here.

Why would a car company want a wooden car?

_____

_____

_____

_____

ACTIVE READING

Lesson Vocabulary
List the terms. As you learn about each one, make notes in the Interactive Glossary.

_____

_____

_____

Signal Words: Sequence
Signal words show connections between ideas. Words that signal sequence include *now*, *before*, *after*, *first*, and *next*. Active readers remember what they read because they are alert to signal words that identify sequence.

What Is ENGINEERING?

From the food we eat and the clothes we wear, to the cars we drive and the phones we talk on, science is at work in our lives every day.

ACTIVE **READING** As you read the next page, circle the main idea of the text, and put brackets [ ] around each detail sentence.

Electrical engineers use their knowledge of physics to build things like this robot.

Knowledge of math and geology allows surveyors to make maps of Earth.

This biomedical engineer uses his knowledge of biology to make glass eyes.

Look around. Many of the things you see are products of engineering. **Engineering** is the use of scientific and mathematical principles to develop something practical. Some engineers use biology. Others use geology, chemistry, or physics.

Engineers use this knowledge to create something new. It might be a product, a system, or a process for doing things. Whatever it is, it's practical. People use it. Engineers develop things that people use.

▶ In the space below, draw a picture of something you can see around you that was probably designed by an engineer.

What Is the DESIGN PROCESS?

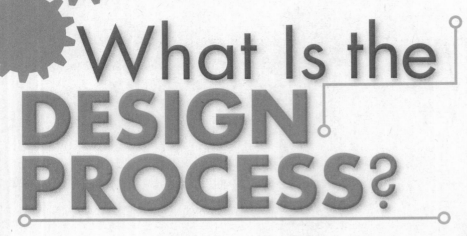

It has been said that necessity is the mother of invention. But once you find a need, how do you build your invention? That's the design process!

ACTIVE **READING** As you read these two pages, draw boxes around clue words or phrases that signal a sequence or order.

What is design? **Design** means to conceive something and prepare the plans and drawings for it to be built. Engineers use the design process to develop new technology, but anyone can follow the design process.

From basic to complex, skateboards have changed over time.

The design process starts with identifying a need or a problem. Next, you brainstorm and write down ideas on how to plan and build a potential solution. Once you have some options, select a solution to try. Usually, engineers test possible solutions using a prototype.

A **prototype** is an original or test model on which a real product is based. If the prototype works, then the real product is made. Usually, after testing a prototype, improvements have to be made. The prototype is then tested again. Finally, a finished product is made.

Design Process Steps

- **Find a problem**
- **Plan and build**
- **Test and improve**
- **Redesign**
- **Communicate**

Even something seemingly simple takes a lot of thought, planning, testing, and improvement.

1 Find a Problem
2 Plan & Build
DESIGN PROCESS STEPS
3 Test & Improve
4 Redesign
5 Communicate

How was it improved?

Look at the skateboards. Describe two design features that have been improved over time.

_____

_____

_____

_____

_____

71

Design
YOU CAN USE

Look around you at all the things you use every day. Do you have ideas about improving them?

ACTIVE **READING** As you read these two pages, find and underline the meaning of the word *prototype*.

Who Needs It?

The first step in any design process is identifying a need or problem. Is there a chore that could be easier, a tool that could work much better, a car that could go faster or be safer? Often, the design process begins with the phrase "What if?"

Prototype!

A prototype is a test version of a design. To build a prototype, a person has to have plans. Early sketches give a rough idea. More detailed drawings provide exact measurements for every piece. Keeping good records and drawings helps to make sure that the prototype can be replicated.

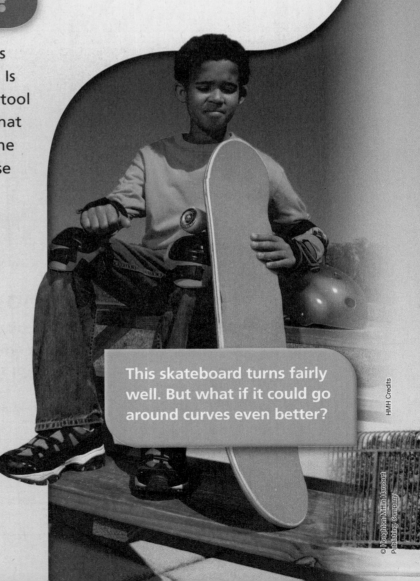

This skateboard turns fairly well. But what if it could go around curves even better?

HMH Credits

Details

Draw a blueprint of a school supply, favorite toy, or tool. Label its parts and include exact measurements.

Sketches and detailed drawings are an important step in planning a product.

wheel

Every part of a product can become an opportunity for a design change.

trucks

deck

Are We DONE YET?

Now that the prototype has been built, can the final product be far behind? Yes, it can. But it might not be. It all depends.

ACTIVE **READING** As you read these two pages, draw a box around the clue word or phrase that signals one thing is being contrasted with another.

Test It and Improve It!

Prototypes are carefully tested. This testing helps answer questions such as, *Does it work the way it should? Is it easy to use? How does it hold up under normal working conditions?*

The first prototype you build may pass all its tests. If so, the prototype can go into production. However, it is more likely that testing shows that the design needs to change. Once the test results are analyzed, it's back to the drawing board. The product may need only a few minor improvements, or it may need to be completely redesigned.

If a prototype works as expected, it will become a finished product.

Redesign and Share

When a prototype fails to meet a design goal, it may be redesigned. Redesign takes advantage of all work done before. Good design features are kept, and those that fail are discarded.

When the final working prototype is done, team members communicate the design. Sketches, blueprints, and test data and analysis are shared. Often, the product details are recorded in a legal document called a *patent*.

Sometimes, one prototype leads to ideas for others.

Spin Off!

Imagine a normal bicycle. Now think of three ways it could be modified to work better in different environments.

_____

_____

_____

_____

_____

New ideas keep the engineering design process constantly moving forward.

Use information in the summary to complete the graphic organizer.

The first step in the design process is to identify a need or a problem to be solved. The next step is to plan and build a prototype. Brainstorming ideas and drawing detailed sketches of potential solutions are important parts of this step. The third step is to test and improve a prototype. After testing, a prototype might need to be redesigned and tested again. A prototype that meets all its design goals is ready for production. The final step in the design process is to communicate to others the details of a working prototype.

1 The design process starts with identifying a need or _____ _____.

3 _____ _____ _____ _____

5 The final step in the design process is to _____ _____.

2 _____ _____ _____ _____ _____

4 _____ _____ _____ _____ _____

Name _____

Vocabulary Review

1 Use the clues to help you write the correct word in each row. Some boxes have been filled in for you.

A. To conceive something and prepare plans to build it

B. The use of scientific and mathematical principles to develop something practical

C. A prototype may undergo many rounds of this.

D. Engineers have to be familiar with these principles.

E. The answer to a problem

F. A test version of something

G. Is identified during the first step in the design process

H. What comes after sketches, plans, and the prototype?

I. Something that people will use is described as this.

J. Engineers have to be familiar with these principles.

Apply Concepts

2 Write numbers in the circles to put the pictures in the correct order.

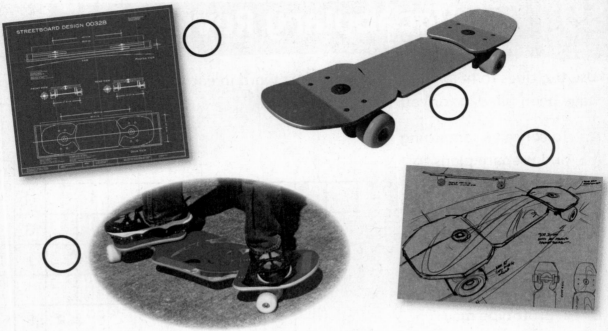

3 How is a prototype different from the finished product?

_____

_____

_____

_____

_____

4 Why is it better to build and test a prototype of a product than to produce tens of thousands of the product and then test it?

_____

_____

_____

5 The owner of a safety apparel company asks an engineer to "design a better helmet for skateboarders." How would you improve this instruction?

_____

_____

_____

_____

_____

_____

_____

_____

_____

6 Which job is more likely to be done by an engineer? Why?

Developing a new material that will be used to make the outer covering of vitamin capsules	Determining how vitamins are absorbed into the bloodstream

_____

_____

_____

_____

_____

_____

7 The engineers at an appliance company have developed a new dishwasher. It looks very different from previous models. The controls look different and work differently. The part of the machine that heats the water has been completely redesigned. Now that the plans are completed, should the company start producing thousands of these dishwashers? Why or why not?

_____

_____

_____

_____

_____

_____

_____

_____

_____

_____

_____

_____

_____

_____

 **Take It Home!**

See *ScienceSaurus*® for more information about science and engineering.

SC.4.N.1.1 Raise questions... conduct both individual and team investigations... and generate appropriate explanations... SC.4.N.1.6 Keep records that describe observations made... SC.4.N.1.7 Recognize and explain that scientists base their explanations on evidence. SC.4.N.1.8 Recognize that science involves creativity in designing experiments.

(i) INQUIRY LESSON 2

Name _____

ESSENTIAL QUESTION

How Can You Design a Solution to a Problem?

Materials

egg
gallon freezer bag
various other materials

EXPLORE

You will design a crash safety device for an egg transportation system.

Before You Begin—Preview the Steps

1 Put your egg inside a gallon freezer bag and zipper the bag shut. You will drop it from 2 meters high. Your safety device must allow the egg to land uncracked.

2 Work with a partner to decide what materials you will use.

3 Make drawings and build a prototype. Test your safety device.

4 Modify your design to improve its performance and then test it again. Use drawings and data to communicate your result.

Set a Purpose

What do you think you will learn from this investigation?

_____

_____

_____

Think About the Procedure

How will the equipment you design be similar to safety belts and airbags in a car?

_____

_____

_____

_____

_____

Why is it a good idea to make sure the plastic bag is tightly sealed before you test your prototype?

_____

_____

_____

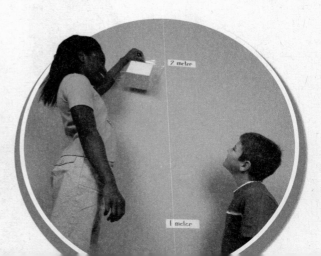

82

Name _____

Record Your Data

In the space below, draw a table to record the materials you used in your prototype and your observations from each test.

Draw Conclusions

What conclusions can you draw as a result of your test observations?

_____

_____

_____

_____

_____

Claims • Evidence • Reasoning

1. Evaluate your design. Was your design successful? Write a claim about the success of your design. Cite evidence to support your evaluation.

   _____

   _____

   _____

2. How could you improve your design? Explain your reasoning.

   _____

   _____

   _____

3. Were there any aspects of someone else's design you might incorporate into your design?

   _____

   _____

4. What is the difference between a successful design and a successful prototype?

   _____

   _____

   _____

5. What other questions would you like to ask about forces and transportation?

   _____

   _____

SC.4.N.1.1 Raise questions about the natural world,... and generate appropriate explanations based on those explorations. SC.4.N.1.6 Keep records that describe observations made, ... SC.4.N.3.1 Explain that models can be three-dimensional, two-dimensional, an explanation in your mind, or a computer model.

LESSON 3

ESSENTIAL QUESTION
What Is Technology?

 Engage Your Brain

Find the answer to the following question in the lesson and record it here.

This robot is riding a bicycle, just like a human, and not falling over. How is this possible?

_____

_____

_____

_____

📖 ACTIVE **READING**

Lesson Vocabulary
List the terms. As you learn about each one, make notes in the Interactive Glossary.

_____

_____

_____

Main Ideas
The main idea of a paragraph is the most important idea. The main idea may be stated in the first sentence, or it may be stated elsewhere. Active readers look for main ideas by asking themselves, What is this paragraph mostly about?

A bulldozer and a shovel serve the same purpose. However, because of a bulldozer's size, it can move huge amounts of material much more quickly than a shovel can.

TOOLS RULE!

Look in your desk. Do you see pens and pencils? Scissors? A ruler? All of these things are tools.

ACTIVE READING As you read these two pages, put brackets [ ] around the sentences that describe a problem. Underline the sentences that describe the solution.

Planting a vegetable garden? You'll need a shovel, a rake, and a spade. All these items are tools. A **tool** is anything that helps people shape, build, or produce things to meet their needs.

Your family's toolbox probably contains a hammer and screwdrivers. Construction workers have similar tools that do the same jobs, only on a larger scale. Instead of hammering nails by hand, construction workers use tools that quickly drive nails into wood with the push of a button. Their tools are sized and powered differently to meet different needs.

Some tools are designed to do one task. You use a pen to write a note to a friend. You keep your science notes organized in a notebook. You talk to your grandmother on the phone. What if you had one tool that could do all these tasks? A smartphone is a tool that can help you send a message, organize information, *and* talk to people.

A smartphone, like all tools, is an example of technology. **Technology** is any designed system, product, or process that people use to solve problems. Technology doesn't have to be complex. The pencil you write with and the cell phone you text with are both technology. Technology changes as the needs of people change.

Suppose you are building a birdhouse. How will you make each side straight? How will you cut through wire? How will you secure the nuts and bolts? Tools can help you solve these problems.

Level

Socket wrench

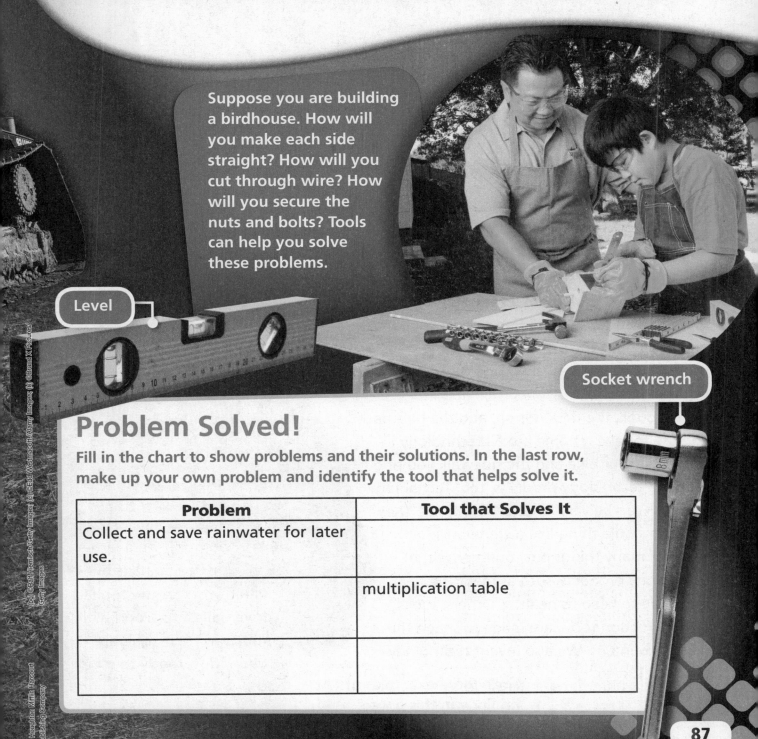

Problem Solved!

Fill in the chart to show problems and their solutions. In the last row, make up your own problem and identify the tool that helps solve it.

Problem	Tool that Solves It
Collect and save rainwater for later use.	
	multiplication table

WHAT IS TECHNOLOGY?

Vending machines, televisions, and video games are examples of technology products you know—but there are more. Technology is all around you.

As you read this page, underline technology products. On the next page, circle the paragraph that describes examples of a technology process.

A video game is the end product of a technology process. Programming a video game involves technology you can't hold in the palm of your hand.

You've learned that technology is any designed system, product, or process. A *technology product* is anything designed to meet a need or desire. Some people think that electronics are the only type of technology product. However, most technology products do not use electricity!

This book, the desk it is on, and the backpack you use to take it home are all technology products. Your bike and the sidewalk you ride it on are technology products, too. Technology products can be very large or very small. They can be a single thing like a stone brick or made of many things put together. Some technology products, such as medicine, are made to keep us healthy. Others, such as construction tools, are made to shape the world around us. We also invent technology products just to have fun.

▶ Circle three examples of technology in this photo.

© Houghton Mifflin Harcourt Publishing Company

(bg) ©Ralf Hiemisch/Getty Images (t) ©Picture Contact BV/Alamy Images

The way a product is made is also a form of technology. A *technology process* is a series of steps used to achieve a goal or make a product. The steps in a technology process are like the steps in a scientific investigation. They are carefully designed for doing something a certain way.

Many things you do are a technology process. You follow a series of steps to make gelatin dessert, tie your shoelaces, and add music to your MP3 player. If you have ever played baseball, you are familiar with its rules. The rules of a game are a technology process.

Safety gear and clothing are types of technology that help baseball players perform. The bleachers and the backstop are types of technology that let spectators watch safely.

Play Ball

The ballpark, scoreboard, rules, and baseball equipment are all examples of technology. How can technology help deliver the game's events to people who aren't at the ballpark?

_____

_____

_____

TECHNOLOGICAL SYSTEMS

The next time you ride in a car, look at how many parts it has. It took many tools and hundreds of steps to produce this technology.

ACTIVE READING As you read this page, underline the sentence that describes what makes a designed system.

Groups of things that work together to achieve a goal make up a *system*. Tools, parts, and processes that work together form a *designed system*. Designed systems help us travel and ship goods. They help us communicate and grow our foods.

You are a part of many designed systems. Whether you ride the bus or walk to school, you are a part of a transportation system. This system is made up of the sidewalks, roads, and traffic signs. It also includes the cars, buses, planes, and trains that move people and materials from place to place.

Designed systems help us shape the world around us. When you ride around your town, you might see cars, roadways, buildings, or farm fields. All these things make up the *designed world*. The designed world is the part of your community that is designed and built by people.

Many designed systems work together in the designed world. For example, the agricultural system produces the food that we need. Ships, trains, and trucks in the transportation system carry food where it is needed.

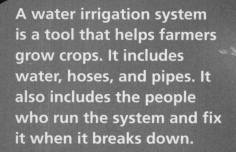

A water irrigation system is a tool that helps farmers grow crops. It includes water, hoses, and pipes. It also includes the people who run the system and fix it when it breaks down.

PARTS OF A DESIGNED SYSTEM

Part	Example: Rail Transportation System
Goal—what the system aims to do	Goal—to move cargo and passengers safely from place to place
Input—what is put into the system to meet the goal	Inputs—fuel for the train, cargo, and people to ride the train
Processes—describe how the goal is to be achieved	Processes—train tracks and departure and arrival schedules
Output—the end product	Output—safe and timely delivery of people and cargo
Feedback—information that tells whether or not the output is successful	Feedback—records of whether trains left and arrived on time

A railroad system includes trains, rails, and safety signals at road crossings. The system also has parts you can't see. Radio signals keep track of where trains are. The signals raise and lower crossing arms, too.

Tech Systems

What do you think would be the goal of a farming system?

_____

_____

_____

THE GOOD AND THE BAD OF IT

A light bulb that can save you $100 a year? What's the catch?

ACTIVE READING As you read this page, draw a box around the main idea.

Compact fluorescent lights (CFLs) and light emitting diodes (LEDs) use less energy than incandescent bulbs. However, CFLs contain mercury, which can be hazardous if the bulbs break open, and LEDs are more expensive than regular light bulbs.

Technology is constantly changing. Anyone can invent or improve a technology product or process. It takes new ideas and knowledge for technology to change. The goal of any new technology is to better meet people's needs. However, new technology can also bring new risks.

Changes in technology often involve making things safer, quicker, easier, or cheaper. For example, people once used candles and lanterns to light their homes. These things helped people see at night, but they could also cause fires. Electricity and incandescent light bulbs helped solve this problem, but this technology also has its risks.

We burn coal to generate electricity. When coal burns, harmful ash and gases are produced. The potential harm these substances can cause leads to negative feedback. Such feedback helps people think of ways to improve technology.

Sometimes the problems with a technology are caused by the way people use technology. For instance, pesticides are helpful technology products. They are used to protect people, crops, and farm animals from harmful organisms. However, when used incorrectly, they can contaminate the soil, the water, and the air. Living things exposed to pesticides by accident can get sick and die.

➕➖✖️➗ DO THE **MATH**

Interpret a Table

Use the data in the table to answer the questions below.

Light Bulb Cost Comparisons		
	60-Watt Equivalent CFL	60-Watt Equivalent Eco-Incandescent
Cost of bulb	$3.00	$1.50
Bulb life	2500 days (about 7 years)	500 days (about 1.4 years)
Energy cost per year	$2.40	$7.00
Total cost over 7 years	$19.80	$56.50

1. How much more is the total cost of incandescent bulbs than a CFL?

_____

2. How much would your yearly energy cost be if you had 20 CFL bulbs in your home?

_____

3. Which bulb lasts longer?

_____

_____

Airplanes can transport a lot of people at one time. However, they burn a lot of fuel and release pollution into the atmosphere. Engineers redesign airplanes to improve their performance.

OUT WITH THE OLD

Computers, cell phones, and flat-screen TVs are fun and useful. But like all technology, electronic gadgets have drawbacks.

Electronic technology seems to change at the blink of an eye. New electronic devices rapidly replace old ones. People benefit from new or improved electronic devices, but they also bring new problems.

Not long ago, most televisions and computer monitors were large, bulky things. New technology has made these large devices a thing of the past. They have been replaced by thin, lightweight flat screens.

But what do we do with old electronics? Some are taken apart and recycled; however, like the devices shown on this page, most end up in landfills. At landfills, electronics may release harmful chemicals into the environment.

Many electronic devices contain lead. Lead can be harmful to people and other organisms in the environment.

Electronics are helpful communication, work, and entertainment tools. They can also be a distraction. Some people spend a lot of time playing video games or on the Internet. They send text messages or listen to MP3 players while they are with other people. Some might even operate electronics while driving and cause a safety hazard for themselves and others.

People can solve these problems. They can set limits on computer and game time. They can put the phone away and pay attention to people and driving. These are ways to be responsible with technology.

► On the chart below, fill in the pros and cons of each electronic technology. Some examples have been provided for you.

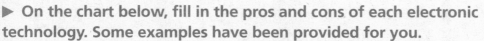

	Pros	Cons
Television	can be educational; can provide breaking news quickly	
Smartphones		can take time away from doing other activities or being social; can cause drivers to be a hazard
Video games	fun; can be social when played with others	

Sum It Up »

Complete the graphic organizer below.

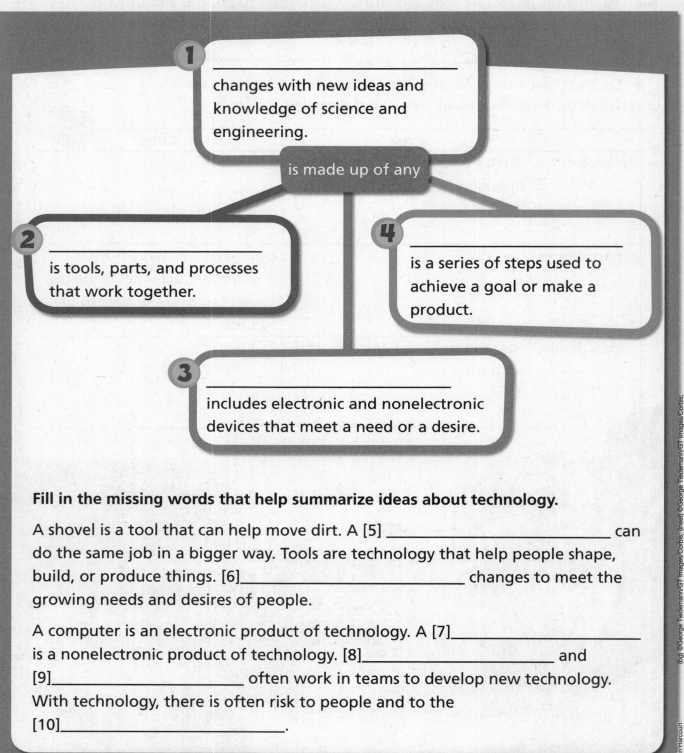

1 _____ changes with new ideas and knowledge of science and engineering.

is made up of any

2 _____ is tools, parts, and processes that work together.

4 _____ is a series of steps used to achieve a goal or make a product.

3 _____ includes electronic and nonelectronic devices that meet a need or a desire.

Fill in the missing words that help summarize ideas about technology.

A shovel is a tool that can help move dirt. A [5] _____ can do the same job in a bigger way. Tools are technology that help people shape, build, or produce things. [6]_____ changes to meet the growing needs and desires of people.

A computer is an electronic product of technology. A [7]_____ is a nonelectronic product of technology. [8]_____ and [9]_____ often work in teams to develop new technology. With technology, there is often risk to people and to the [10]_____.

Name _____

Vocabulary Review

1 **Use the clues below to fill in the words of the puzzle.**

1. Any designed system, product, or process

2. Anything that helps people shape, build, or produce things to meet their needs

3. Tools, parts, and processes that work together

4. Things that are made to meet a need

5. The end product or service of a system

6. Anything that is put into a system to meet a goal

7. Information that tells whether or not the output is successful

8. This is made up of all products of technology

9. A series of steps that result in a product

feedback	input
process	products
output	system
technology*	tool*
designed world	
* Key Lesson Vocabulary	

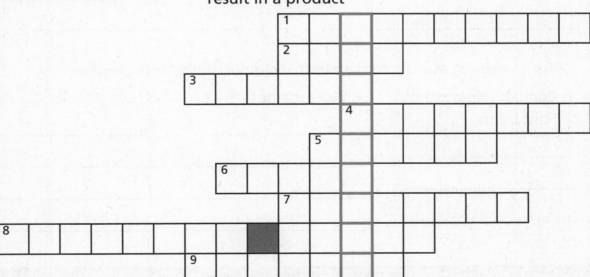

Read down the squares with red borders. The word will answer the question below.

Murata Boy is a bicycling robot. He can ride forward, backward, and stop without falling over. Where does he get the ability to do it?

___ ___ ___ ___ ___ ___ ___ ___ ___

Apply Concepts

Passenger jets can transport people quickly from one place to another. Modern computer electronics help pilots fly these planes.

2 Describe two technological systems that are related to airplanes.

_____

_____

_____

3 What are some of the risks of global airline travel? What are some of the benefits?

_____

_____

_____

4 Write a problem associated with each example of electronic technology.

1. Compact fluorescent light bulbs

_____

_____

_____

2. Video games

_____

_____

_____

_____

3. Cell phones

_____

_____

_____

_____

 Work with a family member to make a list of tools found in your kitchen. Sort the items in your list into simple and complex tools. Share your work with your class. Explain how you categorized the items in your list.

SC.4.N.1.1 Raise questions... use appropriate reference materials... conduct both individual and team investigations... and generate appropriate explanations... **SC.4.N.1.6** Keep records that describe observations made... **SC.4.N.3.1** Explain that models can be three dimensional, two dimensional, ...

INQUIRY
LESSON 4

Name _____

ESSENTIAL **QUESTION**

How Do We Use Technology?

EXPLORE

We use technology all the time. In this activity, you will build and test a tool that could be used to help us do work.

Materials

string
books
spring scale
5 marbles
jar lid
5 cubes

Before You Begin—Preview the Steps

① Tie the string tightly around a stack of four books. Use the spring scale to pull and measure the force needed to move the books across a table. Repeat this step two more times. Record your observations.

② Place the marbles under the jar lid, and then place your book stack on top of the lid. Again use the spring scale to measure the force needed to move the book stack. Repeat two more times. Record your observations.

③ Replace at least three marbles with the same number of cubes under the lid. Test your stack of books again. What happens to the system? Record your observations.

④ Draw a conclusion about how the system works best.

Set a Purpose

What do you think you will you learn from this investigation?

_____

_____

_____

Think About the Procedure

What does the spring scale measure?

_____

_____

Why is it a good idea to repeat each trial in Steps 1 and 2 three times?

_____

_____

_____

What is being modeled when some of the marbles are replaced with cubes?

_____

_____

Name _____

Record Your Data

In the table below, record your observations for Trials 1–3.

_____

Measured Force (N)			
Trial	Bare Table	Marbles	Marbles and Cubes
1			
2			
3			
Average			

Draw Conclusions

Calculate the average force needed to move the book stack in each setup. Show your work and record your answers in the table above.

Which problem did the tool you built help solve?

_____

_____

_____

Which setup required the greatest amount of force to move the book stack? Why?

_____

_____

_____

Claims • Evidence • Reasoning

1. Which products of technology did you use to build your tool? Explain your reasoning.

_____

_____

_____

_____

2. In the space below, draw a bar graph to show the average force needed to move the book stack in each setup.

3. Write a claim about how using worn-down marbles would affect the force needed to move the book. Cite evidence that supports your claim.

_____

_____

_____

4. How could you redesign this tool to move larger things? Explain the reasoning behind your changes to the design.

_____

_____

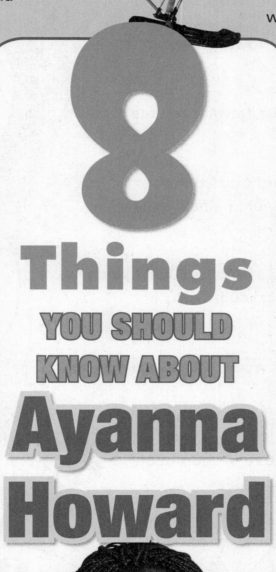

8 Things

YOU SHOULD KNOW ABOUT

Ayanna Howard

1 Dr. Ayanna Howard is a roboticist. She designs and builds robots.

2 Dr. Howard is making robots that will make decisions without the help of people.

3 To get a robot to make decisions on its own, Dr. Howard must teach the robot how to think.

4 Dr. Howard uses computer programs to teach robots. She observes the robots. Then she changes her computer programs to get better results.

5 Dr. Howard studies how robots can help explore outer space and unsafe places on Earth.

6 Dr. Howard taught a robot called SmartNav to move around things in its path. This robot could explore the surface of Mars.

7 Scientists want to understand why the ice in Antarctica is melting. Dr. Howard's SnoMote robots can safely gather data on the cracking ice sheets.

8 Dr. Howard has won numerous awards in engineering, innovation, and education.

Now You Be a Roboticist!

1 What is Dr. Howard investigating?

2 Why does Dr. Howard test the robots?

3 What scientific question does Dr. Howard's SnoMote help answer?

4 If you were a roboticist, what kind of robot would you make?

5 What steps would you take in making your robot?

6 Draw a picture of your robot.

Name _____

Vocabulary Review

Use the terms in the box to complete the sentences.

> design
> designed system
> engineering
> technology process
> prototype
> technology
> technology product
> tool

1. Anything that is made to meet a need or desire is

   a(n) _____.

2. To conceive of something and prepare the plans

   and drawings for it to be built is _____.

3. A designed system, product, or process that people use to solve

   problems is called _____.

4. A series of steps used to achieve a goal or make a product is

   called a(n) _____.

5. The use of scientific and mathematical principles to develop

   something practical is called _____.

6. An original or test model on which a real product is based is

   called a _____.

7. Tools, parts, and processes that work together form

   a(n) _____.

8. Anything that helps people shape, build, or produce things to

   meet their needs is called a _____.

Science Concepts

Fill in the letter of the choice that best answers the question.

9. A group of researchers is working on a way to make winter coats warmer. The first coat the researchers' design is not very warm. What should they do?

   (A) They should try again without using tools.

   (B) They should find a different designed system.

   (C) They should continue their work without using technology.

   (D) They should examine their test data for ways to improve the coat's design.

10. Sylvia works for a car company. She uses her knowledge of math and science to design dashboards that make it easier to operate cars. What is Sylvia's profession?

    (F) analyst

    (G) biologist

    (H) engineer

    (I) geologist

11. Marco is using this object to help him find information for a report.

    Which statement best describes this object?

    (A) It is a technology process.

    (B) It is an engineer.

    (C) It is a prototype.

    (D) It is a tool.

12. Researchers want to build a new type of spaceship for transporting astronauts to the moon. What should they do **first**?

    (F) They should test the prototype.

    (G) They should plan a prototype.

    (H) They should build a model.

    (I) They should evaluate how the prototype worked.

13. Bulldozers, measuring cups, pencils, and hammers are all examples of tools. What else can be said about all of them?

    (A) They are all technology products.

    (B) They are all in the prototype stage.

    (C) They all release harmful gases into the atmosphere.

    (D) They all require power sources other than their users.

14. New solutions to problems often begin with a "What if?" question. Which "What if?" question might an engineer ask after seeing the electrical energy station shown below?

    (F) What if we burned trees instead of coal?

    (G) What if we could find even more coal to burn?

    (H) What if we all threw away all of our electrical appliances?

    (I) What if we could burn coal to make electricity without polluting the air?

Name _____

15. Angie tested a reflector that she hopes will make bicycles safer. Although her first test went well, she repeated the test three more times. Which of these statements is **true**?

Ⓐ She skipped the step of asking "What if?"

Ⓑ She wasted her time by repeating the same test.

Ⓒ She obtained unreliable data, because there were more chances for mistakes.

Ⓓ She obtained more accurate data than if she had only tested the reflector once.

16. You probably use the tools shown below every day.

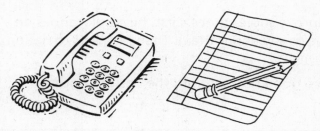

Which statement about these tools is true?

Ⓕ They cost about the same to produce.

Ⓖ They are both examples of technology.

Ⓗ They are examples of identical technology.

Ⓘ They are each designed for many different tasks.

17. Sometimes, a prototype tests poorly or fails completely. What should be done when that happens?

Ⓐ The prototype should be abandoned

Ⓑ A second prototype should be built.

Ⓒ The prototype should be modified, with the good parts of it kept.

Ⓓ The prototype should be examined to see if it has other uses.

18. A fuel-efficient automobile is an example of a designed system. What is an example of feedback for such an automobile?

Ⓕ safe arrival at the destination

Ⓖ fuel for the car and the roads on which it will travel

Ⓗ data on how much fuel the car used to travel 100 km

Ⓘ to move a family of four 100 km using only 2 liters of gasoline

19. Long ago, there were few roads. Now, there are many roads. How has a system of roads changed most communities?

Ⓐ People can easily get from one place to another.

Ⓑ People live closer to where they work and drive less.

Ⓒ People travel less and rarely see family members that live far away.

Ⓓ Use of fossil fuels has decreased with the increase in roads and highways.

Apply Inquiry and Review the Big Idea

Write the answers to these questions.

20. This picture shows solar cells on the roof of a house. These cells take solar energy and convert it into electricity that appliances in the house need to function.

   A. Use reasoning to support the claim that the solar cells are part of a designed system.

   _____

   _____

   _____

   b. Identify the goal, input, output, and feedback of this system.

   _____

   _____

   _____

21. An engineer follows the design process to improve soccer shoes. First, he studies shoes on the market and reads about what people have to say about them. Then he starts to design his prototype.

   a. Why is it important for the engineer to keep good notes during the design process?

   _____

   _____

   b. Why should the engineer build a prototype of the shoes?

   _____

   _____

   c. Describe a part of the design process the engineer should do **after** testing the prototype.

   _____

   _____

   _____

   _____

Earth's Place in Space

Earth in Space and Time

The Soyuz rocket launches to the International Space Station in 2012.

I Wonder Why

People have been exploring space for decades. The space program has changed our lives. Why is this? *Turn the page to find out.*

Here's Why

Space technology has led to many new discoveries about our universe. It has also made possible many inventions here on Earth.

Essential Questions and Florida Benchmarks

LESSON 1
How Does Earth Rotate and Revolve in Space?...........111
SC.4.E.5.1 Observe that the patterns of stars ...
SC.4.E.5.3 Recognize that Earth revolves around the Sun in a year and rotates on its axis in a 24-hour day.
SC.4.E.5.4 Relate that the rotation of Earth (day and night) and apparent movements of the Sun, Moon, and stars are connected.

PEOPLE IN SCIENCE:
Neil deGrasse Tyson/Michael Kobrick.................................123
SC.4.E.6.5, SC.4.N.2.1

 LESSON 2
How Does Earth Move in Space?........................125
SC.4.E.5.3, SC.4.E.5.4, SC.4.N.1.1, SC.4.N.1.7, SC.4.N.3.1

LESSON 3
What Are Moon Phases?..................................129
SC.4.E.5.2 Describe the changes in the observable shape of the moon over the course of about a month.

LESSON 4
How Does Technology Help Us Learn About Space? 139
SC.4.E.5.5 Investigate and report the effects of space research and exploration on the economy and culture of Florida.
SC.4.E.6.5 Investigate how technology and tools help ... humans ....

S.T.E.M. Engineering and Technology
Space Exploration/Design It: Build a Sundial 153
SC.4.N.3.1

 ### Unit 3 Benchmark Review....................................157

Science Notebook

Before you begin each lesson, write your thoughts about the Essential Question.

SC.4.E.5.1 Observe that the patterns of stars in the sky stay the same although they appear to shift across the sky nightly, and different stars can be seen in different seasons. SC.4.E.5.3 Recognize that Earth revolves around the Sun in a year and rotates on its axis in a 24-hour day. SC.4.E.5.4 Relate that the rotation of Earth (day and night) and apparent movements of the Sun, Moon, and stars are connected.

ESSENTIAL QUESTION

How Does Earth Rotate and Revolve in Space?

 Engage Your Brain

Find the answer to the following question in this lesson and record it here.

In what ways do we know that Earth moves in space?

_____

_____

_____

📖 ACTIVE READING

Lesson Vocabulary
List the terms. As you learn about each one, make notes in the Interactive Glossary.

_____

_____

_____

Cause and Effect
Active readers look for ideas that are connected by a cause-and-effect relationship. Why something happens is a cause. What happens as a result of something else is an effect. Active readers look for effects by asking themselves, What happened? They look for causes by asking, Why did it happen?

Day and Night

How can it be morning where you live and yet be nighttime in India? You cannot feel it, but Earth moves in space.

ACTIVE READING As you read this page, draw one line under a cause of day and night. Draw two lines under an effect of day and night.

People once thought the sun moved around Earth. After all, the sun seems to rise in the east and set in the west. Today we know that Earth **rotates**, or spins. This spinning causes day and night. It is the reason that the sun seems to rise, move across the sky, and set.

Have you ever been on a merry-go-round? It turns around a pole in its center. Earth is a little like a merry-go-round with an imaginary pole. This imaginary pole or line is called Earth's **axis**. The axis runs through Earth's center, from the North Pole to the South Pole. Earth rotates on its axis once about every 24 hours. As it rotates, one side of Earth faces the sun. This part of Earth has daytime. The other side of Earth faces away from the sun and has nighttime. As Earth rotates, we have day and night again and again.

 DO THE MATH

Use and Represent Numbers

The time it takes a planet to rotate once on its axis is 1 day. The rate of rotation is different for each planet, so the length of a day is different. Find the difference between a day on Earth and a day on other planets.
(1 Earth day = 24 hours)

Length of Day:

Venus: 243 Earth days _____

Jupiter: 9 Earth hours, 55 minutes _____

Neptune: 16 Earth hours, 6 minutes

_____

Night

Day

Earth rotates on its axis from west to east. It takes 24 hours for Earth to rotate once on its axis.

Seasons

When it is summer in the United States, it is winter in Brazil. How can two places have a different season at the same time of year?

ACTIVE READING As you read this page, draw one line under the cause of the seasons.

Earth rotates on its axis, which is tilted to one side. Earth also moves in another way. It *revolves*, or follows a path, around the sun. The path that Earth takes around the sun is called an **orbit**. Earth takes about 365 days to make one orbit around the sun. As Earth moves around the sun, Earth's axis stays tilted in the same direction. The tilt of Earth's axis and its orbit cause the seasons.

Earth is divided into halves called *hemispheres*. The upper half is the Northern Hemisphere. The lower half is the Southern Hemisphere. In June,

Winter

Spring

the Northern Hemisphere is tilted toward the sun and gets more rays of sunlight. There are more hours of daylight, and it's warmer. It's summer there.

In June, the opposite season is occurring in the Southern Hemisphere. Why? The Southern Hemisphere is tilted away from the sun and gets less sunlight. There are fewer hours of daylight, and it's cooler. It's winter there.

In December, the Northern Hemisphere is tilted away from the sun. It's winter there. At the same time, the Southern Hemisphere is tilted toward the sun. So, it's summer in the Southern Hemisphere.

Home Sweet Home

What season is it where you live? Draw a picture of Earth. Label where you live.

Seasons In the Northern Hemisphere

When the North Pole is tilted away from the sun, that part of Earth has darkness for nearly 24 hours each day. When the North Pole is tilted toward the sun, that part has about 24 hours of daylight!

Fall

Summer

11

Patterns in the Sky

The stars of the Big Dipper form a pattern at night. The pattern looks like a giant spoon.

ACTIVE READING As you read these pages, draw a circle around words or phrases that provide details about constellations.

For thousands of years, people have looked at star patterns. A star pattern, or **constellation**, is a group of stars that seems to form a pattern in the night sky. The early Greeks named constellations after animals or people from stories called myths. The Big Dipper is part of a constellation called *Ursa Major*, or Great Bear. Orion is a constellation named after a hunter in a Greek myth.

As Earth rotates on its axis, constellations seem to move across the night sky. Like the sun, they seem to rise in the east and set in the west. Stars above the North Pole, however, seem to move in a circle.

The positions of the constellations seem to change with the seasons. This is because we see different parts of space as Earth revolves around the sun. The stars in the constellations do change a little over time. However, it might take millions of years for a constellation to change its shape!

Connect the Stars

Connect the stars to draw a constellation. Use all or some of the stars. What is the name of your constellation?

_____

_____

These pictures show stars seen from the same location during summer (at left) and winter (at right). The constellations seem to change their places in the sky.

For thousands of years, people have seen pictures in the stars. They connect the stars to make a pattern or shape.

Sum It Up >>

Read the summary statements below. Each one is incorrect.
Change the part of the summary in blue to make it correct.

1. Day and night are caused by Earth's revolution around the sun.	_____ _____
2. Earth revolves around the sun once every 24 hours.	_____ _____
3. Earth's seasons are caused by Earth's revolution and rotation in space.	_____ _____ _____
4. During winter in the Northern Hemisphere, there are more hours of daylight and it is warmer.	_____ _____ _____
5. When it is spring in the Northern Hemisphere, it is summer in the Southern Hemisphere.	_____ _____ _____
6. Constellations appear to move across the night sky because of Earth's tilt on its axis.	_____ _____ _____

Vocabulary Review

1 Unscramble letters to fill in the blanks with the words from the box below.

Use the hints to help you unscramble the letters.

1. X A I S _ _ _ _
   [Hint: an imaginary line through Earth]

2. T E R A O T _ _ _ _ _ _
   [Hint: Earth's spinning in space]

3. R I B O T _ _ _ _ _
   [Hint: Earth's path in space]

4. E S O A N S S _ _ _ _ _ _ _
   [Hint: caused by Earth's trip around the sun]

5. L E O V R E V _ _ _ _ _ _ _
   [Hint: Earth does this once a year.]

6. S T E L C O N A L I O N T _ _ _ _ _ _ _ _ _ _ _ _ _
   [Hint: a pattern of stars in the night sky]

seasons	revolve	orbit
axis	constellation	rotate

* Key Lesson Vocabulary

Apply Concepts

2 Draw a picture of the sun and Earth. Draw lines to show Earth's axis and rays from the sun. Label which side of Earth has day and which side has night.

3 At sunset, the sun appears to sink down below the horizon. How would a scientist describe sunset?

_____

_____

_____

4 In Florida, the constellation Orion is seen in the night sky during the winter months. During the summer, Orion can't be seen. Why is Orion only visible during part of the year?

_____

_____

_____

_____

_____

_____

5 Imagine you are going on a ride in a spacecraft next to Earth. Your trip takes one whole year. Describe Earth's tilt in the Northern Hemisphere during your trip. What happens as a result of the tilt?

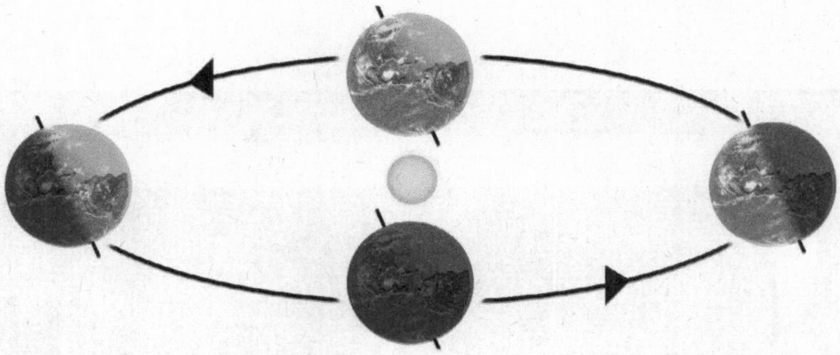

_____

_____

_____

_____

6 Suppose a friend from the Southern Hemisphere plans to visit you in December. Write an e-mail explaining what kind of clothes to pack and why.

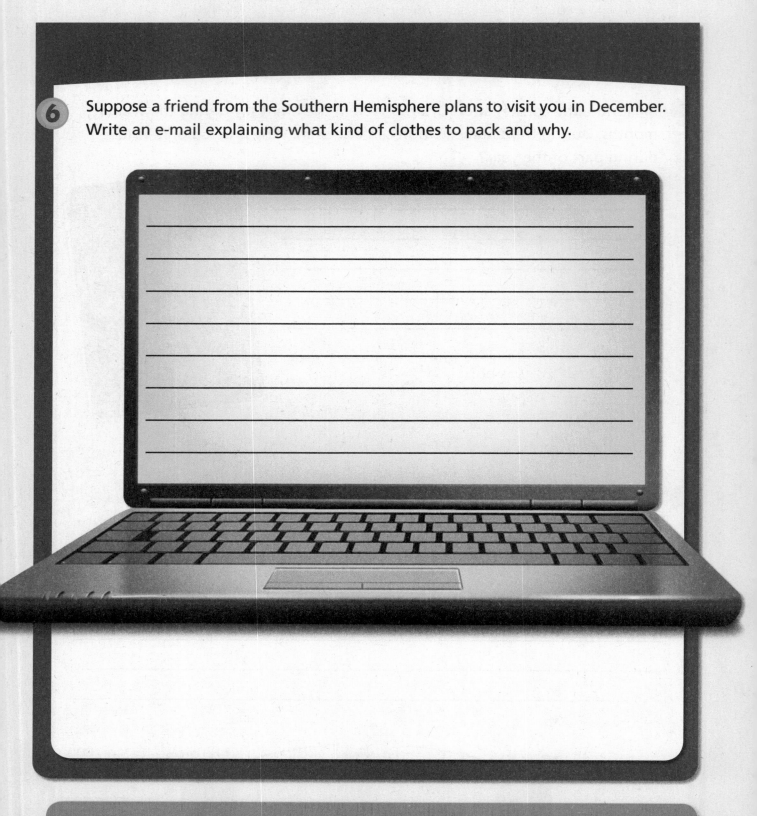

 **Take It Home!**

See *ScienceSaurus*® for more information about the solar system.

SC.4.E.6.5 Investigate how technology and tools help to extend the ability of humans to observe very small things and very large things. **SC.4.N.2.1** Explain that science focuses solely on the natural world.

◇PEOPLE **IN SCIENCE**

Meet the Spacemen on Earth

Neil deGrasse Tyson

Tyson is the director of New York City's Hayden Planetarium. His research uses the Hubble Space Telescope and other telescopes all over the world.

Neil deGrasse Tyson was born in New York City in 1958. His love of stars and space began when he visited the planetarium at age 9. Tyson is an astrophysicist, a scientist who studies the universe. In 1995, Tyson became the director of New York City's Hayden Planetarium. He was twice selected by the government to join a space exploration board. Tyson has written nine books on the universe.

Michael Kobrick

Kobrick's new digital elevation maps give scientists more information about Earth's surface than ever before.

In 2000, a single pass of the shuttle recorded data of Earth's surface using two radar antennas and a 200-foot mast.

Michael Kobrick is a scientist at NASA. His work helped make three-dimensional maps showing Earth's surface. The maps are made using data recorded from space. In 2000, the shuttle recorded data for 80% of Earth's land surface. This important data is used by scientists, engineers, and even businesses. In 2009, new images gave scientists data for 99% of Earth's surface. Kobrick is working to make an even better map of Earth.

Be an Astrophysicist!

Label each satellite photo with the number of the matching description.

1 A satellite sent back a picture of a lake. It is flat, blue, and has land all around it.

2 In a city, many buildings are grouped close to one another. The bright lights also can be seen in the satellite photo.

3 In a satellite photo of a volcano, red streaks of lava from an eruption can be seen. You may see smoke coming from the top.

4 You can tell the ice of a glacier or icecap by its white color in the satellite photo.

5 A satellite photo of a river shows how it winds through the land.

6 The unique shape of Florida is easy to see in its satellite photo.

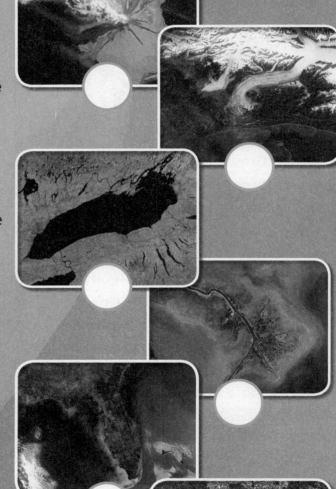

Think About It!

What are some uses for digital three-dimensional maps?

_____

_____

_____

(volcano) ©Image Makers/Getty Images; (glacier) ©Marvin Dembinsky Photo Associates/Alamy; (lake) ©Marshall Ikonography/Alamy; (river) ©NASA/Corbis; (florida) ©NASA/Alamy; (city) ©Disco/Alamy

SC.4.E.5.3 Recognize that Earth revolves around the Sun in a year and rotates on its axis in a 24-hour day. SC.4.E.5.4 Relate that the rotation of Earth (day and night) and apparent movements of the Sun, Moon, and stars are connected SC.4.N.1.1 Raise questions... and generate appropriate explanations... SC.4.N.1.7 Recognize ... that scientists base their explanations on evidence. SC.4.N.3.1 Explain that models can be three dimensional, two dimensional...

i INQUIRY LESSON **2**

Name _____

ESSENTIAL QUESTION

How Does Earth Move in Space?

EXPLORE

Let's travel through space! In this activity, you will investigate how Earth, the sun, and the moon form a system in space.

Before You Begin—Preview the Steps

① Work in a group of four to model Earth, the sun, and the moon in space. One person holds the beach ball to represent the sun. Another person holds the softball to represent Earth. A third person holds the table-tennis ball to represent the moon. A fourth person observes and takes notes for the group.

② The person holding the sun stands far away from Earth and the moon and does not move. The person holding Earth moves around the sun in an almost circular path. At the same time, Earth should also be spinning.

③ The person holding the moon moves around Earth in a circle. At the same time, the moon should spin slowly as it completes each revolution.

Set a Purpose

What do you think you will learn from this experiment?

_____

_____

_____

Think About the Procedure

Why do you think you are using different balls as models to represent the sun, Earth, and the moon?

_____

_____

_____

Why do you think the balls in this investigation are different sizes?

_____

_____

_____

Name _____

Record Your Data

In the space below, make a chart to record what you observed.

Draw Conclusions

Think about the movements you made during the activity. How do these model the way Earth moves in space?

_____

_____

_____

Claims • Evidence • Reasoning

1. What movement represented a year? Explain your reasoning.

_____

_____

2. How is the movement of the moon similar to that of Earth? Explain your reasoning.

_____

_____

3. Write a claim about how the rotation of the moon and Earth compare. Cite evidence that supports your claim and explain why it supports the claim.

_____

_____

_____

_____

_____

_____

4. Could you use only these three balls to model day and night or Earth's seasons? Give evidence to support your claim.

_____

_____

_____

_____

SC.4.E.5.2 Describe the changes in the observable shape of the moon over the course of about a month.

LESSON **3**

ESSENTIAL **QUESTION**

What Are Moon Phases?

 Engage Your Brain

Find the answer to the following question in this lesson and record it here.

What do you observe about the moon in the night sky?

_____

_____

_____

_____

📖 ACTIVE **READING**

Lesson Vocabulary

List the terms. As you learn about each one, make notes in the Interactive Glossary.

_____

_____

_____

_____

Cause and Effect

Many ideas in this lesson are connected by a sequence, or order, that describes the steps in a process. Active readers stay focused on sequence when they mark the transition from one step in a process to another.

Our Moon

Neil Armstrong was the first person to walk on Earth's moon. He said of the moon, "The surface is fine and powdery. I can pick it up with my toe."

The moon is Earth's satellite. A satellite is an object that moves around another larger object in space. Earth's moon is the largest and brightest object in the night sky. It looks large because it is close to Earth. But the moon is small compared to Earth. It is only about one-fourth the size of Earth. The moon has no air, wind, or liquid water. We see the moon because light from the sun reflects from it and back to Earth.

The pull of Earth's gravity keeps the moon in its orbit around Earth. We see only one side of the moon from Earth. That is because the moon takes the same amount of time to rotate once as it does to orbit Earth once.

We can see the moon at night (small photo) and sometimes during the day.

Moon and Earth

Compare the moon and Earth. How are they alike? How are they different? Complete the Venn diagram below.

Moon | Earth

Rocks and chunks of debris from space slammed into the moon and formed its many craters. Craters, or pits in the ground, cover the moon's rocky surface.

There are mountains and large, flat plains. The plains on the moon's surface are called *maria* [mah•REE•uh], a Latin word meaning "seas."

Moon Phases

One night, you might look at the moon and see a tiny sliver in the sky. A few nights later, you might see a bright, round circle. What makes the moon look so different?

ACTIVE **READING** As you read the last paragraph, write numbers next to the sentences to show the sequence of moon phases.

As Earth orbits the sun, the moon also orbits Earth. The moon reflects light from the sun. That is the light we see from Earth. As the moon travels in its orbit, different amounts of the moon's lit side can be seen from Earth.

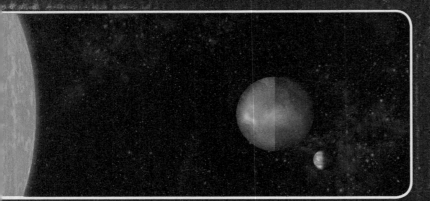

First Quarter

New Moon

During the new moon phase, the moon is between Earth and the sun. We can't see the moon at all. During a first quarter moon, we see one-half of the moon's lit side.

The moon's shape does not change. The changes in the appearance of the moon's shape are known as **moon phases**.

You know that sunlight reflects from the moon to Earth. Yet the sun lights only half of the moon at any time. The motions of Earth and the moon are responsible for the phases you see. As the moon revolves around Earth, the amount of the lit part that we see from Earth changes. These different amounts of the moon's lighted side are the different phases of the moon.

Each phase of the moon has a different shape. It takes about 1 month for the moon to complete all of its phases. Then the cycle repeats.

During the new moon phase, we can't see the moon. That is because the lit part of the moon faces away from Earth. As the moon moves in its orbit around Earth, we see more of the moon's lit part. We see a full moon when all of the lit part of the moon faces Earth. Then we see less and less of the lit part again.

 DO THE **MATH**

Estimate Fractions and Percentages

What fraction and percent of the moon's lit side is seen during each phase? Complete the table.

	Full moon	First quarter	New moon	Third quarter
Fraction		$\frac{1}{2}$		
Percent		50%		

Full Moon

Third Quarter

The lit portion grows larger until we see a full moon. This happens when Earth is between the moon and the sun. As the moon continues in its orbit, we see less of its lit portion. When it is half lit again, it is a third quarter moon.

Lunar and Solar Calendars

For thousands of years, people used the phases of the moon to make calendars and track time. These are called lunar calendars. Earth's orbit around the sun also has been used to make calendars and track time. These are called solar calendars.

The Chinese Zodiac Calendar

The Chinese zodiac calendar is based in part on the phases of the moon. Twelve animals stand for cycles of time on the calendar. Some of these animals are the tiger, rabbit, dragon, and snake. Each year is also given an animal name. For example, in 2026, it will be the "Year of the Horse." The year 2027 will be the "Year of the Sheep".

Chinese New Year comes sometime between late January and early February. It is celebrated with fancy dragon costumes.

The Aztec calendar is based on Earth's orbit around the sun. Each part of the calendar has colorful animals or symbols. These symbols marked important times of the year, such as when to plant crops.

APRIL

Sunday	Monday	Tuesday	Wednesday	Thursday	Friday	Saturday
			1	2	3	4
5	6	7	8	9	10	11
12	13	14	15	16	17	18
19	20	21	22	23	24	25
26	27	28	29	30		

New Year's Day

In the United States, New Year's Day is always January 1. In China, it is on the day of the new moon. Why do you think New Year's Day always falls on a different day each year in China?

_____

_____

_____

_____

Our modern calendar is based on Earth's orbit around the sun. Each month is based roughly on the moon's phases. Once in a while, there are two full moons in one month.

Sum It Up >>

The idea web below summarizes the lesson. Complete the web.

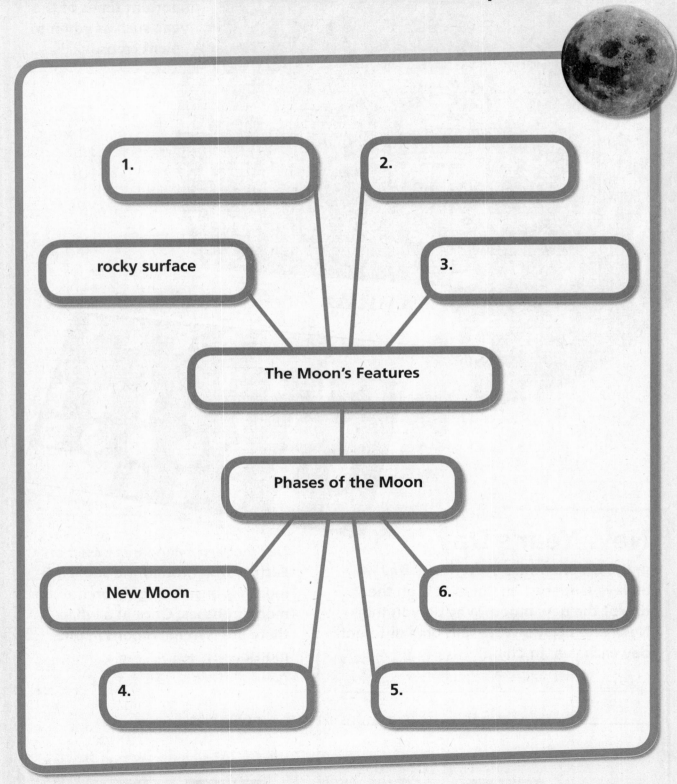

1.

2.

rocky surface

3.

The Moon's Features

Phases of the Moon

New Moon

6.

4.

5.

Name _____

Vocabulary Review

1 Look at the picture and word clues. Write the answer to each clue on the blanks.

1.

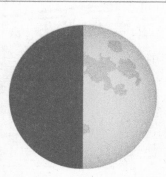

The picture shows a first
— ◯ — ◯ — — — moon.
   1   2

2.

People use this to track time.
— — ◯ — ◯ — — —
      3   4

3.

These are pictures of some moon
— — — — ◯◯.
     5 6

4.

An object that moves around another
object in space is a
◯◯ — — — — — —.
7 8

Look at the letters in circles. Match the letter with the number below each space to solve the riddle.

What kind of cartoons does the moon watch?

— — — — — — — — — — —
3 1 4 7 2   8 1 4 5 6

Apply Concepts

2 Draw a picture of the sun and the moon. Add lines to show light rays from the sun. Shade the part of the moon that is dark.

3 Look at the calendar. One of the moon's phases is missing for January 10th. Draw and label the missing moon phase in the space below.

4 Explain why you drew the moon the way you did in Question 3.

_____

_____

_____

Take It Home! With an adult, use a pair of binoculars to observe the moon. Can you see craters? Draw a picture of what you see.

SC.4.E.5.5 Investigate and report the effects of space research and exploration on the economy and culture of Florida. SC.4.E.6.5 Investigate how technology and tools help to extend the ability of humans to observe very small things and very large things.

LESSON 4

ESSENTIAL **QUESTION**

How Does Technology Help Us Learn About Space?

Engage Your Brain

Find the answer to the following question in this lesson and record it here.

What do you think it would be like to work in space? Explain.

_____

_____

_____

_____

_____

ACTIVE **READING**

Lesson Vocabulary

List the terms. As you learn about each one, make notes in the Interactive Glossary.

_____

_____

_____

Signal Words: Details

Active readers remember what they read because they are alert to signal words that identify examples and facts about a topic. Signal words show connections between ideas. *For example* and *for instance* signal examples of an idea. *Also* and *in fact* signal added facts.

EARLY ASTRONOMERS

People have always looked at the night sky. Early people built monuments based on what they saw in the sky. When writing was developed, people began to record their observations.

ACTIVE READING As you read these pages, circle two clue words or phrases that signal a detail such as an example or a fact.

Ancient Egyptians, Aztecs, and Mayans built pyramids based on their observations of the sky.

This early map of the solar system shows Earth at the center of the universe.

Early Aztec and Egyptian astronomers were limited to observing space with just their eyes. They observed several planets using just their eyes. Early astronomers also believed that Earth was the center of the universe.

Then, in the 1600s, the telescope was invented. A **telescope** is a tool that uses lenses to make faraway objects appear closer and larger. Galileo was one of the first astronomers to study space by using a telescope. The telescope led to many new observations about space. For example, Galileo observed four of Jupiter's moons by using a telescope.

By the early 1600s, astronomers knew that Earth revolved around the sun. However, they still believed that the sun was the center of the universe.

▶ By the 1600s, scientists knew that the sun was the center of the solar system. They had also observed five other planets with telescopes. Draw a diagram of an early solar system.

This early model of the solar system is known as an astrolabe.

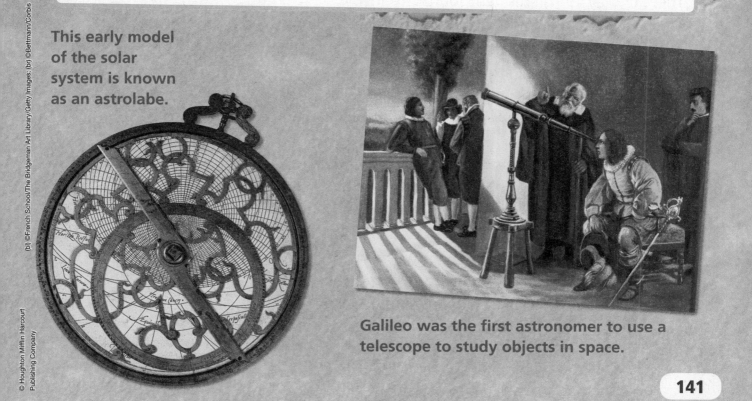

Galileo was the first astronomer to use a telescope to study objects in space.

HUMANS ON THE MOON!

The launch of *Sputnik* was the beginning of the Space Age.

"That's one small step for [a] man, one giant leap for mankind." Neil Armstrong spoke those words from the moon's surface in July 1969. He was the first person ever to be there!

ACTIVE **READING** As you read these pages, draw circles around clue words or phrases that signal a sequence of events.

Before 1960, scientists had already developed the technology to send rockets and people into space. Russia sent the satellite *Sputnik* into space in 1957.

Then, in May 1961, President John F. Kennedy challenged NASA. He wanted the United States to be the first country to put a human on the moon. The space race was on! During the late 1960s and early 1970s, the United States sent nine *Apollo* spacecrafts to the moon. Six of those spacecrafts landed on the moon's surface.

Both the United States and Russia launched space probes. **Space probes** are vehicles that move through space, but are controlled from Earth. They take photos of faraway objects, and send the data back to Earth.

By the early 1960s, large observatories had been built all over the world. These are buildings where huge telescopes are kept. The telescopes are powerful enough to observe distant stars.

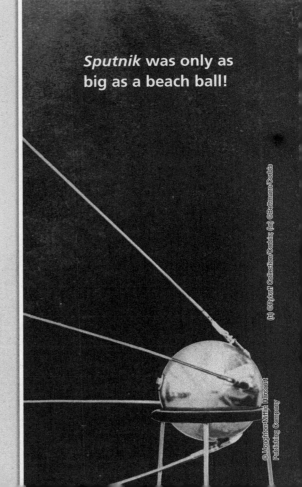

Sputnik was only as big as a beach ball!

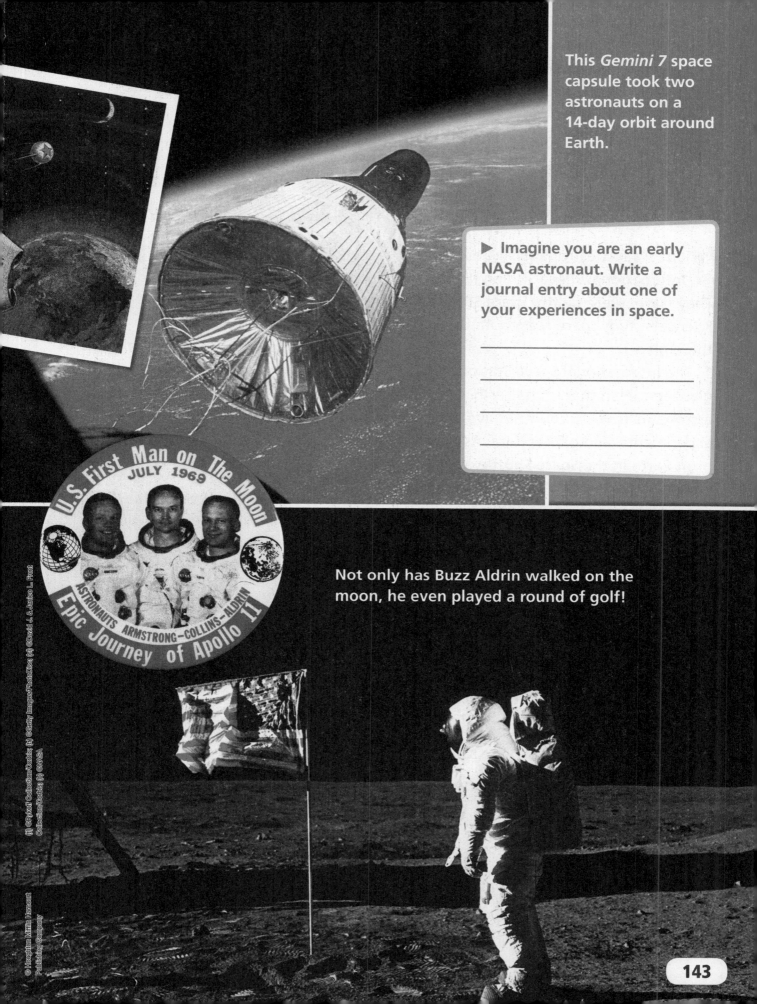

This *Gemini 7* space capsule took two astronauts on a 14-day orbit around Earth.

▶ Imagine you are an early NASA astronaut. Write a journal entry about one of your experiences in space.

_____

_____

_____

_____

U.S. First Man on The Moon
JULY 1969
ASTRONAUTS ARMSTRONG–COLLINS–ALDRIN
Epic Journey of Apollo 11

Not only has Buzz Aldrin walked on the moon, he even played a round of golf!

TECHNOLOGY IN SPACE!

Today, a few astronauts live on the International Space Station (ISS). They travel there on the Space Shuttle. Scientists study space from both of these places.

The International Space Station is a giant space lab that orbits Earth. There, astronauts from 16 countries live, conduct experiments, and gather data. Astronauts orbit Earth in the Space Shuttle, too.

Another example of technology orbits in space. It is the Hubble Space Telescope. It takes pictures of space that are not possible to get from Earth.

People have not traveled any farther than the moon. But space probes have travelled past the edge of our solar system. The first space probes visited nearby planets such as Mars and Venus. Most space probes just fly by planets. They take pictures and send them back to Earth. *Viking I* was the first space probe to successfully land on Mars in 1976. Since then, other space probes have landed on Mars' surface.

> ▶ The International Space Station is covered with solar panels. What do you think they are used for?

_____

_____

_____

Astronauts from space shuttle missions have helped to build the ISS right in space!

The Hubble Space Telescope takes pictures of faraway galaxies. Here are just a few of Hubble's amazing pictures.

▶ **Think about what astronomers could view with early telescopes. How does it compare with what can be viewed with the Hubble Space Telescope? Give three examples.**

_____

_____

_____

_____

FLORIDA'S ROLE IN SPACE

Powerful rockets launch from the Kennedy Space Center in Florida. This huge complex is America's gateway to space.

ACTIVE **READING** As you read these pages, underline sentences that tell the main ideas.

The Space Age began in Florida in the early 1960s. Then, Florida's space center was known as Cape Canaveral. Each of the moon missions launched from Florida's coast. In 1963, NASA's headquarters was renamed in honor of President John F. Kennedy.

Florida is a good location for the space center. Why? Florida has some of the fairest weather in the country. Rockets can't be launched in bad weather.

Beyond the Book

Research ways that space exploration has affected the economy and culture of Florida. Develop a presentation to share with your class.

146

One of the most important buildings at the Kennedy Space Center is the Vehicle Assembly Building. Construction on this giant building began in 1963. Many people came to Florida to help with its construction. Since then, hundreds of rockets have been built here.

Many people work at Kennedy Space Center. Engineers design and build rockets. Scientists study data brought back by astronauts and space probes.

Every year, visitors come to Florida to visit the space center. It's an important tourist attraction.

 ## DO THE **MATH**

Solve a Two-Step Problem

It takes the shuttle about 90 min to make one trip around Earth. About how many trips can it make in 24 hr? (Hint: 1 hr = 60 min)

_____

_____

The Atlas V rocket launches a spacecraft at the Kennedy Space Center.

Scientists build space vehicles in the Vehicle Assembly Building.

The Kennedy Space Center welcomes visitors from all over the world.

SPACE TECHNOLOGY IN EVERY HOME

Much of the technology used in our homes comes from the space program. These technologies are known as space "spin-offs."

Astronauts on the moon needed tools to do many tasks. So scientists developed cordless power tools. Today, we use cordless power tools in our homes.

▶ Why do you think astronauts cannot use a drill with a cord in space?

_____

_____

_____

Did you know that the design of the athletic shoes you wear is a space spin-off? Astronauts needed boots to stay on the surface of the moon where there is no gravity. With the boots, they could walk and jump around on the moon. The soles of today's athletic shoes are based on these moon boots. The soles improve how you jump and run.

Have you ever cooked something in a nonstick frying pan? The material used to coat the inside of pots and pans is another space spin-off.

The beverage cooler you take on picnics is based on a space cooling system. Astronauts also need a way to keep food in space, so along came freeze-dried foods. Just add water and you've got a meal. Perhaps you have some freeze-dried fruit in your cereal!

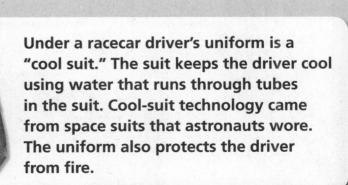

Under a racecar driver's uniform is a "cool suit." The suit keeps the driver cool using water that runs through tubes in the suit. Cool-suit technology came from space suits that astronauts wore. The uniform also protects the driver from fire.

Sum It Up »

Read the summary. Write the numbers from the list below the summary into the correct box at the bottom of the page.

Travel to space and space technology have changed our lives. Early astronomers began to study space with telescopes. Later, technologies put people in space and on the moon. Today, the space program has affected our lives in many ways.

1. athletic shoes
2. the Hubble Space Telescope
3. missions to the moon
4. jobs in the space program
5. Galileo

6. space probes
7. freeze-dried foods
8. International Space Station
9. Space Shuttle

Astronomy	Space Travel	Space in Our Lives

Name _____

Vocabulary Review

1 Use the words in the box to complete each sentence.

1. A person who studies space is an _____.

2. _____ was an early astronomer.

3. A cordless power tool is an example of a _____.

4. The first satellite in space was _____.

5. The _____ is a large telescope that orbits in space.

6. A _____ is a vehicle that moves through space but is controlled from Earth.

7. A tool used to make objects appear larger is a _____.

8. The _____ space center is in Florida.

telescope	space probe	Kennedy	Sputnik
Hubble	**Galileo**	**astronomer**	**spin-off**

* Key Lesson Vocabulary

2 Draw stars you might see with your eyes. Then draw stars that an astronomer might see with the Hubble Space Telescope.

Your Eyes

The Hubble

3 All of the pictures below show space spin-offs. Tell how each one has affected your life.

_____   _____   _____

_____   _____   _____

4 Imagine that it's 1969. You are the first astronaut to land on the moon. What would your first words be? Write them below.

_____

_____

 **Take It Home!** Interview an older relative about what Central Florida was like before NASA and the Kennedy Space Center. How has the area changed? Compare what you learn to what Central Florida is like today.

SC.4.N.3.1 Explain that models can be three dimensional, two dimensional, an explanation in your mind, or a computer model.

S.T.E.M.
ENGINEERING & TECHNOLOGY
Space Exploration

Typically, engineering design problems have many solutions. An engineer often needs to find a balance among many trade-offs to get the best solution. A *trade-off* is the giving up of one design feature to make another design feature better. The charts below show trade-off analyses for spacecraft with and without crew. The benefits and drawbacks of some major design features of each kind of mission are shown. You decide which one should blast off.

Spacecraft with Crew

Design Feature	Benefit	Drawback
living space for crew	people onboard to fix problems and run difficult science experiments	greater cost to build and to fuel; increased weight during liftoff (must store air, food, and water)
heat shield for reentry to Earth's atmosphere	safe return of crew; reusable ship	more fuel needed; less space for everything else

Spacecraft without Crew

Design Feature	Benefit	Drawback
smaller, lighter	less fuel needed; costs less to launch	less room for instruments
no living space for crew	no need to store air, food, water	no one to fix problems or watch experiments
large energy supply to last many years in space	can learn about faraway objects	spacecraft doesn't return to Earth; it cannot be reused

YOU DECIDE

Which type of spacecraft works best for space exploration? Use information from the chart to explain your answer.

_____

_____

_____

© Houghton Mifflin Harcourt Publishing Company

(l) ©StockTrek/Getty (r) ©NASA

153

Analyze Trade-offs

Engineers think about trade-offs before designing a spacecraft. Sometimes, the trade-offs lead them to conclude that a particular solution is not worth trying.

Suppose a crew wants new space suits. Use the features and trade-offs of the old and new space suits to answer the questions below.

Old Space Suit		New Space Suit	
Design Feature	**Trade-off**	**Design Feature**	**Trade-off**
thick space suit protects astronaut against extreme temperatures and debris	hard to move around in	thinner space suit lighter and easier to move around in	may not protect as well as the old suit against extreme temperatures or debris
sturdy material and strong joints	difficult to put on quickly	has newer technologies built in	all technologies may not have been tested in space

What is the most important feature of a space suit?

_____

_____

Do you think the benefits of the new space suit outweigh its trade-offs? Why or why not?

_____

_____

_____

_____

© Houghton Mifflin Harcourt Publishing Company

Design It:
Build a Sundial

What time is it? Most likely, you'll find the answer by looking at a watch or another electronic device. However, thousands of years ago, people used the sun to tell time.

A sundial is a device that uses the position of the sun to tell time. It has an upright rod that casts a shadow onto a number scale that identifies the time of day.

Now that you know about sundials, can you build one, too? Think about how a sundial is used. What materials would work best? A good sundial design should be accurate to within a half hour of the actual time.

Sundial

S.T.E.M. continued

What to Do:

1. Research sundials to learn how they use Earth's motion to tell time.

2. Identify everyday materials you could use to build your sundial.

3. Identify the design criteria your sundial must meet.

4. Draw a diagram of your design.

5. Build and test your design.

6. Use an electronic clock to test the accuracy of your sundial. How can you improve the sundial's performance?

7. If needed, redesign your sundial until it meets your design criteria.

8. Place your sundial outside and use it to tell time.

9. Keep a record of your work in your Science Notebook.

DESIGN PROCESS STEPS

1 Find a Problem
2 Plan & Build
3 Test & Improve
4 Redesign
5 Communicate

Name _____

Vocabulary Review

Use the terms in the box to complete the sentences.

> axis
> constellation
> moon phase
> orbit
> rotate

1. A change in the appearance of the moon's shape is

   known as a(n) _____.

2. When things turn like a top, they _____.

3. Earth turns around an imaginary line called

   a(n) _____.

4. The path that one object takes around another object in space

   is its _____.

5. A group of stars that seems to form a pattern in the night sky is

   a(n) _____.

Science Concepts

Fill in the letter of the choice that best answers the question.

6. One kind of modern calendar is a solar calendar. What is a solar calendar based on?

   (A) daily pattern of the sun

   (B) yearly pattern of the sun

   (C) weekly pattern of the sun

   (D) monthly pattern of the sun

7. A fourth-grader in Florida is doing an experiment in her science class. At the same time, a fourth-grader in China is getting a good night's sleep. What is responsible for it being daytime in Florida while it is nighttime in China?

   (F) Earth's rotation

   (G) Earth's revolution

   (H) moon's revolution

   (I) Earth's path as it orbits the sun

8. As Earth rotates, it is tilted on its axis. Which model correctly shows how much Earth tilts on its axis?

Ⓐ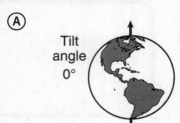
Tilt angle 0°

Ⓑ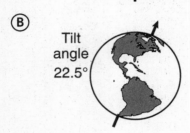
Tilt angle 22.5°

Ⓒ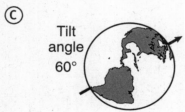
Tilt angle 60°

Ⓓ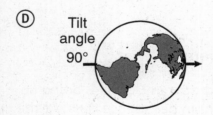
Tilt angle 90°

9. One day on Earth is 24 hours. Some planets have shorter days. Other planets have longer days. What determines the length of a planet's day?

Ⓕ moons   Ⓗ rotation
Ⓖ revolution   Ⓘ tilt

10. The data table shows how long it takes each planet to make one complete rotation and revolution. The numbers are in Earth days.

Planet	Time needed to make one complete rotation (Earth days)	Time needed to make one complete revolution (Earth days)
Mercury	58.6	87.96
Venus	243	224.7
Earth	1	365.26
Mars	1.02	687

According to the data table, which is correct?

Ⓐ Earth takes less time to orbit the sun than Mars.

Ⓑ Venus takes more time to orbit the sun than Mars.

Ⓒ Venus takes less time to orbit the sun than Mercury.

Ⓓ Mercury takes more time to orbit the sun than Earth.

Name _____

11. Ashley notices changes in the moon over the course of a month. Which of the following sequences could Ashley have seen?

Ⓕ

Full moon   New moon   Third quarter moon   First quarter moon

Ⓖ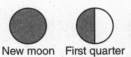

New moon   First quarter moon   Full moon   Third quarter moon

Ⓗ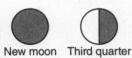

New moon   First quarter moon   New moon   Third quarter moon

Ⓘ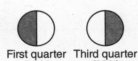

Full moon   New moon   First quarter moon   Third quarter moon

12. A modern Earth solar calendar year has 365 days divided into 12 months. Each month is about 30 days. On an imaginary moon of planet X, a month is 3 days shorter than an Earth month. About how many planet X lunar months will fit into an Earth calendar?

Ⓐ about 12.5   Ⓒ about 14.5

Ⓑ about 13.5   Ⓓ about 15.5

13. Sheena makes a list of different jobs people have in Florida. Which of these types of jobs probably increased the most when the space program was located in Florida?

Ⓕ school teaching

Ⓖ deep-sea fishing

Ⓗ citrus fruit farming

Ⓘ aircraft engineering

14. Technology developed for use in space can help us in other ways. Which type of technology on Earth is a spin-off of technology originally developed for space exploration?

Ⓐ radio   Ⓒ automobiles

Ⓑ cordless drill   Ⓓ light bulb

15. The illustration below shows an instrument used by many scientists. It was first used in the Netherlands in about 1608.

What types of objects can be seen with this instrument?

Ⓕ objects that are far away

Ⓖ objects that produce sound

Ⓗ objects that are very small

Ⓘ objects that move very fast

16. Some constellations are visible from different places on Earth only during part of the year. Why are certain constellations not visible everywhere on Earth all year long?

Ⓐ sun's rotation

Ⓑ Earth's rotation

Ⓒ sun's revolution

Ⓓ Earth's revolution

Apply Inquiry and Review the Big Idea

Write the answers to these questions.

17. The diagram below shows Earth, the moon, and the sun. This diagram is not drawn to scale.

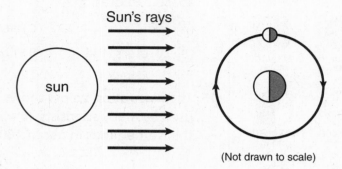

Sun's rays

sun

(Not drawn to scale)

Use the diagram to explain why you can see the moon from Earth.

_____

_____

_____

18. In the United States, how does the temperature on an August day and a January day usually compare? State a claim and explain your claim with reasoning.

_____

_____

_____

_____

_____

_____

Rocks, Minerals, and Resources

FLORIDA **BIG IDEA** 6

Earth Structures

Sand dunes form on Florida beaches.

© Dreamstime

I Wonder Why

The wind blows sand into formations called sand dunes. How did the sand form? *Turn the page to find out.*

Here's Why

Over time, wind and rain break down rock, forming these small particles that we call sand.

Essential Questions and Florida Benchmarks

LESSON 1
How Do Weathering and Erosion Shape Earth's Surface? 163
SC.4.E.6.4 Describe differences between physical weathering ... and erosion....

LESSON 2
What Are Minerals? 177
SC.4.E.6.2 Identify the physical properties of common earth-forming minerals, ... and recognize the role of minerals in the formation of rocks.

LESSON 3
What Are Properties of Minerals? 187
SC.4.E.6.2, SC.4.N.1.1, SC.4.N.1.3, SC.4.N.1.4, SC.4.N.1.5

LESSON 4
How Can Rocks Be Classified? 191
SC.4.E.6.1 Identify the three categories of rocks....

S.T.E.M. Engineering and Technology
Tools that Rock/Improvise It: Separating by Size 207
SC.4.N.1.8 Recognize that science involves creativity in designing experiments.

LESSON 5
Which Resources Are Found in Florida? 211
SC.4.E.6.3 Recognize that humans need resources found on Earth and that these are either renewable or nonrenewable.
SC.4.E.6.5 Investigate how technology and tools help ... humans to observe....
SC.4.E.6.6 Identify resources available in Florida....

PEOPLE IN SCIENCE
Elvia Niebla & Lena Qiying Ma 223
SC.4.E.6.5, SC.4.N.2.1

Unit 4 Benchmark Review 225

Science Notebook

Before you begin each lesson, write your thoughts about the Essential Question.

SC.4.E.6.4 Describe the basic differences between physical weathering (breaking down of rock by wind, water, ice, temperature change, and plants) and erosion (movement of rock by gravity, wind, water, and ice).

LESSON **1**

ESSENTIAL **QUESTION**

How Do Weathering and Erosion Shape Earth's Surface?

 Engage Your Brain

Find the answer to the following question in this lesson and record it here.

How do you think this arch formed?

_____

_____

_____

 ACTIVE **READING**

Lesson Vocabulary

List the terms. As you learn about each one, make notes in the Interactive Glossary.

_____

_____

_____

_____

Cause and Effect

Some ideas in this lesson are connected by a cause-and-effect relationship. Why something happens is a cause. What happens as a result of something else is an effect. Active readers look for effects by asking themselves, What happened? They look for causes by asking why it happened.

What can Break a Boulder?

When you think of rocks, words like *hard* and *solid* may come to mind. You may think rocks can't ever break, but that's not true. Rocks can be cracked and crushed by mere wind and rain.

ACTIVE **READING** As you read these pages, underline all of the different things that can cause a rock to break down.

The roots of this tree broke apart the rock.

When it rains, water can get into the cracks of rocks.

When water freezes, it expands. This widens the cracks.

When water freezes again, it pushes the cracks in the rocks even wider. When this happens many times, the rock breaks apart.

The process of rock breaking apart is called **weathering**. Many different things can cause weathering. Gravity can cause rocks to fall down a cliff and break apart. Flowing water can cause rocks to tumble and scrape against each other. Sand blown by wind can scrape against rocks.

Living things can also cause weathering. A tree's roots can grow in a small crack in a rock. As the roots grow, it can push the rock apart until the rock breaks. Animals may dig up rocks, causing the rocks to be exposed to wind and rain.

Chemicals in water and rain that flow through and around rocks can also cause weathering. These chemicals can combine with the rock and change it so that it crumbles and wears away. Look at the statues on this page. Chemical weathering has already changed one of the statues.

WEATHERED

How will weathering change what this statue looks like?

Draw a picture to show the changes.

Rocks on the Move

Don't rocks just sit around in the sun all day?
No! Rocks can move—find out how.

Weathering is the beginning of a series of changes that often occurs to rocks on Earth's surface. The same wind and water that can cause weathering also can carry the broken bits of rock away. The process of moving weathered rock from one place to another is called **erosion** [uh•ROH•zhuhn].

The erosion of rock can be caused by many different natural processes. Moving water is one of the most common causes of erosion. The fast-moving water in this stream can shift or move large rocks near the top of the mountain. Together with gravity, water can cause the rocks to move downhill.

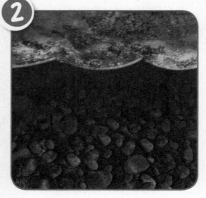

The water pulls the larger pieces of weathered rock along the river's bottom. As the water slows down, it has less energy. It cannot move the largest rocks and pebbles. These are left behind as the water moves on. The dropping of weathered rock by wind or moving water is known as **deposition** [dep•uh•ZISH•uhn].

What happens next?

These pictures show the Yangtze River before and after a dam was built across the river. How do you think the dam affects the movement of sediment?

BEFORE

_____

_____

_____

_____

AFTER

3

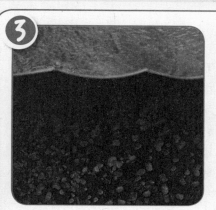

As the water in a river continues to slow down, more bits of weathered rock are dropped. This happens because slow-moving water has less energy than fast-moving water. So, slow-moving water can carry only very small pieces of rock, such as sand and silt. These bits of rock are called sediment.

4

When rivers reach the ocean, they slow down even more. As they slow down, much of the remaining sediment in the water is dropped. Over time, the sediment piles up near the mouth of the river. It forms a landform called a _delta_.

3

4

Wind

The wind is just moving air, so what can it do? A lot—wind blows sand and other sediment away.

Wind can carry away soil and other sediment. Where does all of it go? Some particles are not carried very far. Others can be carried thousands of miles away. Sand from the Sahara Desert, in Africa, is sometimes carried all the way across the Atlantic Ocean to the United States!

Winds may deposit a lot of sand in one area. Over time, the sand builds up and forms dunes. Sand dunes are often found near sandy beaches.

▶ Do you think the mushroom rock shown below formed quickly or slowly? Explain.

_____

_____

_____

_____

_____

_____

This rock, called a mushroom rock, began as a big boulder. Wind slowly eroded the rock, leaving the mushroom shape behind.

EXPOSED BY WIND!

Ice

Can you imagine an ice cube the size of a city? Some chunks of ice are even larger than that!

ACTIVE READING As you read the text, circle two effects glaciers have on Earth's surface.

Huge sheets of ice are called *glaciers*. Glaciers are found in very cold places. You may think that because a glacier is made of ice, it does not move. However, the ice flows like a very slow river. As the glacier flows, it can pick up rocks as large as boulders.

It also picks up the rock and soil under it, causing erosion. When a glacier begins to melt, the rocks and sediment drop out. The dropped-off sediment forms many different features, including hills called *moraines* [muh•RAYNZ].

A glacier made these grooves in the rock.

CARVED BY ICE!

Glacier Bay, Alaska

Gravity

Gravity pulls a ball thrown into the air down, it pulls you down, it pulls rain and snow down—it can even pull rocks down.

Just as gravity causes a ball to fall back to the ground, it causes rocks and sediment to slide down mountains and cliffs. Gravity can even cause huge chunks of rock and soil to slide down a slope all at once. This is called a *landslide*. Landslides happen a lot in mountain ranges.

A hill's slope affects how gravity will act on it. If the slope is steep, rocks are much more likely to fall than if it is not steep.

 DO THE **MATH**

Measure Angles

The steepness of a slope is measured in degrees. Use a protractor to measure the three slopes. Record their angles and draw a star next to the steepest slope.

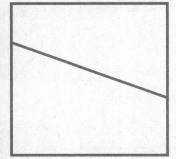

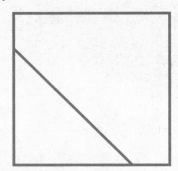

_____   _____   _____

Water

Water carries dirt down the drain when you wash your hands. It also carries rocks and sediment down a river or along a beach.

ACTIVE READING As you read the text, circle two effects of water erosion.

Flowing water has energy. That energy can carry sediment down a river. Ocean waves have a lot of energy. Waves crash on rocks along a shore, causing rocks to break apart. The waves cut cliffs and cause caves to form. Waves can also carry away sediment and deposit it in other places. Over time, a beach may form.

This shape of rock is called a *sea arch*. It forms when waves erode rock, cutting all the way through it.

WASHED AWAY BY WATER!

Sum It Up »

Use the information in the summary to complete the cause-and-effect graphic organizers

Over time, wind, water, ice, gravity, plants, and animals cause rocks to break down into smaller pieces. Bits of broken-down rock, or sediments, are eroded away by such agents as wind and flowing water. Eventually, the sediments are deposited. Deposited sediments form landforms, such as deltas and sand dunes.

1

1. Water enters the cracks in a rock and freezes into ice.

→ _____
_____

2

_____
_____
_____

→ Sediments are deposited at the mouth of the river and form a delta.

Name _____

Vocabulary Review

1 Use the words in the box to complete the puzzle.

1. | grineatewh | ———————— the process that causes rocks to break down into smaller pieces

2. | ndoeiitosp | ———————— the process that causes eroded sediments to be dropped off in another place

3. | aoldmnfm | ———————— a land feature such as a delta or a sand dune

4. | tnseidem | ———————— broken-down pieces of rock

5. | neroiso | ———————— the process that carries away weathered rock

6. | iceglar | ———————— a large sheet of flowing ice

7. | ytarvig | ———————— a force that causes landslides to occur

| deposition* | erosion* | glacier |
| gravity | landform | sediment* |
| weathering* |

* Key Lesson Vocabulary

Apply Concepts

2 Make a list of things that can weather rock.

_____   _____

_____   _____

_____   _____

_____   _____

_____   _____

3 Explain how a plant can cause a rock to weather.

_____

_____

_____

_____

4 Circle the body of water that could erode the largest sediments.

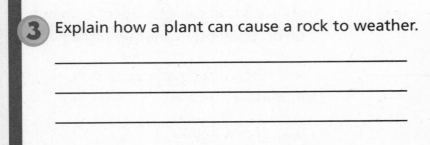

5 For each landform shown, write the word that tells what caused the landform to form. Choose from the list of words below.

wind   *ice*   *gravity*   *water*

_____   _____

_____   _____

_____   _____

6 For each landform below, write whether the landform was formed by erosion or by deposition. Describe how you know your answer is correct.

_____
_____
_____
_____

_____
_____
_____
_____

_____
_____
_____
_____

_____
_____
_____
_____

 See *ScienceSaurus*® for more information about weathering and erosion.

SC.4.E.6.2 Identify the physical properties of common earth-forming minerals, including hardness, color, luster, cleavage, and streak color, and recognize the role of minerals in the formation of rocks.

LESSON **2**

ESSENTIAL **QUESTION**

What Are Minerals?

Engage Your Brain

Find the answer to the following question in this lesson and record it here.

You find a clear mineral that can't be scratched by any other minerals. It has a glassy luster. What mineral did you probably find?

_____

_____

_____

_____

📖 ACTIVE **READING**

Lesson Vocabulary

List the terms. As you learn about each one, make notes in the Interactive Glossary.

_____

_____

_____

_____

Visual Aids

Charts, diagrams, and photos add information to the text that appears on the page with them. Active readers pause their reading to review each visual aid and decide how the information in the visual aid adds to what is provided in the running text.

What Are Minerals?

What do copper, table salt, and diamonds have in common? They are all minerals!

A **mineral** [MIN•er•uhl] is any nonliving solid that has a crystal form. All minerals form in nature—under the ground, in caves, and even in the air. Plastic and bricks are not minerals; they are made by people. There are over 4,700 different minerals found on Earth.

When you think of crystals, you may think of ones like those in caves. Yet not all crystals look like those. Mineral crystals come in different shapes, but there is something that is the same. The particles in a crystal combine to form a shape that is repeated over and over again. It is this repeated structure that defines a crystal.

Minerals are the same in another way. Each mineral is made up of the same set of nonliving things called elements. For example, the mineral calcite is always made of the elements calcium, carbon, and oxygen. Rubies are always made of aluminum and oxygen. Diamonds are always made of carbon.

 DO THE **MATH**

Identify Shapes

One characteristic that can help you identify minerals is crystal shape. Draw a line from the name of each shape to the crystal that best matches that shape.

Square Pyramid   **Square Prism**   **Hexagonal Prism**

Pyrite   Fluorite   Beryl

Which Mineral Is Which?

With more that 4,700 minerals in the world, how can you tell one mineral from another?

ACTIVE READING On this page, underline two mineral properties.

Hardness is one property used to identify minerals. *Hardness* is a mineral's ability to scratch another mineral. In 1812, a scientist named Friedrich Mohs [mohz] developed a scale to compare the hardnesses of different minerals.

On the Mohs scale, a mineral with a higher number can scratch another mineral with a lower or equal number. The softest minerals score a 1. Every other mineral can scratch minerals with a hardness of 1. The hardest mineral—a diamond—scores a 10 on the Mohs scale. A diamond can't be scratched by any mineral except another diamond.

Another property used to tell one mineral from another is luster. *Luster* describes how minerals reflect light. The minerals copper, gold, and silver each have a metallic luster. Talc and gypsum [JIP•suhm] each have an earthy luster.

The Mohs Scale

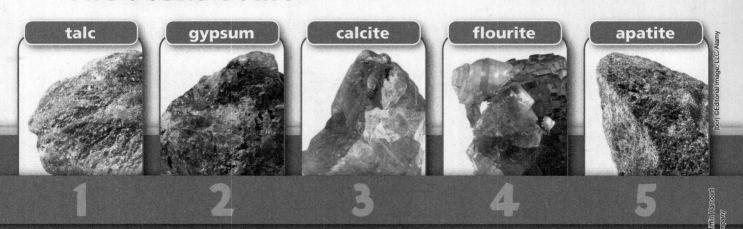

talc	gypsum	calcite	flourite	apatite
1	2	3	4	5

▶ Suppose you found this bright purple mineral. How would you describe its luster?

_____

_____

The mineral can be scratched by diamond but not by feldspar. What could the mineral's hardness be?

_____

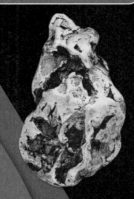

metallic luster

earthy luster

Luster can be described using words such as *metallic*, *earthy*, and *glassy*.

glassy luster

You can scratch minerals with a hardness of 2 or less with a fingernail. You can scratch minerals with a hardness of 6 or less with a steel nail.

feldspar	quartz	topaz	corundum	diamond

6	7	8	9	10

Magnetite attracts things that have iron in them.

Unique Properties of Minerals

You can use all sorts of properties to identify minerals. Some are more useful, some less. But use all of them, and you'll probably identify the mineral.

ACTIVE **READING** Underline the name of the mineral that has a greenish-black streak.

The color of a mineral may vary, but its streak is always the same.

You've learned that mineral crystals come in different shapes. Mineral crystals also break in a certain way. The way a mineral breaks can be used to identify it. When some minerals break, the broken sides are smooth and straight. Minerals that break this way have *cleavage*. Minerals that do not break along smooth lines have *fracture*.

To identify a mineral, you can rub the mineral against a white tile called a streak plate. The color left behind is called the mineral's *streak*. Sometimes a streak is the same color as the mineral itself. But this is not true for many minerals. Pyrite has a gold color, but its streak is greenish-black.

A mineral can come in different colors. Corundum [kuh•**RUHN**•duhm] crystals can be red, blue, green, yellow, purple, or brown. Yet no matter what color the corundum crystal is, its streak is always white. Because of this, streak color is useful when identifying a mineral.

Some minerals have other properties. Calcite and fluorite glow under a black light. Calcite also fizzes when you put a drop of vinegar on it. Quartz can conduct electricity.

This piece of mica [MY•kuh] has cleavage. It breaks into thin, flat sheets.

Confused by Color?

Look at the minerals shown here. They are all quartz. How could you show that they are all quartz? What tests could you use?

_____

_____

_____

_____

Sum It Up »

Read the summary statements. Then match each statement with the correct image.

1 Minerals are nonliving solids that have crystal shapes. Garnet crystals are shaped almost like soccer balls. ____

A

2 A mineral's hardness can help to identify it. Fluorite has a hardness of 4. It can be scratched with a steel nail. ____

B
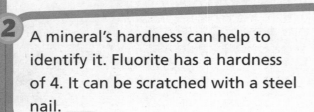

3 Different minerals reflect light in different ways. This property is called luster. Gold has a metallic luster. ____

C

4 Minerals that break in straight lines have cleavage. The mineral mica breaks into thin, flat sheets. ____

D

5 You can see a mineral's streak color using a streak plate. Each mineral has a characteristic streak color. Graphite has a black to gray streak. ____

E

Vocabulary Review

1 Use the words in the box to complete each sentence. Then use the circled letters to answer the question below.

| cleavage | crystal | hardness | luster | minerals* | streak |

* Key Lesson Vocabulary

1. You can find out a mineral's (O)_ _ _ _ _ _ _ _ by seeing what other minerals it can scratch.

2. A nonliving solid that has a _ _ _ _ _ (O)_ form is called a mineral.

3. Gold, silver, copper, and pyrite each have a metallic (O)_ _ _ _ _ _ .

4. Fluorite, talc, diamond, gold, and quartz are all examples of _ (O)_ _ _ _ _ _ _.

5. The color left behind when a mineral is rubbed across a white tile is its _ (O)_ _ _ _ _ .

6. A mineral that breaks along straight, smooth lines is said to have _ _ _ (O)_ _ _ _ _ .

Question:

Which mineral is also known as table salt?

O O O O O O

I "ROCK" AT WORD PLAY!

Apply Concepts

2 Make a list of the different properties that can be used to identify a mineral.

_____   _____

_____   _____

_____   _____

_____   _____

3 Magnetite has a metallic or earthy luster, a gray-black streak, and a hardness of 5–7. Circle the mineral that is most likely magnetite.

Mohs Hardness Scale	
1	Talc
2	Gypsum
3	Calcite
4	Fluorite
5	Apatite
6	Feldspar
7	Quartz
8	Topaz
9	Corundum
10	Diamond

This mineral can scratch talc but not calcite.

This mineral can scratch apatite but not quartz.

This mineral can scratch apatite but not quartz.

4 Which part of the description helped you identify the mineral?

_____

_____

_____

5 Which mineral did you rule out first? How?

_____

_____

 Using building blocks, chenille sticks, or other items, build a model of a crystal. Your crystal can be any shape, but remember that crystals have a repeating shape.

SC.4.E.6.2 Identify the physical properties of common earth-forming minerals...
SC.4.N.1.1 Raise questions... and generate appropriate explanations... SC.4.N.1.3 Explain that science does not always follow a rigidly defined method... SC.4.N.1.4 Attempt reasonable answers to scientific questions and cite evidence in support. SC.4.N.1.5 Compare the methods and results... done by other classmates.

INQUIRY
LESSON 3

Name _____

ESSENTIAL **QUESTION**

What Are Properties of Minerals?

Materials

mineral samples
streak plate
steel nail
penny

EXPLORE

If minerals look the same to you, then it's time to take a closer look! In this activity, you will classify some minerals by their properties.

Before You Begin—Preview the Steps

① Observe each mineral sample. Write a word that best describes each sample's luster.

② Use each mineral to draw a line across the streak plate. Record the color of the streak.

③ **CAUTION:** Handle the nail carefully. It's sharp! Observe each mineral sample. Write a word that best describes each sample's luster. Classify each mineral sample based on luster, streak, and hardness. Test the hardness of each mineral. Try to scratch each one with your fingernail, the steel nail, the penny, and the other mineral samples. Record your observations. (Note: A fingernail has a hardness of 2, a penny has a hardness of 3, and a steel nail has a hardness of 5.).

④ Classify each mineral sample based on luster, streak, and hardness.

Set a Purpose

Why is it important to know how to classify things?

_____

_____

_____

Think About the Procedure

Name three mineral properties you will be using in this activity.

_____

Record Your Data

In the table below, record your observations. Beneath the table, describe how you would classify the minerals into groups, using one of the properties in the table.

Mineral Sample	Luster	Streak	Hardness

Name _____

Draw Conclusions

How did you classify the mineral samples?

_____

_____

_____

_____

_____

_____

Did you classify your minerals in the same way as other students? Why or why not?

_____

_____

_____

_____

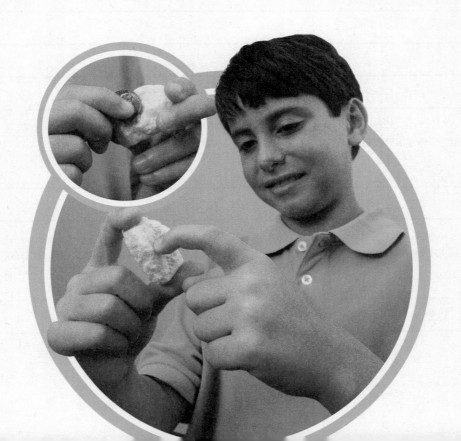

Claims • Evidence • Reasoning

1. Interpret your data. Write a claim about which mineral that you tested is the hardest and which is the softest. Cite evidence that supports your claim and explain why it supports the claim.

_____

_____

_____

_____

2. Based on your observations, write a claim about which property, or properties, are most helpful in identifying a mineral.

_____

3. Give evidence and reasons that support your claim and explain how they support the claim.

_____

_____

_____

_____

_____

4. What are some other ways minerals can be classified?

_____

_____

5. What other questions would you like to ask about the properties of minerals?

_____

_____

SC.4.E.6.1 Identify the three categories of rocks: igneous (formed from molten rock); sedimentary (pieces of other rocks and fossilized organisms); and metamorphic (formed from heat and pressure).

LESSON 4

ESSENTIAL QUESTION

How Can Rocks Be Classified?

 Engage Your Brain

Find the answer to the following question in this lesson and record it here.

Mount Rushmore National Memorial in South Dakota was carved out of granite that formed from cooled magma. What type of rock matches this description?

_____

_____

_____

_____

 ACTIVE **READING**

Lesson Vocabulary

List the terms. As you learn about each one, make notes in the Interactive Glossary.

_____

_____

_____

_____

Sequence

Many ideas in this lesson are connected by a sequence, or order, that describes the steps in a process. Active readers stay focused on the sequence when they mark the transition from one step in a process to another. Focus on the sequence of formation as you read about different classifications of rocks.

Gabbro forms below Earth's surface as magma cools slowly. It contains large crystals of the mineral quartz.

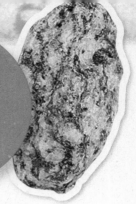

Like gabbro, granite forms below Earth's surface and has large mineral crystals.

Igneous Rock

A volcano erupts. Hot lava sprays into the air and flows over the ground. As lava cools, it hardens. It's a rock factory in production mode. What type of rock forms this way?

ACTIVE **READING** As you read these two pages, **underline** the sentences that describe how igneous rocks form.

Just what is a rock? A **rock** is a natural solid that is made of one or more minerals. Rocks are classified by how they form. The three types of rocks are igneous, sedimentary, and metamorphic.

One way that rock forms is when melted rock, called magma or lava, cools and hardens. Rock that forms when magma or lava harden is called **igneous rock** [IG•nee•uhs]. Igneous rock can form deep inside Earth as magma slowly cools. It can also form on Earth's surface when a volcano erupts and the lava cools.

Basalt has very small mineral crystals. It forms at Earth's surface and is the most common igneous rock on Earth.

Basalt columns in Ireland

Rhyolite forms as lava cools quickly at Earth's surface. It has small mineral crystals.

An igneous rock's appearance gives clues about where it formed. When magma cools slowly beneath Earth's surface, large mineral crystals form. The rock that forms from these minerals has crystals that you can see with the unaided eye. Gabbro and granite are examples of rocks that form this way. When lava at Earth's surface cools quickly, mineral grains do not have time to grow. As a result, igneous rocks that form at Earth's surface, such as rhyolite and basalt, contain small mineral crystals. To study the small crystals in basalt, you need a magnifying glass or, sometimes, a microscope.

Clues from Crystals

Look at the two igneous rocks shown here. Which rock cooled more quickly? How do you know? Infer how each rock formed.

Porphyry   **Obsidian**

_____

_____

_____

_____

_____

_____

Lava cools very quickly at Earth's surface. Mineral crystals have little time to form and remain small.

The temperature of magma can range from 700 °C (1,292 °F) to 1,200 °C (2,192 °F). Below Earth's surface, magma cools more slowly than it does at or near the surface. Because it cools more slowly, mineral crystals have time to form and become large.

Sedimentary Rock

Rocks are broken by ice, wind, and water. The pieces are moved from place to place and fall like a gentle rain out of the water and wind that carry them. How can those pieces form another kind of rock?

ACTIVE READING As you read the next page, write *1*, *2*, and *3* in the margin next to the sentences that give the sequence in which sedimentary rock forms.

What would happen if you placed a flower under a stack of books? Eventually, the weight of the books would flatten the flower. The same thing happens to deposited sediment. *Sediment* is particles of weathered rock. **Sedimentary rock** [sed•uh•**MEN**•tuh•ree] forms from sediment that gets cemented together under pressure.

Sediment from weathered and eroded rock collects in loose layers.

More layers of sediment are deposited on top. The additional weight presses on the layers underneath.

Over time, the sediment at the bottom becomes cemented, or glued, together.

Rock salt forms from salt left behind when salt water evaporates. The main mineral in rock salt is halite. It is one source of the salt you sprinkle on your food.

(bg) ©Kerrick James/Alamy

Conglomerate forms from pebble-sized particles with smooth, round edges.

As layers of sediment are deposited, bottom layers get pressed together by the weight of the layers above. Air and water in the spaces between the sediment layers are squeezed out. Over time, sediment becomes cemented together and forms sedimentary rock.

Sandstone, shale, and conglomerate are distinguished by the size of the sediment they contain. Shale is made of very fine sediment. Sandstones have larger sediment than shale does.

Conglomerates contain even larger sediment. Sometimes sedimentary rock contains fossils, too. A *fossil* is the remains or the signs or trace of a living thing, such as a bone, a shell, a leaf imprint, or a fossil footprint.

Some sedimentary rock forms through chemical processes. Rock salt and limestone are two types of sedimentary rock that form when minerals dissolved in water come out of solution.

Limestone is often formed from the shells of animals that live in the sea. These shells are made up of the mineral calcite. When the animals die, the shells are left behind. They are crushed into sand-sized particles, which become cemented together. Sometimes within the limestone, you can find whole shell fossils.

Where Are Fossils Found?

Why aren't fossils found in igneous rock?

_____

_____

_____

Metamorphic Rock

Squeeze and squeeze and squeeze and squeeze—then add a little, or a lot, of heat—and you get a different kind of rock. How do pressure and temperature change the rock?

ACTIVE **READING** As you read these two pages, write a P next to the paragraph that explains how metamorphic rocks form.

Rock that forms when earth processes change the texture and the mineral content of rock is called **metamorphic rock**. Metamorphic rock can form as a result of high pressure, high temperature, a combination of high temperature and high pressure, or when super-hot fluids such as water come into contact with rock. The word *metamorphic* [met•uh•**MAWR**•fik] comes from the Greek word that means "to change form." The temperature at which metamorphic rock forms is never high enough to melt the rock.

Marble and quartzite are examples of metamorphic rocks. Marble forms when increased temperature and pressure act on the sedimentary rock limestone. Marble is used in buildings and carved sculptures. Quartzite can form when sandstone is exposed to heat and pressure. Quartzite is used in construction of roof tiles or floors.

Most of the changes that cause rock to become metamorphic rock happen deep inside Earth. That is why most rocks you find are igneous or sedimentary, not metamorphic.

Shale is a type of sedimentary rock that forms from very fine sediment.

With high pressure and somewhat increased temperature, the layers of shale are flattened and the structures and minerals within the rock change. Shale becomes the metamorphic rock slate.

With even greater temperatures and pressure, minerals in slate can become other minerals. The way they are arranged in the rock can change. The rock can break easily along the planes where the minerals have lined up. In this way, slate can become schist, another type of metamorphic rock.

Mountains can form when two large pieces of Earth's crust push against each other. The force that pushes the mountains up also causes rocks in the growing mountains to change. Pressure builds up. Rock layers may bend, twist, and break under the pressure. Over time, many of the rocks become metamorphic rocks. You can see such metamorphic rock exposed in some mountain ranges and in areas like the Piedmont in the eastern United States.

Under intense pressure, the minerals in schist separate into bands. New minerals may form, too. This new metamorphic rock is called gneiss [NYS].

DO THE MATH

Use Fractions and Percentages

This circle graph shows the relative amounts of different kinds of rock on Earth's surface.

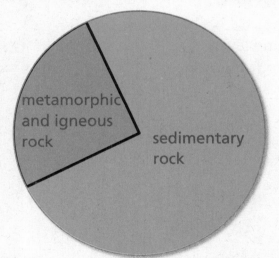

metamorphic and igneous rock

sedimentary rock

1. What fraction of Earth's surface is sedimentary rock?

_____

_____

2. Ninety-five percent of igneous rocks and metamorphic rocks are below Earth's surface. Why is this true?

_____

_____

_____

The twisted rock in this landform was formed by heat and pressure.

The Rock Cycle

Once a rock, always a rock? Well, not exactly. After rock forms, it does not stay the same forever. The rock may be broken down by water and wind. It may be heated and squeezed or melted by pressure inside Earth.

ACTIVE **READING** On the diagram, draw a star next to the arrow that shows the sequence of how an igneous rock becomes a sedimentary rock.

Any type of rock can become any other type of rock. Let's take sedimentary rock as the example. After molten rock has cooled to form igneous rock, weathering and erosion can break down the rock to form sediment. The sediment is deposited and layers build up and become cemented over time to form rock.

© Houghton Mifflin Harcourt Publishing Company

Metamorphic rock can be broken down in the same way and become sediment, which in turn becomes rock. Not even sedimentary rock is safe! It too can be broken down, transported, and deposited to become new sedimentary rock.

In the same way, temperature and pressure can act on any type of rock to transform it into metamorphic rock. Any type of rock can be melted and then cooled to become igneous rock. The continuous process of rock changing from one type to another is known as the *rock cycle*.

The rock cycle diagram summarizes the processes that work to transform Earth's rock.

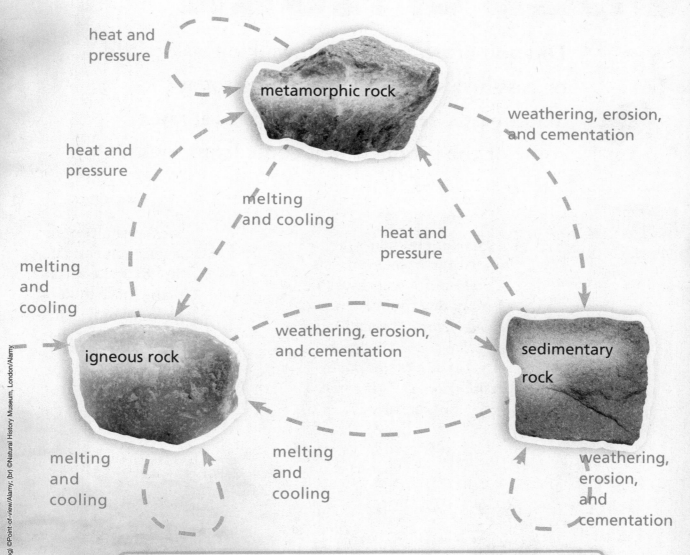

heat and pressure

metamorphic rock

weathering, erosion, and cementation

heat and pressure

melting and cooling

heat and pressure

melting and cooling

weathering, erosion, and cementation

igneous rock

sedimentary rock

melting and cooling

melting and cooling

weathering, erosion, and cementation

Changing Rocks

In the rock cycle diagram, trace all the arrows that show melting in red. Trace the arrows that show heat and pressure in green. Trace the arrows that show weathering, erosion, and cementation in brown.

Polished stones are used in jewelry and decorations.

Uses of Rock

Did you brush your teeth, walk on a sidewalk, or pass by a stone-faced building today? Toothpaste, cement, and buildings are just some of the products that come from rocks.

Many monuments are made of marble. Marble is a metamorphic rock used for building because it is relatively soft. The Taj Mahal in India, shown here, and the Lincoln Memorial in Washington, D.C., are made of marble.

Toothpaste contains several minerals that are extracted from rocks. These minerals have natural cavity-fighting properties.

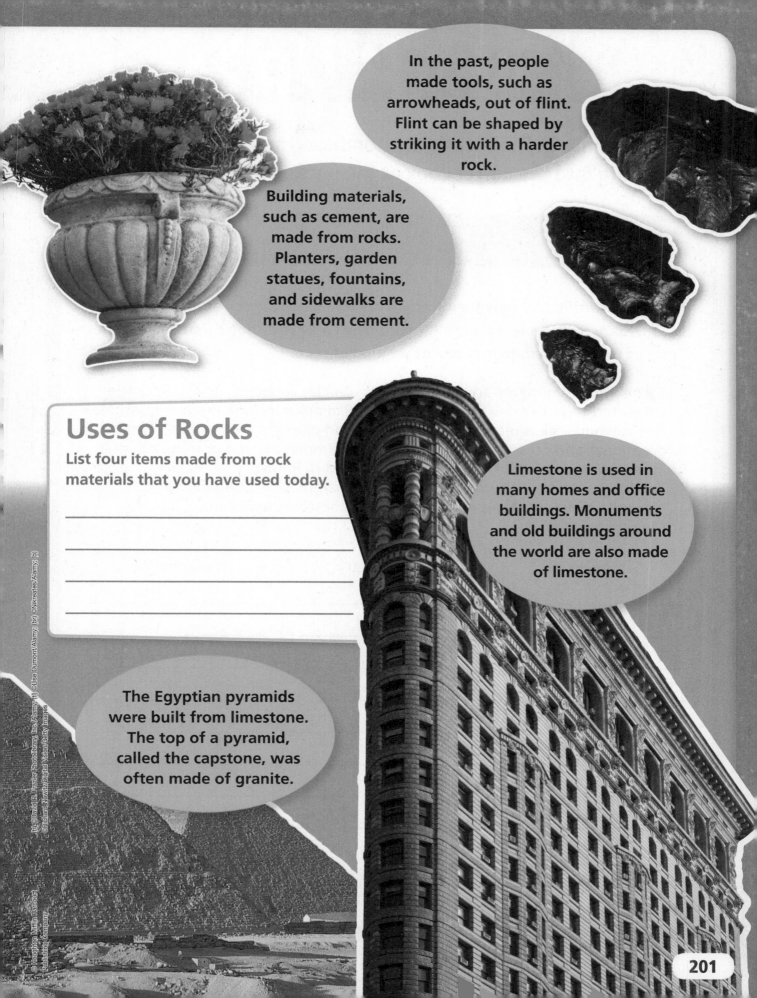

In the past, people made tools, such as arrowheads, out of flint. Flint can be shaped by striking it with a harder rock.

Building materials, such as cement, are made from rocks. Planters, garden statues, fountains, and sidewalks are made from cement.

Uses of Rocks

List four items made from rock materials that you have used today.

_____

_____

_____

_____

Limestone is used in many homes and office buildings. Monuments and old buildings around the world are also made of limestone.

The Egyptian pyramids were built from limestone. The top of a pyramid, called the capstone, was often made of granite.

Sum It Up »

Read the summary. Then place the numbered statements below the summary into the correct box at the bottom of the page.

Rocks are classified by how they form. The three kinds of rock are igneous rock, sedimentary rock, and metamorphic rock. The rock cycle shows that each of these kinds of rock can change into any other kind of rock.

1. Forms when sediments are cemented together
2. Forms when rock is placed under great heat and pressure
3. Forms when magma or lava cools
4. The longer it took to form, the larger its mineral crystals will be
5. May contain fossils

6. Can be found in mountain ranges
7. Examples include marble, quartzite, and gneiss
8. Examples include granite, obsidian, and rhyolite
9. Examples include sandstone, limestone, and shale

Igneous	Sedimentary	Metamorphic
_____	_____	_____
_____	_____	_____
_____	_____	_____
_____	_____	_____
_____	_____	_____
_____	_____	_____
_____	_____	_____

Name _____

Vocabulary Review

1 Draw a line from each term to its definition.

1. Rock

2. Igneous rock

3. Sedimentary rock

4. Metamorphic rock

5. Sediment

6. Rock cycle

7. Magma

8. Fossil

A. A rock that forms from bits of weathered rock

B. A rock that forms by great heat and pressure deep within Earth

C. A rock that forms from magma or lava

D. The natural processes that cause one kind of rock to change into another kind

E. Remains or traces of a once-living thing sometimes found in sedimentary rock

F. Bits of weathered rock

G. Melted rock below the ground

H. Made up of one or more minerals

Riddle

Why did the rock collector like his collection of metamorphic rocks so much?

_____

_____

Apply Concepts

2 What is the relationship between minerals and rocks?

_____

_____

_____

3 Draw a picture of a place on Earth where you think igneous rock would form.

4 Circle the rock below that is most likely a sedimentary rock. How do you know?

_____

5 In the three boxes below, draw and label diagrams showing how sedimentary rock forms.

Diagram 1　　　　　　Diagram 2　　　　　　Diagram 3

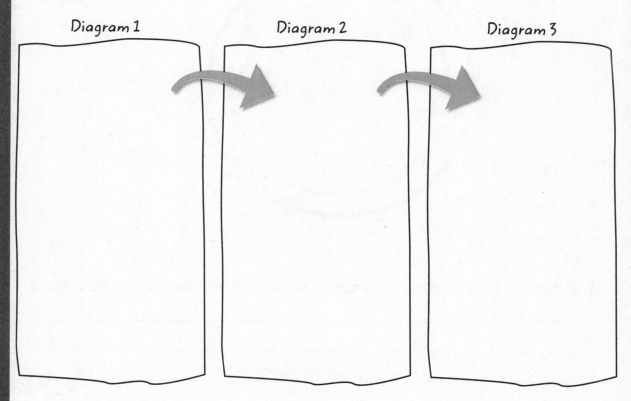

6 Circle the rock below that is most likely a metamorphic rock. How do you know?

_____

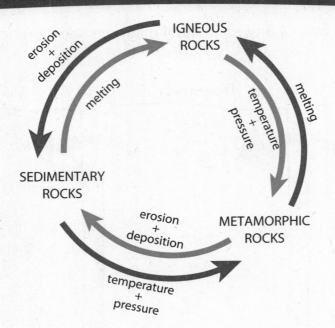

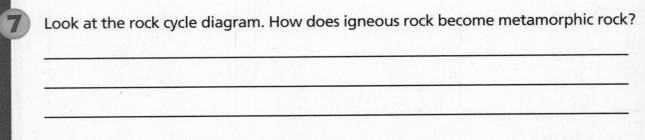

7 Look at the rock cycle diagram. How does igneous rock become metamorphic rock?

_____

_____

_____

_____

8 How does sedimentary rock become igneous rock?

_____

_____

_____

_____

Go on a hike or take a "walk" on the Internet with your family. Observe rocks you find. Try to identify the rocks as being igneous, sedimentary, or metamorphic.

SC.4.N.1.8 Recognize that science involves creativity in designing experiments.

S.T.E.M.

ENGINEERING & TECHNOLOGY

Tools That Rock

Geologists study Earth materials and often work outdoors. They use some tools you are probably familiar with, but they might use them in unexpected ways.

Hand held GPS device

Geologists use physical tools such as this rock hammer to collect rock samples. They also use electronic technology, such as GPS for mapping and computers for recording and processing data.

CRITICAL THINKING

Name three tools a geologist uses that are not shown here. Describe what each tool is used for.

_____

_____

_____

S.T.E.M.

After collecting rocks, a geologist uses different tools to identify the samples.

How can a geologist use each of these tools below to identify a rock sample? Do research to find out, and write your explanations below.

Vinegar

Hand lens

Streak plate

One new technology geologists use is GPS. Research how they use GPS, and write about why it is useful for geologists.

Improvise It:
Separating by Size

Geologists often collect rock material that contains a mixture of different-sized particles. To process their collection, they first separate the material by size. This is accomplished by using a set of sieves. Each sieve has a metal screen with a different-sized opening. The opening determines which sized particles pass through the sieve and which collect on the screen.

Suppose you are on a dig and forgot to bring screen sieves to the site. Do you think you can improvise this geologist's tool using screening, fabrics, and cups? It's time to find out.

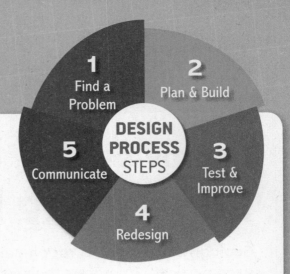

DESIGN PROCESS STEPS

1 Find a Problem
2 Plan & Build
3 Test & Improve
4 Redesign
5 Communicate

What to Do:

1 Examine a mixture of sand, gravel, and pebbles.

2 Try to sort these different-sized particles without using any tools. What do you find?

3 Learn more about screen sieves and how they are used in geology. Improvise a set of sieves using household screening and fabrics. Identify the additional materials you'll need to construct this tool.

4 Draw your design.

5 Then build your design. Test your screen sieves. What improvements can you make?

6 Keep improving or redesigning your design until you are satisfied with your final product.

7 Keep a record of your work in your Science Notebook.

SC.4.E.6.3 Recognize that humans need resources found on Earth and that these are either renewable or nonrenewable. SC.4.E.6.5 Investigate how technology and tools help to extend the ability of humans to observe very small things and very large things. SC.4.E.6.6 Identify resources available in Florida (water, phosphate, oil, limestone, silicon, wind, and solar energy).

LESSON 5

ESSENTIAL **QUESTION**

Which Resources Are Found in Florida?

 Engage Your Brain

Find the answers to the following questions in this lesson and record them here.

What is the resource we use to clean clothes? Is the resource renewable or nonrenewable?

_____

_____

_____

ACTIVE **READING**

Lesson Vocabulary

List the terms. As you learn about each one, make notes in the Interactive Glossary.

_____

_____

_____

Compare and Contrast

Many ideas in this lesson are connected because they explain comparisons and contrasts—how things are alike and different. Active readers stay focused on comparisons and contrasts when they ask themselves, How are these things alike? How are they different?

211

Resources You Can Rely On

Soap, water, clothes, wood, bricks, pencils, paper. What do all these things have in common? They're all uses of Earth's resources or things made from Earth's resources.

ACTIVE **READING** As you read the next page, circle examples of renewable resources.

These pictures show resources. Resources are materials found in nature that are used by living things. Can you identify the resources shown?

> ▶ **What are some renewable resources shown in the picture?**
>
> _____
>
> _____
>
> _____
>
> _____

Some resources, such as water and air, are used again and again. Other resources form quickly in nature and are easy to replace. If a tree is cut to make paper, for example, a new one can be grown in a short time. The new tree replaces the old tree. Resources that can be replaced quickly are called **renewable resources**. Scientists also consider sunlight a renewable resource.

People need to use renewable resources wisely. The wise use of resources is called _conservation_ [kahn•ser•VAY•shuhn]. Why is conservation important? People can use up renewable resources. Think about this: What would happen to fish if people ate more fish than could be replaced? Soon there would be no fish left!

213

nonrenewable Resources

Not all resources are replaced quickly. Some resources take thousands or millions of years to form.

ACTIVE READING On this page and the next, circle phrases that show how nonrenewable resources are different from renewable resources.

Resources that aren't replaced easily are called **nonrenewable resources**. One example of a nonrenewable resource is fossil fuels. Coal, oil, and natural gas are fossil fuels. Some are used to produce electricity. Some are used to run planes, cars, and other vehicles.

Because they form so slowly, there is a limited amount of fossil fuels and other nonrenewable resources. Once these resources are used up, they cannot be replaced. If people keep using fossil fuels at the same rate they do today, these fuels will be gone very soon.

Oil is found deep underground. It is pumped to the surface and then refined before it can be used.

Soil takes hundreds of years to form. It is made of weathered rock and once-living plants and animals.

Limestone and aluminum are mined. Limestone is used to make cement, and aluminum is used to make cans.

We all need to conserve fossil fuels. To conserve fossil fuels, think of things that you can do. For example, you could turn off lights when you leave a room. What else could you do?

Other nonrenewable resources are rocks and minerals. Many rocks and minerals are mined. Once they have been removed from a mine, there are none left. It takes a long time for more rocks or minerals to form.

Another nonrenewable resource is soil. People use soil to grow crops. Soil can be washed away if it is used improperly or left uncovered. Because of this, it is important for people to conserve soil.

(l) ©Grant Faint/Getty Images; (r) ©walter_bilotta/Fotolia

© Houghton Mifflin Harcourt Publishing Company

 DO THE **MATH**

Interpret a Graph

The graph shows the percentage of different resources used to produce electricity in the U.S. How much comes from nonrenewable resources?

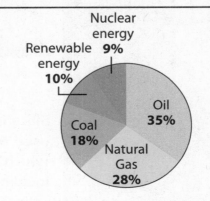

Nuclear energy **9%**

Renewable energy **10%**

Oil **35%**

Coal **18%**

Natural Gas **28%**

Resources in Florida

You've learned about many different kinds of resources. What are some resources found in Florida?

Florida has a large amount of minerals containing phosphate. Phosphate is used to make fertilizers and detergents.

Silica is found in Florida. It is used to make solar panels, which help produce electricity in some areas.

Every day, you use resources from your state. You breathe fresh air and drink water pumped from the ground. You may visit a beach for fun. You may also live in a house made from Florida limestone.

Many people in Florida use its resources to make a living. Some people use Florida's soil to grow oranges, sugarcane, and other crops. Other people fish in Florida's waters. Still others do business with people who come to enjoy Florida's environment. Can you see why it is important for the people of Florida to conserve its resources?

> ► **Which resources shown here are renewable? Which are nonrenewable?**
>
> _____
>
> _____
>
> _____

4 Plants and animals are some of the most important resources in Florida. People from all over the world come to see Florida's wildlife.

5 The most common rock in Florida is limestone. Limestone is used in buildings and to make cement.

Keeping It Clean

Using up resources too quickly is a problem. Another problem is pollution, or harmful materials in the environment. Pollution is harmful to resources. How can you help to conserve resources and prevent pollution?

Pollution can harm air, water, and soil. It can also harm plants and animals.

Many communities have cleanup projects to make the environment healthier for everyone.

Reasons to Recycle

What happens to trash? It ends up in a landfill. Throwing resources away is wasteful. Instead, many resources can be reused. You can reuse paper bags to make gift wrap, for example. Some resources, such as paper, glass, plastic, and metal, can be recycled and made into new products.

How Can You Help?

What can you do to help cut down on air pollution caused by cars and trucks? Draw your solution in the space above.

Sum It Up »

Read the summary statements below. Each one is incorrect. Change the part of the summary in blue to make it correct.

1 Nonrenewable resources can be quickly replaced or renewed after they are used.

_____

_____

_____

2 Examples of renewable resources are rocks and coal.

_____

_____

_____

3 Oil, minerals, and soil are all renewable resources that will be gone forever once they are used up.

_____

_____

_____

4 Nonrenewable resources can take 10 or 20 years to be replaced.

_____

_____

_____

5 You conserve resources so that they disappear faster.

_____

_____

_____

Name _____

Vocabulary Review

1 Use the words in the box to complete each sentence.

conservation	**fossil fuels**	nonrenewable resources*	**pollution**
recycling	resources*	**renewable resources***	

*Key Lesson Vocabulary

Materials found in nature and used by living things are _____ .

Reducing the use of resources is one way to practice _____ .

When _____ are burned, they cause pollution.

Resources that are limited and cannot be replaced quickly are called _____ .

Fish, trees, and other similar resources should be protected because if they are used too quickly, they will no longer be _____ .

Resources such as plastic, metal, glass, and paper can be conserved by _____ them.

Harmful materials in the environment are forms of _____ .

Apply Concepts

2 Circle the renewable resource.

3 List four different resources and products made from those resources.

_____   _____

_____   _____

_____   _____

_____   _____

4 Name three things you could do with a cereal box, instead of throwing it away.

_____

_____

_____

5 Circle the nonrenewable resource.

Take It Home! For a whole day, make a list of all of the resources you use. Find out with your family where each of these resources comes from. For example, where does the cotton used to make a T-shirt come from?

SC.4.E.6.5 Investigate how technology and tools help to extend the ability of humans to observe very small things and very large things. SC.4.N.2.1 Explain that science focuses solely on the natural world.

⬡ PEOPLE **IN SCIENCE**

Meet the Soil Scientists

Elvia Niebla

Elvia Niebla grew up in Arizona. Niebla studied hard in school and became a soil scientist. As a soil scientist, she helped seven states maintain their adobe buildings from the 1700s. Adobe is made of clay and sand. In 1984, Niebla started working for the government. She helped make rules to stop pollution in soil from getting into the food we eat. Now, Niebla studies how changes in the world's climate affect living things in our forests.

Pollution from industrial garbage can enter the soil on farms. People or animals can eat the plants that take in these poisons.

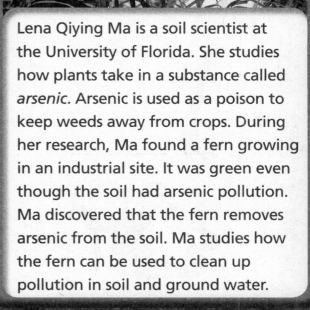

Lena Qiying Ma

Brake ferns collect arsenic in their leaves.

A measurement called pH can affect the amount of nutrients in soil. Scientists can test soil for the correct nutrients and pH.

Lena Qiying Ma is a soil scientist at the University of Florida. She studies how plants take in a substance called *arsenic*. Arsenic is used as a poison to keep weeds away from crops. During her research, Ma found a fern growing in an industrial site. It was green even though the soil had arsenic pollution. Ma discovered that the fern removes arsenic from the soil. Ma studies how the fern can be used to clean up pollution in soil and ground water.

Be a Soil Scientist!

A farmer is planting his crops. He tests the pH of the soil from different fields on his farm. He wants to know what crop to plant in each field.

Use the pH scale to *match* the soil from each field with the best crop to plant in that field. Write the name of the crop on the line for the correct soil.

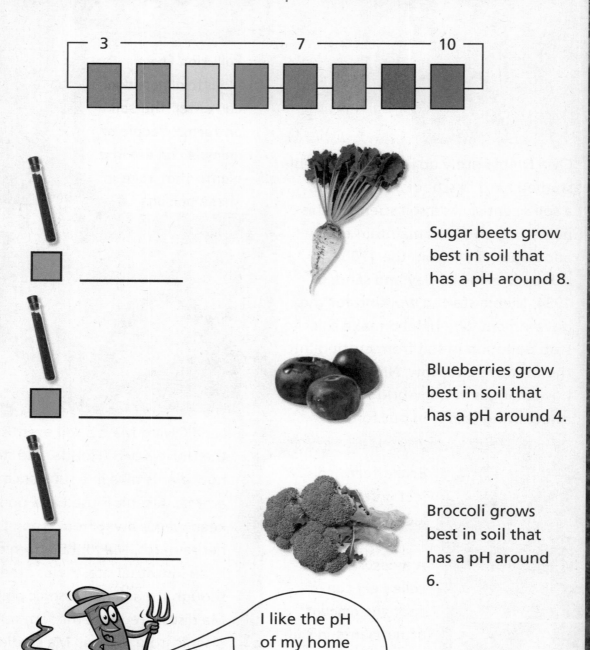

Sugar beets grow best in soil that has a pH around 8.

Blueberries grow best in soil that has a pH around 4.

Broccoli grows best in soil that has a pH around 6.

I like the pH of my home to be right in the middle!

Name _____

Vocabulary Review

Use the terms in the box to complete the sentences.

1. Weathering by wind, water, and ice

   produces _____.

2. The process of wearing away rock is known

   as _____.

3. A landslide quickly erodes sediment on a steep hill. When the landslide reaches the bottom of the hill, it slows down and finally comes to rest. The sediments it leaves are

   called _____.

4. Any nonliving solid with a crystal form is called

   a(n) _____.

5. A rock that forms from lava or magma is classified as

   a(n) _____.

6. A rock that forms when heat or pressure changes an existing rock

   is classified as a(n) _____.

Science Concepts

Fill in the letter of the choice that best answers the question.

7. At one time, limestone quarried in Florida was used to build large, important buildings. Today, most of the limestone mined in Florida is used in road construction. What type of resource is limestone?

   Ⓐ new

   Ⓑ renewable

   Ⓒ reservable

   Ⓓ nonrenewable

8. Wind power is an energy source that causes very little pollution. Large mod wind turbines are turned by the wind to produce electricity. What type of resource is wind power?

   Ⓕ nonrenewable

   Ⓖ recyclable

   Ⓗ renewable

   Ⓘ reusable

9. The Mohs H... scale is shown below.

Min...	Hardness
	1
	2
	3
	4
	5
	6
	7
	8
	9
	10

...ness of a steel nail is about 5.5.
...n mineral scratches a steel nail
...s not scratch quartz. What is the
...ss of the mineral?

(C) 6

(D) 7

...nerals are identified and sorted by
...fferent characteristics. Luster is one
...ay to sort minerals into different types.
What is a mineral's luster?

(F) the way that light reflects from its surface

(G) the mineral's elements and their arrangement

(H) the color that it makes when rubbed on a tile

(I) the way that it breaks when you strike it with a wedge

11. Tamika creates a visual display for her science project on metamorphic rocks. She draws this diagram to show how metamorphic rock is formed.

What natural forces cause rocks to change into metamorphic rocks?

(A) heat and pressure from the magma

(B) pressure from above and heat from the magma

(C) pressure and weathering in the layers above the rock

(D) transportation and heat in the layers below the rock

12. Weathering is one of the forces that drives the rock cycle. What is one direct result of weathering?

(F) decrease in acid rain

(G) increase in flooding

(H) increase in the amount of soil

(I) decrease in the amount of plant life

Name _____

13. Elements in nature such as rock and ice affect one another.

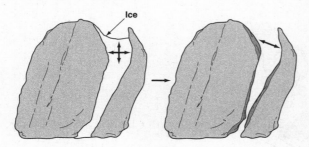

Ice

Which statement describes the process shown in the diagram?

(A) Ice changes to rock.

(B) Ice prevents erosion.

(C) Ice causes the rock to break.

(D) Ice seals the break in the rock.

14. Alluvial fans are fan-shaped deposits of sediment that are created by the flow of water at the base of a mountain.

Which kinds of materials make up the sediment that forms an alluvial fan such as the one in the picture?

(F) boulders and plants

(G) ice and snow

(H) trees and branches

(I) sand and gravel

15. Water erosion can change landforms. Which of the following is a landform caused by water erosion?

(A) dust bowl   (C) moraine

(B) landslide   (D) sand dune

16. Tyrone was given a sample of four minerals. To test the hardness of each mineral, he tried to scratch each mineral with his fingernail, a copper penny, and a steel nail. The results of his experiment are shown in the table below.

Mineral	Fingernail	Copper penny	Steel nail
Calcite	no	yes	yes
Fluorite	no	no	yes
Gypsum	yes	yes	yes
Quartz	no	no	no

Which mineral tested is the hardest?

(F) calcite   (H) gypsum

(G) fluorite   (I) quartz

17. Lila is looking at a map that shows where Florida's major resources are located. Which of these resources is she most likely to see on the map?

(A) air

(B) gold

(C) sunlight

(D) phosphate

Apply Inquiry and Review the Big Idea

Write the answers to these questions.

18. Anish is doing a science activity. Her setup is shown here.

Identify two Earth processes being modeled. Describe what will happen when Anish pours the water over the sand. Make a claim about what would happen if Anish propped up one end of the pan before she poured the water over the sand. Explain your reasoning.

_____

_____

_____

_____

_____

19. Sedimentary rock often forms at the bottom of oceans. Describe the process of the formation of this rock.

_____

_____

_____

Matter and Its Properties

FLORIDA **BIG IDEA 8**

Properties of Matter

A diver explores a ship off Florida's coast.

(tg) ©George Tiedmann/GT Images/Corbis (inset) ©George Tiedmann/GT Images/Corbis; (border) ©NDisc/AgB Fotostock

I Wonder Why

A ship, a manatee, and ocean water are different kinds of matter. How do scientists describe them? *Turn the page to find out.*

Mifflin Harcourt
Company

Here's Why

Everything around you is matter. Color, state, and texture are physical properties of matter. Scientists use properties to describe and compare kinds of matter, such as ocean water, ships, and manatees.

Essential Questions and Florida Benchmarks

LESSON 1 **What Are Physical Properties of Matter?** 231
SC.4.P.8.1 Measure and compare objects and materials ....

LESSON 2 **How Are Physical Properties Observed?** 247
SC.4.P.8.1, SC.4.N.1.1, SC.4.N.1.6

CAREERS **IN SCIENCE**
Medical Chemist.. 251
SC.4.E.6.5 Investigate how technology and tools help ... humans ....
SC.4.N.2.1

LESSON 3 **What Is Conservation of Mass?** 253
SC.4.P.8.3 Explore the Law of Conservation of Mass ....
SC.4.N.1.1, SC.4.N.1.4, SC.4.N.1.8

LESSON 4 **What Are the States of Water?** 257
SC.4.P.8.2 Identify properties and common uses of water ....

S.T.E.M. **Engineering and Technology**
Baby, It's Cold Inside: Refrigeration/
Improvise It: Build a Rubber Band Scale 267
SC.4.N.1.5

LESSON 5 **What Are Magnets?** 271
SC.4.P.8.4 Investigate and describe ... magnets ....
SC.4.P.8.1

LESSON 6 **How Do Magnets Attract Objects?** 285
SC.4.P.8.4, SC.4.N.1.1, SC.4.N.1.3, SC.4.N.1.4

Unit 5 Benchmark Review................................. 289

SC.4.P.8.1 Measure and compare objects and materials based on their physical properties including mass, shape, volume, color, hardness, texture, odor, taste…

LESSON 1

ESSENTIAL QUESTION
What Are Physical Properties of Matter?

 Engage Your Brain

Find the answer to the following question in this lesson and record it here.

How is the chocolate shell on the outside of the bar different from the ice cream on the inside?

_____

_____

_____

_____

_____

 ACTIVE **READING**

Lesson Vocabulary
List the terms. As you learn about each one, make notes in the Interactive Glossary.

_____ _____

_____ _____

_____

Main Idea and Details
Detailed sentences give information about a topic. The information may be examples, features, characteristics, or facts. Active readers stay focused on the topic when they ask, What fact or information does this sentence add to the topic?

Use Your Senses

See

You can see shapes in the sandwich. What other property can you see?

_____

You can use your senses to describe a sandwich. What does it look, taste, and smell like?

Hear

When you bite into a sandwich, you might hear the crunch of the crust.

Matter

Is this sandwich made of matter? Anything that takes up space and has mass is **matter**. A characteristic of matter that you can observe or measure directly is a **physical property**.

The amount of matter in an object is its mass. You use a pan balance to measure **mass**. Less massive objects are measured in grams (g). More massive objects are measured in kilograms (kg).

Taste

You can taste sweet, sour, salty, and bitter. Which would you taste in this sandwich?

_____

_____

Smell

You may smell mustard, onion, or pepper. You may even smell the fresh bread.

Feel

The bread feels soft. The dressing may feel oily. Salt and pepper feel grainy.

You start by placing the object to be measured on one side of the balance. You add known masses to the other pan until the sides balance. You add up the masses to find the mass of the object.

Describe That!

You can use all the words you see here to describe matter. You can use your senses to find an object's hardness, color, taste, size, shape, odor, or texture.

ACTIVE READING As you read these two pages, circle words or phrases that signal a detail about physical properties.

Hardness

A walnut shell is hard. The grapes are soft. Hardness describes how easily something can bend or dent.

Size

A silver dollar takes up more space than other coins. Pennies are larger than dimes.

Color

The words we use for color describe the way light bounces off an object. What colors do you see below? green and Red

Taste

Crackers are salty. Candy can taste sweet or sour. Can you think of something that tastes bitter?

▶ **List five properties that describe this banana.**

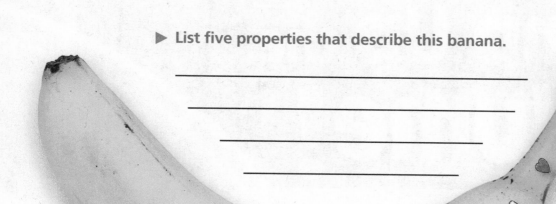

_____

_____

_____

_____

Texture

Texture describes what something feels like. The pinecone has a rough texture. The leaf feels smooth.

Odor

These shoes are stinky! Perfume has a nice smell. How can odor tell you if milk has gone bad?

_____

Shape

Objects can be long, short, flat, tall, or irregular like these keys. Shape describes an object's form. How can you describe the cell phone?

_____

Pump Up the Volume!

You can measure mass with a pan balance. What is another property of matter that we can use tools to measure?

ACTIVE READING As you read these two pages, underline the definition of *volume*. Circle units used to measure volume.

Volume

Volume is how much space an object takes up. The beaker on the left measures the volume of water in milliliters (mL). The beaker on the right measures the volume of an object with an irregular shape plus the volume of the water. To find the volume of just the orange, you must use subtraction:

{ volume of water and orange
− volume of water
――――――――――――――――
volume of orange }

n Mifflin Harcourt Company

DO THE **MATH**

Measure the Volume of Objects

A
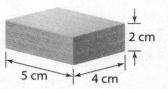
2 cm
5 cm   4 cm

B
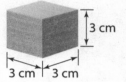
3 cm
3 cm   3 cm

Find It!

The volume of a rectangular solid is found by multiplying the width by the length by the height. Find the volume for each box. The units are cubic centimeters.

Volume of Box A:

Volume of Box B:

To find the volume of both boxes together, you add their individual volumes.

A+B =

Displacement

The dog in this tub takes up space. To make room for him, water was pushed out of the tub.

Don't Be So Dense!

Why does the hook sink? Why doesn't it float? You must use mass and volume to find the answers.

ACTIVE **READING** As you read these pages, underline the sentence that gives the main idea about density.

Density is a physical property of matter. It tells how much space (volume) a certain amount (mass) of matter takes up. In other words, **density** is the amount of matter present in a certain volume of a substance.

Density indicates how close together the particles in an object are. The density of a substance is always the same, no matter how much of the substance there is. A small piece of an eraser, for example, has the same density as a whole eraser.

This Part Floats
Objects that are less dense than water float. This fishing float is made of plastic.

This Part Sinks
The hook and weights are metal. The density of metal is greater than water.

▶ Name three objects that are more dense than water.

_____

_____

label: foam

label: sand

label: pumice

label: obsidian

Different Densities

The density of the foam balls is different than the density of sand. Which is less dense? How do you know?

_____

_____

_____

_____

More About Density

These rocks have different properties. One rock is more dense than the other. Which rock has particles that are closer together? Which rock has the greater density?

_____

_____

_____

Let's Sort Things Out

Shape

Study this example. Then sort using the other properties!

round   rectangular   other

Mass

Texture

Imagine going into a store or a library and finding that nothing is organized. How would you find anything? How can you find your homework in a messy backpack? Organizing makes life easier. Sorting things helps us find things faster.

We can use properties to sort everything, including food, books, and clothes. The items shown are at the bottom of a closet. Sort them by each of the properties listed.

▶ Name another property you could use to sort these items.

_____

Color

_____

Odor

_____

Hardness

_____

Sum It Up »

Use the information in the summary to complete the graphic organizer.

All matter has physical properties. Physical properties can also be called characteristics. Some properties can be described by using your senses. You can feel hardness and see shape or color. You can feel texture and smell odor. Other properties can be measured using tools. You can measure volume with a graduated cylinder. You can measure mass with a pan balance. All matter has density. To measure an object's density, you must know its mass and volume.

[1] Main Idea: All matter has _Physical Properties_.

[2] Detail: Some properties can be _Describe by using your senses_.

[3] An example of one of these properties is _Shape and color_

[4] Other properties must be _measured by using tools_.

[5] An example of one of these properties is _volume_

[6] To find an object's density, you divide its _mass_

[7] by its _volume_

Name _____

Vocabulary Review

1 Which word describes each photo best? Use each word only once.

mass	volume	density
hard	size	shape
texture	odor	taste

_____   _____   _____

_____   _____   _____

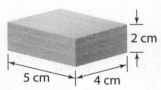

_____   _____   _____

243

Apply Concepts

② Use the chart below to sort the objects into two groups. Label the groups at the top of the chart.

What properties did you use to sort the objects?

_____

_____

Can you sort the same objects into three groups?
Don't forget to label the groups at the top of your chart.

Did you use the same properties to sort the objects the second time?

_____

3 Look at each pair of objects. Tell which one has the greater mass, volume, or density.

greater mass?

greater volume?

greater density?

_____   _____   _____

4 Choose a type of matter that you had for breakfast today. List as many physical properties as you can to describe it. Trade your list with a partner, and see if you can identify the matter your partner chose based on its properties.

_____

_____

_____

_____

_____

_____

5 Work with a group to make a list of ten favorite television shows, songs, or movies. Tell how you can sort them into groups.

_____

_____

_____

_____

6 How could you use physical properties to sort the objects in a desk drawer?

_____

_____

_____

_____

_____

_____

_____

Take It Home! See *ScienceSaurus®* for more information about matter.

SC.4.P.8.1 Measure and compare objects and materials based on their physical properties...
SC.4.N.1.1 Raise questions... use appropriate reference materials... conduct both individual and team investigations... and generate appropriate explanations... **SC.4.N.1.6** Keep records that describe observations made...

INQUIRY
LESSON 2

Name _____

ESSENTIAL **QUESTION**

How Are Physical Properties Observed?

EXPLORE

Time to get hands-on! In this activity, you and your classmates will explore the physical properties of matter.

Before You Begin—Preview the Steps

(1) Spread the objects out on a table.

(2) Make a table to record your observations of each object. You should observe color, mass, shape, texture, hardness, and odor. What else could you add to the table?

(3) Use a pan balance to find the mass of each object. Record the mass in your table.

(4) Find three ways to sort the objects into groups.

Set a Purpose

What skills will you learn from this investigation?

_____

_____

_____

Think About the Procedure

How can you find the mass of an object?

_____

_____

_____

_____

Why do you add up the masses on the other pan?

_____

_____

_____

_____

Name _____

Record Your Data

Make a table in which you record your results.

Draw Conclusions

What are three ways that you can sort the objects?

_____

_____

_____

_____

Claims • Evidence • Reasoning

1. Explain why you need a tool to help you observe an object's mass.

   _____

   _____

2. What other tool could you use to measure objects? How could this tool help you sort the objects? Explain your reasoning.

   _____

   _____

   _____

   _____

3. How can sorting objects help you in everyday life?

   _____

   _____

4. Compare the different ways groups sorted objects. Write a claim about which methods of sorting objects were most popular and least popular.

   _____

   _____

5. Cite evidence that supports your claim and explain why the evidence supports the claim.

   _____

   _____

6. What other questions would you like to ask about sorting objects by physical properties?

   _____

   _____

   _____

SC.4.E.6.5 Investigate how technology and tools help to extend the ability of humans to observe very small things and very large things. **SC.4.N.2.1** Explain that science focuses solely on the natural world.

◯CAREERS **IN SCIENCE**

Ask a Medical Chemist

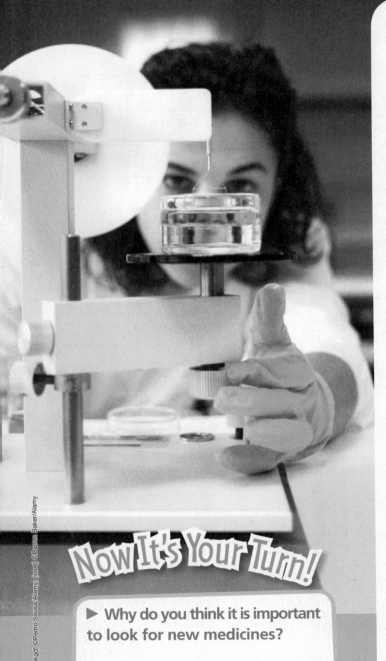

Now It's Your Turn!

▶ Why do you think it is important to look for new medicines?

_____

_____

_____

_____

Q. What is a medical chemist?

A. A medical chemist is a person who discovers new medicines to treat diseases and illnesses. I make the medicines that improve a person's health.

Q. Where do you find the things you use to make medicines?

A. The things used to make medicine can come from nature, such as plants, animals, and fungi. They can also be *synthetic*. Synthetic means that they are made by people.

Q. What are some of the things you do in your job?

A. Sometimes I work with a miscroscope looking at the properties of medicines and what they do. At other times I use computer models to show how a medicine will behave in your body.

251

Medical Discoveries

Use the information below to make a time line of medical discoveries. Write a sentence to fill in each blank box.

1953 Polio is a serious disease. Many people in the United States used to get polio until a vaccine was made. Jonas Salk made the first successful vaccine to protect people against polio in 1953.

1897 Aspirin, a medicine used to treat pain and fevers, was invented in 1897. An ingredient of aspirin came from the bark of a willow tree.

1928 Penicillin was discovered by Sir Alexander Fleming in 1928. Penicillin is a medicine used to treat diseases caused by bacteria.

1798 The first vaccine was made in 1798 by Edward Jenner. It protected people against a disease called smallpox.

1750 ─┼─

2000 ─┼─

Think About It!

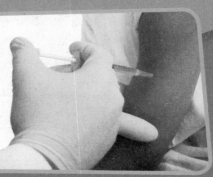

▶ **After which event on the time line should you add this?**
The number of people diagnosed with polio in the United States has greatly decreased.

_____

© Houghton Mifflin Harcourt Publishing Company

(aspirin pill) ©Wendy White/Alamy; (thermometer) ©Image Source/Getty Images; (b) ©Artville/Getty Images; (bl) ©Stewart Cohen/Getty Images

SC.4.P.8.3 Explore the Law of Conservation of Mass by demonstrating that the mass of a whole object is always the same as the sum of the masses of its parts. SC.4.N.1.1 Raise questions... use appropriate reference materials... conduct both individual and team investigations... and generate appropriate explanations... SC.4.N.1.4 Attempt reasonable answers to scientific questions and cite evidence in support. SC.4.N.1.8 Recognize that science involves creativity in designing experiments.

ⓘ INQUIRY LESSON **3**

ESSENTIAL **QUESTION**

Name _____

What Is Conservation of Mass?

> **Materials**
>
> pan balance
> 1 object that can be taken apart

EXPLORE

You can change matter into a new form. But, does this form have the same mass as the old form? Let's see!

Before You Begin—Preview the Steps

① Use a pan balance to find the mass of the object. Record the mass in a table.

② Pull the object apart into several pieces.

③ Find the mass of each piece. Record each mass in your table.

④ Add the masses of the pieces together. Compare this sum to the mass of the whole object.

Set a Purpose

The **law of conservation of mass** says that you cannot make or destroy matter. You can change matter into a new form. However, the new form will have the same amount of mass as the old form.

What do you expect to show in this experiment?

_____

_____

_____

Think About the Procedure

How can you change the object?

_____

_____

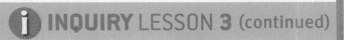

Name _____

Record Your Data

Make a table in which you record your results.

Was the mass of the whole object the same as the mass of the object broken apart?

_____

_____

_____

Draw Conclusions

How is this investigation a good example of the law of conservation of mass?

_____

_____

_____

Claims • Evidence • Reasoning

1. Write the law of conservation of mass in your own words. Can you think of another example of this law?

_____

_____

_____

2. Imagine you are investigating the physical change of melting. You find the mass of an ice cube. Then, after the ice cube melted, you find the mass of the liquid water. Write a claim about whether this demonstrates the law of conservation of mass.

_____

_____

3. What evidence would support your claim? Why would this evidence support the claim?

_____

_____

4. Imagine you are investigating the physical change of evaporation. Use reasoning to explain how you could demonstrate the law of conservation of mass during this change.

_____

_____

5. What other questions would you like to ask about the law of conservation of mass?

_____

_____

SC.4.P.8.2 Identify properties and common uses of water in each of its states.

LESSON 4

ESSENTIAL QUESTION

What Are the States of Water?

 Engage Your Brain

Find the answer to the following question in this lesson and record it here.

How is the snow in this picture like an ice cube?

_____

_____

_____

_____

📖 ACTIVE **READING**

Lesson Vocabulary

List the terms. As you learn about each one, make notes in the Interactive Glossary.

_____ _____

_____ _____

_____ _____

_____

Compare and Contrast

Many ideas in this lesson are connected because they explain comparisons and contrasts—how things are alike and how they are different. Active readers stay focused on comparisons and contrasts when they ask themselves, How are these things alike? How are they different?

Solids, Liquids, and Gases

Matter exists in different forms. The air around us is a gas. The water we drink is a liquid. Your book is a solid.

ACTIVE READING As you read these two pages, underline the contrasting characteristics of each state of matter.

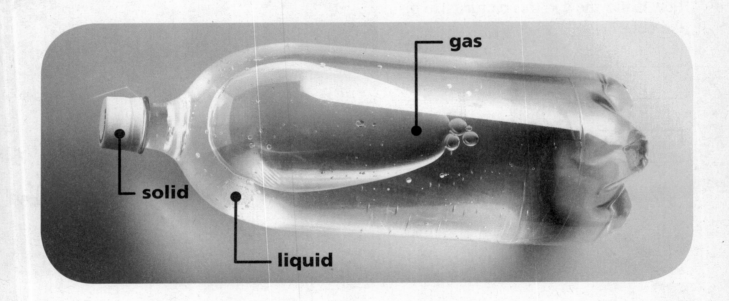

gas

solid

liquid

Solids, liquids, and gases are three **states of matter**. Most matter on Earth is classified as one of these forms.

A **solid** has a definite volume and shape. Your desk, book, pencil, and chair are all solids. Solids stay solid unless something, such as heat, changes them.

A **liquid** has a definite volume but not a definite shape. A liquid takes the shape of whatever container holds it. Water, shampoo, and fruit juice are liquids.

A **gas** doesn't have a definite volume or shape. It expands to take up all the space in a container. If you blow up a balloon, you can see that air spreads out to fill the space. The air we breathe is a mixture of gases.

▶ **Label each item as a solid, a liquid, or a gas.**

helmet

outside of bottle

sweat

water inside bottle

breath

teeth

bone

muscle

outside of ball

inside of ball

You are nearly 70% water! The rest of your body is made of gases such as oxygen and solids such as fats.

Water's Forms

Water can be a solid, a liquid, or a gas. This ice cube is solid water. It melts into a liquid. When water is a gas, it is called water vapor.

Water is made of tiny particles. We can learn what state water is in by knowing how fast the particles in it move.

Solid

Water in the solid state has a definite volume and shape. You can make square or round ice cubes. You can make big ones or little ones.

The particles in solids are close together. They are moving, but stay in the same spot, much like the strings of a guitar vibrating back and forth.

Liquid

Liquid water has a definite volume but not a definite shape. Pouring water from a glass into a bowl changes its shape, but not its volume.

Generally, particles are a bit farther apart in a liquid than in a solid. They move around more, too. The particles slide past each other.

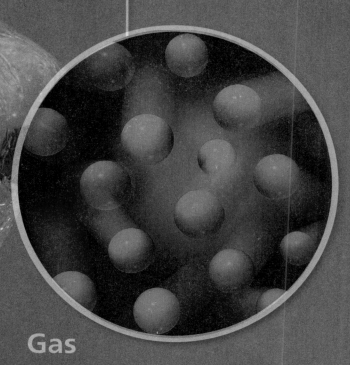

Gas

The air around the ice cube has water vapor in it. We can't see the water vapor, but it's there. A gas doesn't have a definite volume or shape.

Particles in a gas are far apart. They are much farther apart than the particles in a liquid. They move very quickly in all directions.

▶ **Use what you have learned to fill in the chart.**

	Physical Properties	How We Use It
ice		
liquid water		
water vapor	no definite volume or shape	steam cleaning

Freezing

At a certain temperature, water can freeze as heat energy is removed. Particles slow down and get closer together. They begin to lock into place. Water changes from a liquid to a solid. A **change of state** occurs when matter changes from one state to another.

Melting

Adding heat energy causes ice to melt. Particles speed up until they overcome the attractions that hold them in place. Water melts when it changes from a solid to a liquid.

Water changes Form

Anything made out of snow will melt if it gains enough heat energy. Energy from the sun causes the snow to change to a liquid.

ACTIVE READING As you read these two pages, compare changes of state. Draw a circle around changes that happen when heat is added.

Evaporation

When heat energy is added to water, its particles speed up. Particles that gain enough energy enter the air as water vapor. **Evaporation** is the process by which a liquid changes into a gas. Water evaporates from oceans, lakes, and rivers every day.

Condensation

When heat energy is removed from a gas, its particles slow down and clump together. **Condensation** is the process by which a gas changes into a liquid. Clouds form when water vapor condenses on particles of dust in the air.

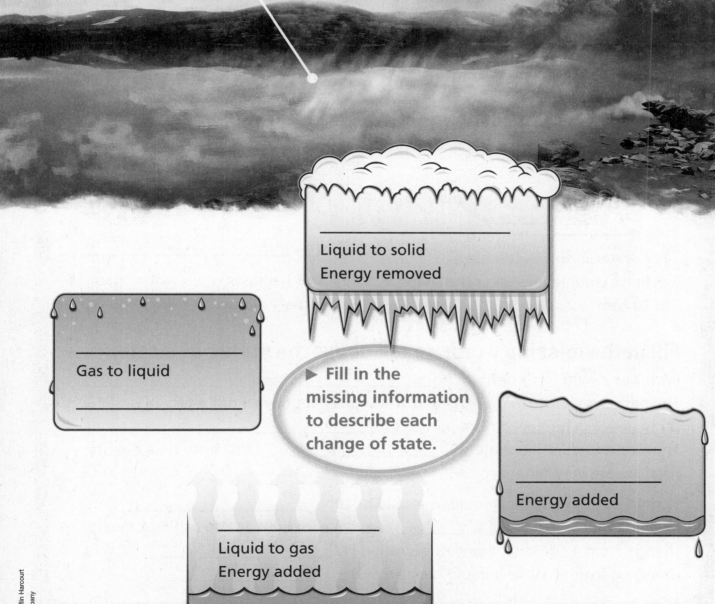

_____
Liquid to solid
Energy removed

_____
Gas to liquid
_____

▶ Fill in the missing information to describe each change of state.

_____
_____
Energy added

_____
Liquid to gas
Energy added

Sum It Up »

Write the vocabulary term that matches each photo and caption.

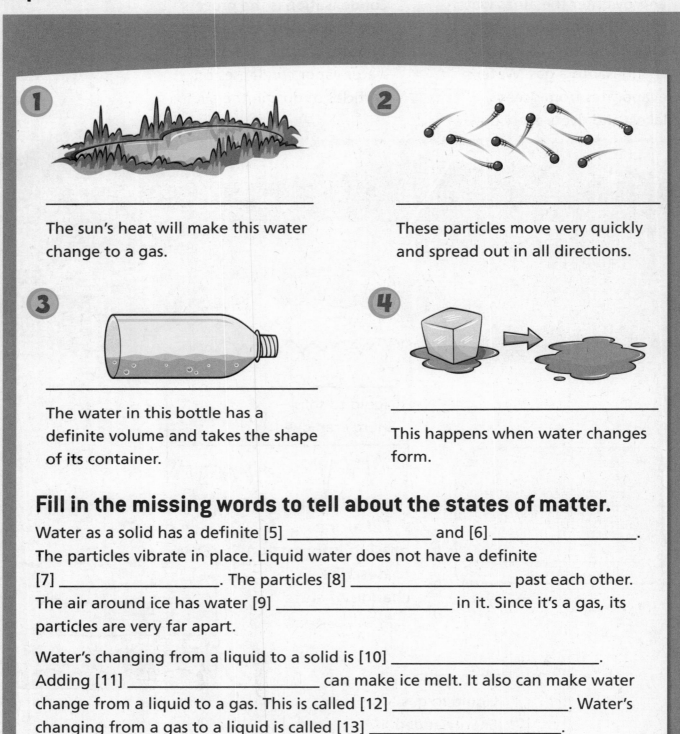

1. _____

The sun's heat will make this water change to a gas.

2. _____

These particles move very quickly and spread out in all directions.

3. _____

The water in this bottle has a definite volume and takes the shape of its container.

4. _____

This happens when water changes form.

Fill in the missing words to tell about the states of matter.

Water as a solid has a definite [5] _____ and [6] _____. The particles vibrate in place. Liquid water does not have a definite [7] _____. The particles [8] _____ past each other. The air around ice has water [9] _____ in it. Since it's a gas, its particles are very far apart.

Water's changing from a liquid to a solid is [10] _____. Adding [11] _____ can make ice melt. It also can make water change from a liquid to a gas. This is called [12] _____. Water's changing from a gas to a liquid is called [13] _____.

Name _____

Vocabulary Review

1 Unscramble these words. Use the highlighted letters to find the answer below.

sag

disol

qiludi

stianodocnne

rvapnotieao

ngecha fo ttase

ttases fo tmaert

tware

povra

We can find out what state water is in by finding how fast these move. What are they?

_____

Draw a star next to each word that names a state of matter.

2 Make a menu for a meal. The meal will have 3 solids and 3 liquids.

Solids

_____

_____

_____

Liquids

_____

_____

_____

3 Draw and label a diagram to show what happens to the particles of a substance as it changes from a solid to a liquid to a gas.

4 Name an example of condensation.

_____

5 Name an example of evaporation.

_____

_____

Make "Sunshine on a Stick"! Put an ice cube tray filled with orange juice into the freezer. When partly frozen, place a toothpick in each section. When the juice is a solid, you can eat it off the toothpicks!

S.T.E.M.
ENGINEERING & TECHNOLOGY

Baby, It's Cold Inside
Refrigeration

Have you ever thought about how refrigeration has changed the way we live? We can store foods without having them rot as quickly. Spoiled foods can make people ill.

1900s
By the early 1900s, many homes had iceboxes. Ice was placed in the bottom to cool the air inside the box. It became easier to cool food for longer periods of time until it could be used. These iceboxes were like coolers we use today but larger.

1800s
People put food on blocks of ice to keep it cold. The ice was cut from lakes or ponds, packed in straw, and stored in warehouses. This ice had to be replaced often.

1920s
In the 1920s, electric refrigerators became available for home use. The inside of this refrigerator stayed cold without needing blocks of ice. It used an electric motor and a gas compressor to remove heat from its wooden or metal box.

CRITICAL THINKING

In addition to slowing food spoilage, what is another advantage of refrigerating food?

_____

_____

_____

Make Some History

If you look closely, you will find that many of your home appliances have an *Energy Star* label. Do research to find out more about this label. Draw the Energy Star label in the space below on the timeline. Then, describe what it is and when it was first used on refrigerators.

2010s

Today's refrigerators are larger but use less energy. They have electronic controls that can be adjusted to set different parts of the refrigerator at different temperatures. Some modern refrigerators can alert people when a particular food supply is running low!

Design Your Future

Think of another household appliance that helps you save time. Describe how it helps you. Then, explain what you would do to improve its design.

Food Scale

Improvise It:
Build a Rubber Band Scale

When you stand on a bathroom scale, a spring inside it compresses. This change in the spring's length is shown as a weight measurement on the scale's dial.

Like a spring, a rubber band can also change length. When a mass is placed on one end of the rubber band, it stretches.

Think about it. Can you use this stretching property of a rubber band to construct a tool to measure weight? It's time to find out.

Have you ever wondered how a bathroom scale works? If you had the chance to look inside, you'd discover a simple spring.

S.T.E.M. continued

What to Do:

DESIGN PROCESS STEPS
- 1 Find a Problem
- 2 Plan & Build
- 3 Test & Improve
- 4 Redesign
- 5 Communicate

1 Research different scales and balances to learn how they work.

2 Use caution as you explore how a rubber band stretches and contracts.

3 Think about how this physical property can be used to build a scale to measure weight.

4 Identify the design criteria your rubber band scale must meet.

5 Draw your design.

6 Build and test your design.

7 Compare your design to a classroom scale. How can you improve your scale's performance?

8 If needed, redesign your scale until it meets your design criteria.

9 Keep improving or redesigning your design until you are satisfied with your final product.

10 Keep a record of your work in your Science Notebook.

SC.4.P.8.1 Measure and compare objects and materials based on their physical properties… SC.4.P.8.4 Investigate and describe that magnets can attract magnetic materials and attract and repel other magnets.

ESSENTIAL **QUESTION**

What Are Magnets?

 Engage Your Brain

Find the answer to the following question in this lesson and record it here.

Why do these rings seem to float?

_____

_____

_____

_____

📖 ACTIVE **READING**

Lesson Vocabulary

List the terms. As you learn about each one, make notes in the Interactive Glossary.

_____   _____

_____   _____

_____   _____

Cause and Effect

Some ideas in this lesson are connected by a cause-and-effect relationship. The reason that something happens is a cause. The event that takes place as a result of a cause is an effect. Active readers look for effects by asking themselves, What happened? They look for causes by asking, Why did it happen?

Magnets Are Everywhere

You use magnets every day. They are in computers, televisions, speakers, and even microwaves.

ACTIVE READING As you read these two pages, draw circles around two things that affect a magnet's pull.

Barriers

Weak

A barrier between a magnet and iron items weakens a magnet's pull. The barrier here is paper.

Even Weaker

You can make the pull weaker by making the barrier bigger. Paper was added, so fewer objects are stuck to the magnet.

© Houghton Mifflin Harcourt Publishing Company

A **magnet** is an object that attracts iron and a few other metals. Magnetism is a physical property. Only some kinds of matter are magnetic. The magnets in these pictures are made of iron. They pull objects that also contain iron.

Do you see that in two of the pictures the pull is stronger? Different things affect the strength of a magnet's pull. The pictures show how two factors—barriers and distance—affect a magnet's pull.

Does It Have Pull?

▶ Place each item from the box in the correct column.

iron nail, paper clip, pencil, crayon, rubber band, screw

Attracted by magnets	Not attracted by magnets

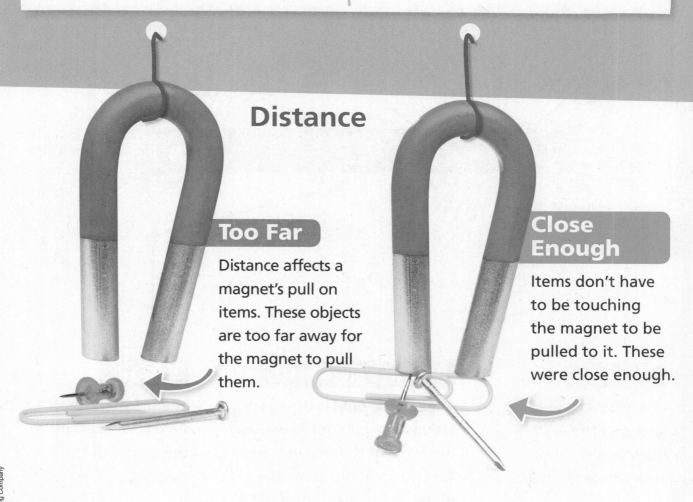

Distance

Too Far

Distance affects a magnet's pull on items. These objects are too far away for the magnet to pull them.

Close Enough

Items don't have to be touching the magnet to be pulled to it. These were close enough.

Magnetic Fields and Poles

You can feel the force between two magnets. You feel magnets pull together, and you feel them push apart. Why do they push and pull?

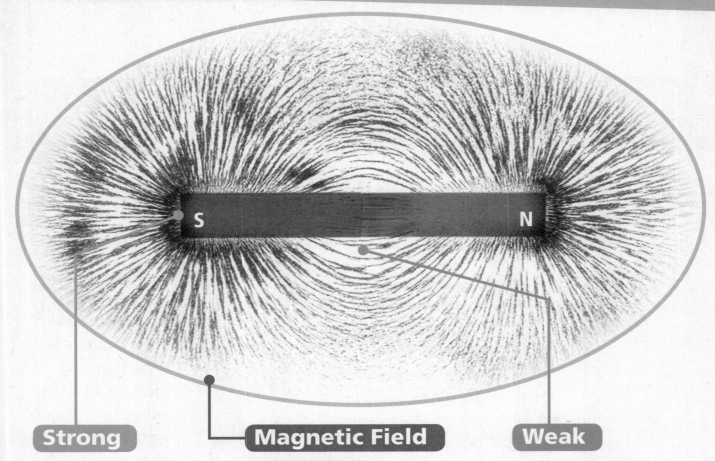

Strong

The magnetic field is strong at the ends of the magnet. These ends are called poles.

Magnetic Field

A **magnetic field** is the space around the magnet in which the force of the magnet acts. These iron filings show the shape of the magnetic field.

Weak

The magnetic field is weakest in the center of the magnet.

274

Each magnet has two ends, or poles. A **magnetic pole** is the part of the magnet where the force is the strongest. One is called the "south-seeking" pole, or *S* pole. The other end is the "north-seeking" pole, or *N* pole.

Earth has an *N* pole and an *S* pole. As a result, the whole planet is a magnet. Two *N* poles or two *S* poles are *like poles*, or similar poles. An *N* pole and an *S* pole are *unlike poles*.

Label This!

Label the poles on the magnets below so that the magnets will stay together.

Unlike Poles

If you bring unlike poles of two magnets together, they will attract, or pull toward, each other. Unlike poles attract.

Like Poles

The *S* pole of one magnet will repel, or push away, the *S* pole of another magnet. Two *N* poles will also repel each other. Like poles repel.

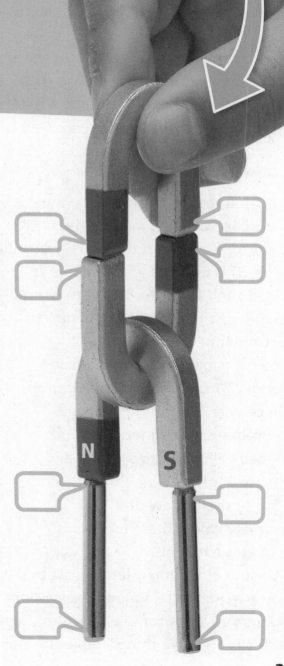

Magnetic Force

The electromagnets on these pages show how closely electricity and magnetism are related.

ACTIVE READING As you read this page, underline the cause of a magnetic field around a wire. Circle the effect this wire can have on a nail.

What makes an electromagnet? Look at the photo on the right. Electricity flows from the battery through a wire. This makes a weak magnetic field around the wire. The wire wraps around a nail. This makes the nail an **electromagnet**.

Can the magnetic field be made stronger? Yes, it can. Wrapping more coils of wire around the nail will strengthen the magnetic field. The nail will attract iron objects more strongly.

Suppose the flow of electricity stops. Then, the nail is no longer a magnet.

We use electromagnets every day. They are used in telephones, televisions, and motors. A **motor** is a device that uses electricity to make things move.

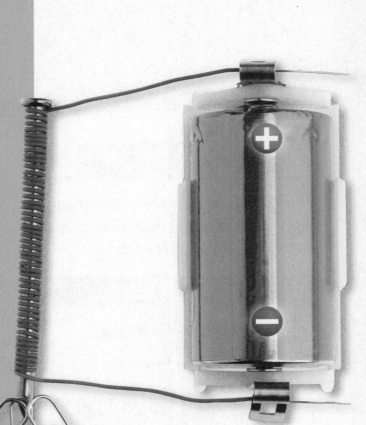

Electromagnet

You can make an electromagnet, like this one, with a D-cell battery.

DO THE **MATH**

Graph the Data

A student recorded these numbers during an experiment with an electromagnet.

Number of Coils	Number of Paper Clips
10 coils	5 clips
20 coils	10 clips
30 coils	15 clips

Graph this information.

What do you conclude?

_____

_____

Mega Electromagnet

An electromagnet like this one can be strong enough to pick up lots of metal!

Magnetic Planet

Our whole planet acts like a giant bar magnet. It has poles that attract and repel. It also has a magnetic field.

Finding North

This compass has a needle with a magnetic tip. The tip points north because its north-seeking pole is unlike the magnetic pole near Earth's geographic North Pole. They attract.

Which Pole Is Which?

Earth's magnetic poles and geographic poles aren't in the same place. The north magnetic pole is about 700 km away from the geographic North Pole.

South Pole

Earth's magnetic force extends out from both poles. The magnetic field around Earth is like the magnetic field of much smaller bar magnets.

(c) CNSA

What Else?

How do we use magnets every day? These are just some of the ways we use magnetic force.

Computer

Hard drives use magnets to spin. The speakers use magnets, too.

Train

Maglev trains can go hundreds of miles an hour and never touch the tracks. Magnets lift up the trains and push them forward.

MRI

An MRI shows a picture of things inside a patient's body. It shows much more than an x-ray. The machine that takes the picture uses magnets.

Junkyard

These huge magnets are turned on to pick something up and then turned off to drop it. They're electromagnets.

Magnetic Field

Earth has iron inside it that moves around as Earth rotates each day. This makes a magnetic field. You can detect this force from anywhere on the planet.

▶ What magnets do you use at home?

_____

_____

_____

Sum It Up »

Use the information in the summary to complete the graphic organizer.

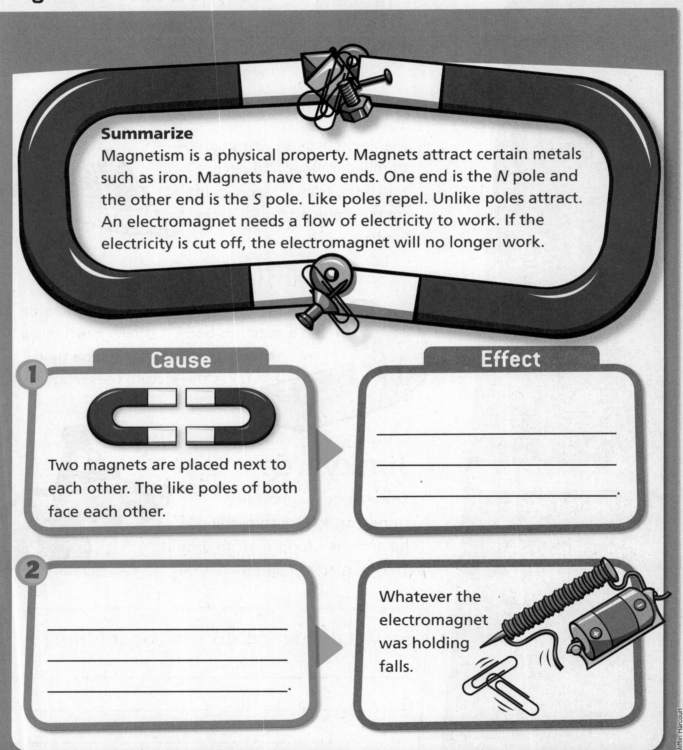

Summarize

Magnetism is a physical property. Magnets attract certain metals such as iron. Magnets have two ends. One end is the *N* pole and the other end is the *S* pole. Like poles repel. Unlike poles attract. An electromagnet needs a flow of electricity to work. If the electricity is cut off, the electromagnet will no longer work.

Cause

Effect

1. Two magnets are placed next to each other. The like poles of both face each other.

_____
_____
_____ .

2. _____
_____
_____ .

Whatever the electromagnet was holding falls.

Vocabulary Review

1 Use the clues to unscramble the words in the box. Use the word bank if you need help.

Name _____

1. **eeltronmcetag**: a magnet made with a battery	
2. **elop**: The end of a magnet	
3. **delif**: The force that wraps around a magnet	
4. **teamgn**: a material that pulls iron to it	
5. **pleer**: two like poles do this	
6. **catrtta**: two unlike poles do this	
7. **tronh** and **stouh**: what the two poles are called	
8. **rootm**: a device that uses electricity and is used to make things move	

WORD BANK:

pole	repel	north	south	motor
attract	electromagnet	magnet	field	

Apply Concepts

2 Circle the objects that can be magnetic. Draw a box around the objects that are not magnetic.

paper

scissors

rock

iron key

Earth

3 Make a list of things in your classroom that have magnets in them.

_____   _____   _____

_____   _____   _____

_____   _____   _____

4 Draw and label a diagram of a bar magnet. Show the poles and the magnetic field.

5

The two magnets below are next to each other. You try to press them together, but they will not touch. Label the magnetic poles N and S.

6

The two magnets below are next to each other. They move toward each other. It's hard to pull them apart. Label the magnetic poles N and S.

7

Describe what is happening in each of the pictures. Which picture shows like poles? Which picture shows unlike poles?

_____

_____

_____

8 Suppose you put a magnet in a drawer filled with nails. It doesn't pick up any of the nails. What does this tell you about the nails in the drawer?

_____

9 Why does a compass point north? Explain.

_____

_____

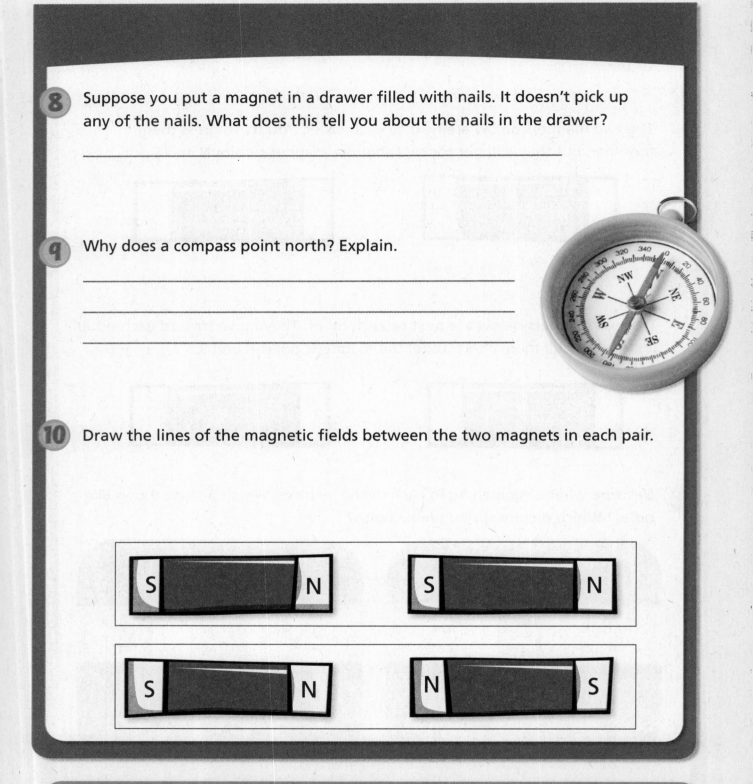

10 Draw the lines of the magnetic fields between the two magnets in each pair.

Take It Home! With a family member, find an object that uses magnets in your home. Use the Internet to research what the magnet does. Together, draw a diagram to explain how the object works.

SC.4.P.8.4 Investigate and describe that magnets can attract magnetic materials and attract and repel other magnets. **SC.4.N.1.1** Raise questions... use appropriate reference materials... conduct both individual and team investigations... and generate appropriate explanations...
SC.4.N.1.3 Explain that science does not always follow a rigidly defined method...
SC.4.N.1.4 Attempt reasonable answers to scientific questions and cite evidence in support.

INQUIRY
LESSON 6

Name _____

ESSENTIAL QUESTION

How Do Magnets Attract Objects?

Materials

bar magnet
iron or steel nail
small objects

EXPLORE

You have seen that magnets attract some items, but not others. Do you think you can make something into a magnet? Find out!

Before You Begin—Preview the Steps

(1) Work in pairs or in small groups. Spread out the objects.

(2) Move a magnet near each object. Observe what happens as the magnet gets close to each object. Record your observations in a data table.

(3) CAUTION: Handle the nail carefully! Stroke the nail 30 times with one end of the magnet. Stroke in one direction only. What do you think will happen when the nail gets close to each object? Record your predictions.

(4) Move the stroked nail near each object. Record your observations.

(5) Move the magnet near the stroked nail. Record your observations.

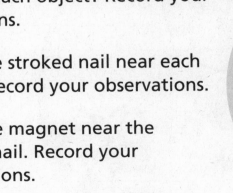

Set a Purpose

What do you want to find out from this investigation?

_____

_____

_____

State Your Hypothesis

Write your hypothesis, or testable statement, about what types of objects are attracted by a magnet.

_____

_____

Think About the Procedure

Why doesn't the magnet have to touch each object?

_____

_____

_____

Name _____

Record Your Data

Make a table in which you record your results.

[blank boxed area for table]

Draw Conclusions

Which objects did the magnet attract?

_____

_____

_____

What happens to a nail when you stroke it with a magnet?

_____

_____

Claims • Evidence • Reasoning

1. Did your results support your hypothesis about the kinds of objects that magnets will attract? Give evidence that supports your answer.

_____

_____

_____

2. Write a claim about whether all metals are attracted to magnets. Cite evidence that supports your claim and explain why it supports the claim.

_____

_____

_____

_____

3. Some paints are magnetic. You can paint a wall and use magnets to hold things on the wall. What do you think these paints contain? Explain your reasoning.

_____

_____

4. Some screwdrivers are magnetized so that they can hold small screws. Write a claim about how you could magnetize a screwdriver. Cite evidence that supports your claim and explain why the evidence supports the claim.

_____

_____

_____

5. What other questions would you like to ask about magnets?

_____

_____

Name _____

Vocabulary Review

Use the terms in the box to complete the sentences.

| condensation |
| density |
| evaporation |
| law of conservation |
| of mass |
| mass |
| matter |

1. Anything that takes up space and has mass

   is _____.

2. The amount of matter in an object is

   its _____.

3. The amount of matter present in a certain volume of a substance

   is its _____.

4. The idea that you cannot make or destroy matter is called

   the _____.

5. The process by which a liquid changes into gas

   is _____.

6. The process by which gas changes into liquid

   is _____.

Science Concepts

Fill in the letter of the choice that best completes the statement.

7. Jalil has a magnet and two needles. The magnet attracts both needles, but the needles do not attract each other. He strokes one needle with the magnet. What happens when he moves the two needles near each other?

   (A) They do not move.

   (B) They move away from each other.

   (C) They both move toward the magnet.

   (D) They move toward each other and stick.

8. Certain magnets are permanent. Others are temporary and can be turned on and off. Which of these magnets is temporary?

   (F) bar magnet

   (G) donut magnet

   (H) electromagnet

   (I) horseshoe magnet

9. Lyle performs a science activity in which he wants to describe certain properties of a substance. Which of the following properties should Lyle use to measure the space taken up by the substance?

Ⓐ density   Ⓒ volume

Ⓑ mass   Ⓓ weight

10. Look at the illustration of the two bar magnets below.

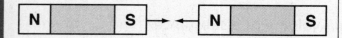

What will happen when the two magnets are moved closer together?

Ⓕ Magnetic force will pull the magnets together.

Ⓖ One magnet will slide under the other magnet.

Ⓗ You will be unable to push the magnets together.

Ⓘ The two magnetic fields will cancel each other out.

11. Shayna classifies a group of objects by their physical properties. She puts a soccer ball, a blue marble, and an orange in one group. What property did she **most likely** use to classify these objects?

Ⓐ color   Ⓒ shape

Ⓑ hardness   Ⓓ size

12. A student is describing the properties of an unknown substance. Which of the following words could he use to describe texture?

Ⓕ oval   Ⓗ gritty

Ⓖ floral   Ⓘ shiny

13. Tiko is washing the dishes and puts the wet dishes on the drying rack. Tiko knows that, over time, the water on the dishes will disappear and the dishes will be dry. What causes the water on the clean dishes to disappear?

Ⓐ The water melts.

Ⓑ The water condenses.

Ⓒ The water evaporates.

Ⓓ The water is absorbed.

14. The diagrams below show the particles that make up water. Which diagram shows how the particles are arranged when the water is solid?

Ⓕ 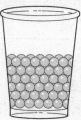   Ⓗ

Ⓖ    Ⓘ

Name _____

15. The three states of matter are solid, liquid, and gas. Which process turns liquid water into water vapor?

Ⓐ condensation

Ⓑ evaporation

Ⓒ freezing

Ⓓ melting

16. The three states of matter are solid, liquid, and gas. Which process turns liquid water into ice?

Ⓕ melting

Ⓖ freezing

Ⓗ condensing

Ⓘ evaporating

17. Some materials are magnetic, but most are not. Which of the following is magnetic?

Ⓐ aluminum

Ⓑ gold

Ⓒ steel

Ⓓ tin

18. Cherie changed water from a solid to a liquid. What did Cherie do to the water?

Ⓕ She froze the water.

Ⓖ She melted the water.

Ⓗ She condensed the water.

Ⓘ She evaporated the water.

19. Water is found in all three states of matter. Which shows the change of state involved when water condenses?

Ⓐ solid → gas   Ⓒ gas → liquid

Ⓑ solid → liquid   Ⓓ liquid → solid

20. Lien has a new box of eight crayons. Each crayon is identical. The mass of the box of crayons is 53 g. The mass of just one crayon is 6 g. What is **most likely** the mass of the box alone?

Ⓕ 2 g

Ⓖ 3 g

Ⓗ 4 g

Ⓘ 5 g

21. Aiden uses a balance to measure the mass of an apple. He finds that it is 224 g. He then cuts up the apple into four parts of varying sizes. What can he conclude?

Ⓐ The mass of each part is 56 g.

Ⓑ The sum of the masses of the parts is 224 g.

Ⓒ Each part has a mass that is slightly less than 56 g.

Ⓓ Each part has a mass that is slightly greater than 56 g.

Apply Inquiry and Review the Big Idea

Write the answers to these questions.

22. Jason wanted to find the volume of two rocks. How could he use the tools shown below to find the volume of these irregularly shaped rocks?

_____

_____

_____

_____

_____

23. You have a red box and a black box that are exactly the same size. The red box is heavier than the black one. Based on this data, make a claim about the densities of the two boxes. Then use reasoning and evidence to support the claim.

_____

_____

_____

24. Suppose you wanted to describe an object to someone but you could not name it. Which properties could you include in your description if you could only share information that you can determine with your senses?

_____

_____

_____

Matter and Its Changes

FLORIDA BIG IDEA 9

Changes in Matter

Art Deco Building
Miami, Florida

I Wonder Why

The walls of this building have changed with age. How?
Turn the page to find out.

Image Ideas/Jupiterimages/Getty Images

Here's Why

Over time, the building might be painted a different color. The outside walls may crack. Windows may even break. These are some familiar changes that matter undergoes. It might look different, but the building is still a building.

Essential Questions and Florida Benchmarks

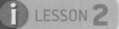 **LESSON 1**
What Are Physical and Chemical Changes? 295
SC.4.P.9.1 Identify some familiar changes in materials that result in other materials with different characteristics, such as decaying animal or plant matter, burning, rusting, and cooking.

 LESSON 2
How Can You Tell When a New Substance Forms? 311
SC.4.P.9.1, SC.4.N.1.3, SC.4.N.1.4, SC.4.N.1.7

PEOPLE **IN SCIENCE**
Héctor Abruña/Ruth Rogan Benerito 315
SC.4.E.6.5 Explain how technology and tools help ... humans ....
SC.4.N.2.1

S.T.E.M. Engineering and Technology
What's It Made Of? Body Armor/
Build in Some Science: Making Carbon Dioxide 317
SC.4.N.1.1

Unit 6 Benchmark Review 321

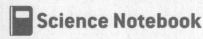Science Notebook

Before you begin each lesson, write your thoughts about the Essential Question.

SC.4.P.9.1 Identify some familiar changes in materials that result in other materials with different characteristics, such as decaying animal or plant matter, burning, rusting, and cooking.

LESSON 1

ESSENTIAL QUESTION

What Are Physical and Chemical Changes?

 Engage Your Brain

Find the answer to the following question in this lesson and record it here.

Sometimes we eat raw food, such as a freshly picked apple, but many times we change food before we eat it. How did this food change as it was prepared?

_____

_____

_____

_____

📖 ACTIVE **READING**

Lesson Vocabulary

List the terms. As you learn about each one, make notes in the Interactive Glossary.

_____

_____

Main Idea and Details

Detail sentences give information about a main idea. The information may be examples, features, characteristics, or facts. Active readers stay focused when they ask, What fact or other information does this sentence add to the main idea?

Physical Changes Are All Around

Matter can be changed in many ways. In how many ways can you change a piece of paper?

As you read, draw a line under the main idea of each paragraph.

Stacked

You can describe the physical properties of this paper, such as its size and color.

Soaked

What a mess! It is soggy, but the paper hasn't turned into a new substance.

Shredded

Does shredding the paper make a new substance? No, it just changes the shape of the paper into tiny pieces.

Think of a piece of clay. Can it be changed like paper can? If you pull bits from the clay, you change its size. If you flatten the clay, you change its shape. The size or shape may be different, but it is still clay. Changing size and shape is a physical change. A **physical change** is a change in which a new substance is not formed.

You can scratch a piece of clay until it is rough. It has a new texture, but it is still clay. You can add bits to it. It is heavier, but adding clay does not make a new substance. Changing a physical property, such as size, shape, texture, or mass, is a physical change.

▶ **What are some different ways that you can make a physical change to a piece of string?**

_____

_____

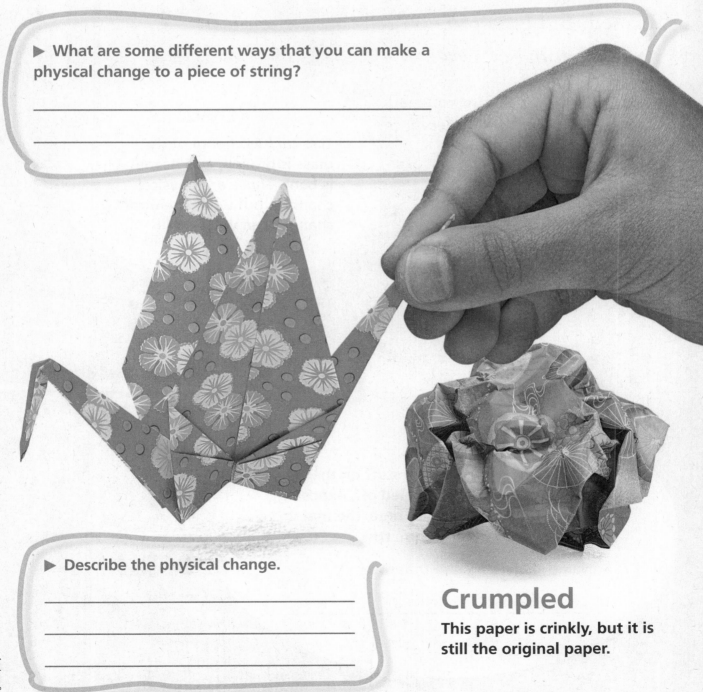

▶ **Describe the physical change.**

_____

_____

_____

Crumpled

This paper is crinkly, but it is still the original paper.

297

Chemical Changes Are All Around

During a chemical change, new substances are formed. But how can you tell that a chemical change has happened?

As you read these pages, underline the sentence that tells how rust is formed.

Wow!

This car has changed! Its glass is broken, and its metal is bent. These are physical changes, but what chemical changes can you find?

Rust

What is that reddish brown stuff on the car? It is rust. The paint peeled off, exposing the car's metal frame. Over time, the metal reacted with oxygen to form rust.

▶ Name something else that rusts.

_____

Picture the wick of a candle. If you twist it or cut it, it is still a wick. But what happens when you light it with a match? Smoke is given off as the wick burns. Was the smoke there before? No, it's a new substance. The burning of the wick is a chemical change. A **chemical change** occurs when one or more substances are changed into entirely new substances. When you blow out the flame, you can see that the wick turned black, so it is no longer the same substance.

Did you know that rusting is a chemical change? What happens if you leave your bicycle outside for a long time? Nothing changes at first. But if the bicycle gets wet, it could rust. Was there rust on the bike before? No, the rust is a new substance.

▶ Fill in the table to describe two chemical changes.

Before	After
In autumn, leaves fall to the ground.	
	Your sister blows out a candle and the wick has become black and brittle.

Rubber

A chemical change happens when light causes the rubber in the tire to break down.

Rot

Have you ever smelled rotting leaves? As the leaves break down and form a new substance, they release a gas that smells.

Chemical vs. Physical

How do you decide if something is a physical change or a chemical change?

ACTIVE READING As you read these two pages, find and underline the definition of *decay*.

Think about an orange that has been left in the refrigerator too long. Mold begins to grow on the orange. It gets very soft. White fuzz appears on the skin. It begins to smell funny.

A fungus is causing the orange to decay, or break down into simpler substances. That is why the orange gets so soft. The white fuzz you see and the rotten gas you smell also show that new substances are forming.

The decay of the orange is an example of a chemical change. But pulling apart a fresh orange is a physical change.

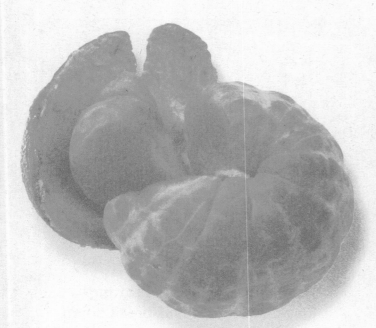

Physical Change

The orange is cut into segments, but it is still the same sweet, juicy orange.

Chemical Change

You don't want to eat this orange! The mold is causing a chemical change.

▶ Label each result as either a
physical change or a chemical change.

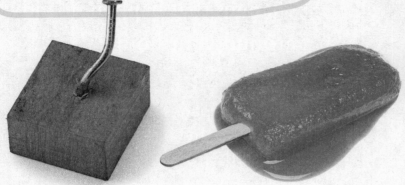

_____   _____   _____

_____   _____   _____

_____   _____   _____

Chemical Changes at Home

Some chemical changes happen in science labs, but there are also many chemical changes that happen in and around your home.

ACTIVE **READING** As you read these two pages, find and underline four clues that a chemical change has occurred.

From Yuck to Useful

Many people place their food waste into compost piles. These piles undergo chemical changes and fertilize soil.

COMPOST

Did a chemical change occur? Look for the following clues:

- Smell: As plants or animals decay, they release gases. You may want to hold your nose, because these gases stink!

- Color: When you toast bread, it turns brown—or black if you burn it!

- Heat: Firewood gets hot as it burns.

- Substance given off: When you light a birthday candle, smoke rises into the air.

These clues aren't foolproof. Think of what happens when you boil water. As the water bubbles, steam is released into the air. Is this a chemical change? Nope! Remember that in a chemical change, a new substance is made. Steam is not a new substance. It is still water but in a different state. The boiling of water is a physical change.

► Find three chemical changes around your home, and tell why you think each is a chemical change.

① _____
_____
_____
_____
_____
_____
_____

Fireworks

Fireworks are the result of chemical changes. Fireworks start off inside shells. A fuse is lit. The fuse sets some gun powder on fire, and the shells explode. The explosion causes other chemicals to burn, which causes the sparkles that you see.

② _____
_____
_____
_____
_____

③ _____
_____
_____
_____
_____
_____
_____
_____

Is the Dark Coin Dirty?

No. That is tarnish. Copper and other metals react with substances in the air to form tarnish.

Making Pizza!

Pizza comes in many varieties: thin-crust, thick-crust, pepperoni, and veggie. Can you keep track of all the physical and chemical changes that go into making one of these pizzas?

① Start with the Dough

Mix flour and water until the mixture is gooey. Next add some yeast and a little sugar. The yeast acts on the sugar to form new substances, including carbon dioxide gas. The gas makes bubbles in the dough, causing it to rise. (**Hint:** The bubbles tell you that there is a chemical change.) The dough is now ready to push, pull, and shape into a crust. (**Hint:** These are a physical changes.)

② Add the Toppings

Make the sauce by crushing tomatoes and mixing in spices. (**Hint:** Because you can separate the spices from the tomatoes, this is a physical change.) Spread the sauce, and shred some cheese on it. (**Hint:** The cheese is still cheese, so this is another physical change.) You can cut up some of your favorite vegetables to put on top. (**Hint:** No new substance is formed because cutting is a physical change.)

3 Bake the Pizza

Now it is time to bake the pizza. The dough gets hot and turns brown. It changes from dough into a crust that is nice and crispy. (**Hint:** You can smell the dough baking and see the change in color and texture, so you know chemical changes are happening.)

4 Dig In!

Slice the pizza. (**Hint:** Slicing is a physical change.) Then take a big bite. As you eat the pizza, it reacts with the juices in your stomach. Your body uses it for energy. (**Hint:** Chemical changes are occurring.)

➕➖ DO THE MATH
✖️➗

Equivalent Fractions

You can cut a pizza in many different ways. Any way you slice it, it is a yummy treat!

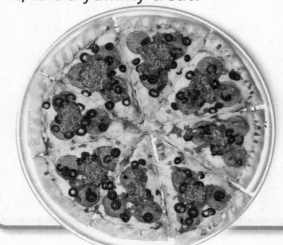

1. Color the first circle to show that $\frac{2}{8}$ of the pizza has been eaten. Color the second to show $\frac{1}{4}$ has been eaten.

2. Use the drawings to compare $\frac{2}{8}$ and $\frac{1}{4}$.

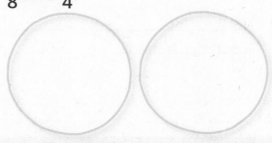

Sum It Up »

Read the two summaries below. Draw a picture to show each type of change.

1 Objects can be changed physically and chemically. A physical change occurs when the size, shape, or state of an object is changed. Cutting and folding paper are examples of physical changes. Even though the paper may look different, it is still paper.

2 In a chemical change, an object reacts with something else. A new substance is formed. Clues that a chemical change has happened include changes in smell, color, and heat. In all cases, a new substance appears.

Physical Change

3 Two examples of physical changes

are _____

and _____ .

4 No _____
substance is made.

Chemical Change

5 Two clues that a chemical change

has occurred are _____

and _____ .

6 A _____
substance is made.

Name _____

Vocabulary Review

1 Draw a line from each term to its definition or description.

1. physical

2. chemical

3. react

4. rust

5. decay

6. smoke

A. In a chemical change, one substance will ___ with another.

B. a change that does not result in a new substance

C. this forms when iron gets wet and reacts with oxygen

D. what dead plants and animals do over time; they are broken down into simpler substances

E. The result of this type of change is a new substance.

F. what you see when you light a campfire that is a sign of a chemical change

Apply Concepts

2 Label each of the following as a physical change or a chemical change.

_____   _____   _____

3 Label each of the following as a physical change or a chemical change.
Explain how you knew the answer.

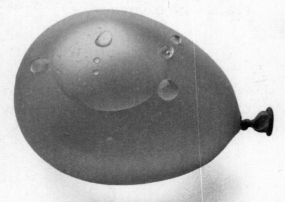 

You fill a balloon with water.
Then you pop it.

You forget your bananas in the car for a
week. Now they are squishy and brown.

_____   _____

_____   _____

_____   _____

_____   _____

4 Look at each picture. Tell how you could change what is shown.

Physical Change	Chemical Change
_____	_____
_____	_____
_____	_____
_____	_____
_____	_____
_____	_____
_____	_____
_____	_____
_____	_____
_____	_____
_____	_____
_____	_____
_____	_____
_____	_____
_____	_____
_____	_____

5 Read the steps in the cake recipe. Then answer the questions below it.

Place 2 cups of flour and 1 teaspoon of baking powder into a bowl.

Measure $1\frac{1}{2}$ cups of milk, and add it to the flour.

Break open 3 eggs. Add them to the bowl one at a time.

Add $\frac{3}{4}$ cup of sugar to the mixture.

Pour the batter into a pan.

Bake the mixture at 325 °F for 45 minutes.

Carefully remove the cake from the oven, and let it cool.

Name one step that describes a physical change.

_____

_____

Name one step that describes a chemical change.

_____

_____

When you bake a cake, how do you know a chemical change has occurred?

_____

_____

Take It Home! See *ScienceSaurus*® for more information about physical and chemical changes.

SC.4.P.9.1 Identify some familiar changes in materials that result in other materials with different characteristics, such as decaying animal or plant matter, burning, rusting, and cooking. **SC.4.N.1.3** Explain that science does not always follow a rigidly defined method. . . **SC.4.N.1.4** Attempt reasonable answers to scientific questions and cite evidence in support. **SC.4.N.1.7** Recognize and explain that scientists base their explanations on evidence.

INQUIRY
LESSON 2

Name _____

ESSENTIAL QUESTION

How Can You Tell When a New Substance Forms?

EXPLORE

In this activity, you and your classmates will explore what happens when steel wool gets wet.

Materials

2 small pieces of steel wool
water
2 small plates
plastic bowl
hand lens
forceps
safety goggles
plastic gloves

Before You Begin—Preview the Steps

① **CAUTION:** Wear safety goggles and gloves. Put one piece of steel wool on a plate. Soak another piece of steel wool in water. Then put it on the other plate.

② Place both samples in the same area, away from direct sunlight. Examine them every day for a week. Record your observations.

③ On the last day, observe both samples with a hand lens. Draw or describe what you see.

④ Use the forceps to pull apart the strands in both samples. Record your observations.

Set a Purpose

What will you learn from this experiment?

_____

_____

_____

State Your Hypothesis

Write your hypothesis, or testable statement.

_____

_____

_____

_____

_____

Think About the Procedure

What does each sample test?

_____

_____

_____

Name _____

Record Your Data

Make a chart to record your observations.

Draw Conclusions

What two clues tell you that a chemical change occurred?

_____

_____

_____

_____

Claims • Evidence • Reasoning

1. Could a scientist use your samples as evidence that a chemical change has occurred? Explain your reasoning.

_____

_____

_____

2. Write a claim about whether your hypothesis was correct. Cite evidence that supports your claim and explain why the evidence supports the claim.

_____

_____

_____

_____

3. Given what you have learned, what kind of warning might you place on a box of steel wool pads?

_____

_____

4. From what you have learned, describe two uses for steel wool—one that won't cause it to rust, and one that will cause it to rust. Explain your reasoning.

_____

_____

_____

5. Think of other questions that you would like to ask about rusting.

_____

_____

SC.4.E.6.5 Investigate how technology and tools help to extend the ability of humans to observe very small things and very large things. SC.4.N.2.1 Explain that science focuses solely on the natural world.

PEOPLE IN SCIENCE

Meet the Chemists

Benerito invented wash-and-wear cotton. It doesn't need ironing.

Ruth Rogan Benerito

Ruth Rogan Benerito's work as a chemist gave us wash-and-wear cotton clothing. Before the 1950s, clothing made from cotton wrinkled after washing. So, many people switched to synthetic cloth. The cotton farmers began to suffer. Benerito discovered a way to treat the cotton particles so that they were chemically joined. In doing so, she made a cloth that had few wrinkles. Benerito taught college classes for many years.

Héctor Abruña

Dr. Héctor Abruña is a chemist. He studies fuel cells. A fuel cell makes electricity from chemical changes. Unlike energy from burning fossil fuels, there is very little pollution from a fuel cell. Fuel cells can provide energy for cars, buildings, and even cell phones. Abruña has taught chemistry at Cornell University for nearly 30 years. He works to help more women and minorities become scientists.

Dr. Abruña studies ethanol as a possible fuel source for fuel cells. Ethanol is made from corn or other plants.

Chemistry Is All Around You!

Read the chemistry clues. Then **label** each item with the number of the matching clue.

1. It can make things stick almost instantly. A chemical change creates the bond.

2. It is lightweight. Garbage bags and water pipes are some of the many things made from this.

3. A chemical change makes milk into this tangy food.

4. This synthetic fabric is used to make clothing and tents. It is made from a chemical change.

5. Without it, you would be in the dark. A gas-filled tube uses a chemical change to make light.

6. A chemical change lets us see pictures on a screen.

7. A chemical change inside of this object makes electricity so objects can turn on or move.

LCD monitor

batteries

super glue

nylon

yogurt

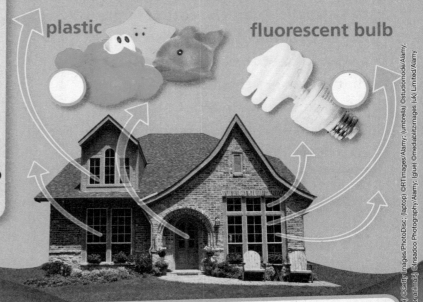

plastic

fluorescent bulb

Think About It!

You may find some or all of the items above in your home. Name five other things in your home that chemistry helped make.

_____

_____

_____

SC.4.N.1.1 Raise questions about the natural world, use appropriate reference materials that support understanding to obtain information (identifying the source), conduct both individual and team investigations through free exploration and systematic investigations, and generate appropriate explanations based on those explorations.

What's It Made Of?
Body Armor

Do you skate? Play football? Or play catcher for a softball team? If so, then you know how hard, bulky, and heavy sports safety gear can be. Not to worry—change is coming. Members of the U.S. Olympic ski team have worn suits with safety pads made of a new kind of body armor!

These light-weight, flexible, shock-absorbing safety pads mold to the wearer's body. Long chains of carbon and hydrogen particles make up the pads.

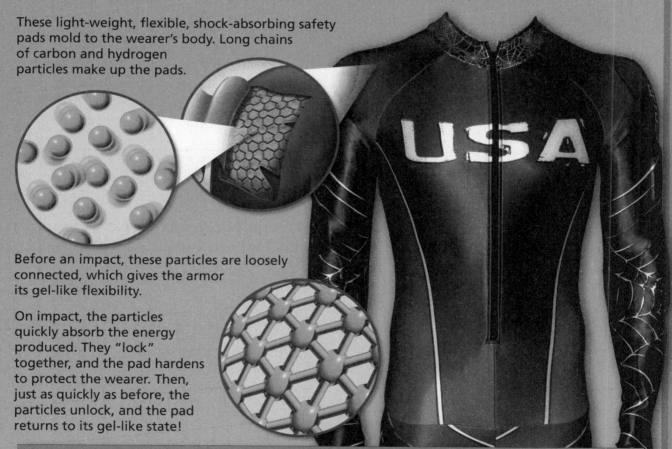

Before an impact, these particles are loosely connected, which gives the armor its gel-like flexibility.

On impact, the particles quickly absorb the energy produced. They "lock" together, and the pad hardens to protect the wearer. Then, just as quickly as before, the particles unlock, and the pad returns to its gel-like state!

TROUBLESHOOTING

Over time, sunlight can make the new safety pads hard and breakable. Suppose safety gear made from this material will be worn in full sun. How would you change its design?

_____

_____

What Else Could It Do?

Think about the properties of this new material. What other uses could it have? Suppose it was used to make a hammock. How would it work?

_____

_____

_____

_____

_____

Design Your Future

What are some other uses of this type of material? Draw a picture of your idea. Include labels to show when the material is flexible and when it is hard. Then, describe how your idea works.

_____

_____

_____

_____

_____

Build in Some Science:
Making Carbon Dioxide

When baking soda and vinegar are mixed, they react. If you look closely, you can see bubbles forming. Each bubble contains carbon dioxide gas.

Can you think of ways to put this reaction to good use? You may want to capture the carbon dioxide, allow it to fill a container, and use it to push against a surface or move an object. Or you might find out more about the useful properties of carbon dioxide gas.

Fzzzzzz. Carbon dioxide bubbles let you see and hear when baking soda and vinegar react. Carbon dioxide is a common gas. It is in the air that you breathe in and out. It is also dissolved in carbonated beverages.

DESIGN PROCESS STEPS

1 Find a Problem
2 Plan & Build
3 Test & Improve
4 Redesign
5 Communicate

What to Do:

1. Put on your safety equipment. Place 1/2 teaspoon of baking soda in the center of a plate.

2. Add drops of vinegar—one drop at a time—to the baking soda. What happens?

3. Research the properties of carbon dioxide. List some properties you think would be useful.

4. Based on your research, suggest ways this reaction might be part of a useful product.

5. Draw diagrams to illustrate your thoughts and designs. Then share your ideas with the class.

6. Keep a record of your work in your Science Notebook.

Name _____

Vocabulary Review

Use the terms in the box to complete the sentence.

| chemical change |
| chemical property |
| chemical reaction |
| physical change |

1. A change in matter in which a new substance is not formed is a _____.

2. A characteristic that describes how a substance will interact with another substance is a _____.

3. Any change in matter in which a new and different substance forms is called a _____ or a _____.

Science Concepts

Fill in the letter of the choice that best answers the question.

4. Blake will cook some pasta for dinner. He puts a pot of water on the stove to boil.

What best describes the type of physical change of boiling water?

Ⓐ change in size   Ⓒ change in color

Ⓑ change in state   Ⓓ change in shape

5. Winnie wants to make a tossed salad. She chops lettuce, tomatoes, carrots, and other vegetables. Then she puts them into a large bowl and mixes them up. Winnie takes a bite of salad and chews it. When she swallows, her stomach digests the vegetables.

Which of the actions is a chemical reaction?

Ⓕ chopping carrots

Ⓖ mixing the salad

Ⓗ biting the food

Ⓘ digesting the vegetables

6. Ian pushes the mower around the yard, cutting the grass to about 2 in. tall. When he stops the mower, he removes the grass catcher and pours the clippings into the compost pile. The grass will eventually decompose. Finally, Ian sweeps the grass clippings off the sidewalk. Which statement is true?

(A) Cutting the grass is a chemical change.

(B) Composting the grass is a physical change.

(C) Sweeping the sidewalk is a physical change.

(D) Pushing the mower is a chemical change.

7. Before swimming, Kiera covers her arms and legs with sunscreen. She blows up an inner tube to float on and jumps into the pool. After an hour, Kiera notices that her face has become sunburned. Which action is a chemical change?

(F) putting sunscreen on her arms and legs

(G) blowing up an inner tube

(H) jumping into the pool

(I) becoming sunburned

Apply Inquiry and Review the Big Idea

Write the answers to these questions.

8. Franco wants to test the effects of water on steel wool. He sets up two plates. Steel Wool J is dry and exposed to air. Steel Wool K is wet and exposed to air.

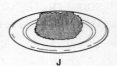 

J
Dry Steel Wool on Plate

K
Wet Steel Wool on Plate

a. Franco makes some observations about the steel wool before he starts the test. What are two observations that he can make? Make a claim about what tools should he use to make those observations.

_____

_____

b. What changes is Franco likely to observe after one week? Make a claim about whether these changes are chemical or physical. Cite evidence to support your claim.

_____

_____

_____

Energy and Its Uses

FLORIDA **BIG IDEA** 10

Forms of Energy

Daytona, Florida

I Wonder Why

A band has to plan how it will be seen and heard before a concert. Why? *Turn the page to find out.*

Here's Why

A lot of energy is used at concerts. Bands use lights and sound to put on a great show.

Essential Questions and Florida Benchmarks

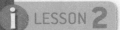 **LESSON 1**

What Are Some Forms of Energy? 325

SC.4.P.10.1 Observe and describe some basic forms of energy, including light, heat, sound, electrical, and the energy of motion.
SC.4.P.10.2 Investigate and describe that energy has the ability to cause motion or create change.

S.T.E.M. Engineering and Technology

How It Works: Piezoelectricity/Design It: Solar Water Heater 341
SC.4.N.3.1

 **LESSON 2**

Where Does Energy Come From? 345

SC.4.P.10.1, SC.4.P.10.2, SC.4.N.1.1, SC.4.N.1.5

CAREERS IN SCIENCE

Civil Engineer 349
SC.4.E.6.5, SC.4.N.2.1

 LESSON 3

What Is Sound? 351

SC.4.P.10.3 Investigate and explain that sound is produced by vibrating objects and that pitch depends on how fast or slow the object vibrates.
SC.4.N.1.1, SC.4.N.1.4, SC.4.N.1.6

 LESSON 4

How Do We Use Wind and Water for Energy? 355

SC.4.P.10.4 Describe how moving water and air are sources of energy and can be used to move things.

Unit 7 Benchmark Review 367

Science Notebook

Before you begin each lesson, write your thoughts about the Essential Question.

SC.4.P.10.1 Observe and describe some basic forms of energy, including light, heat, sound, electrical, and the energy of motion. SC.4.P.10.2 Investigate and describe that energy has the ability to cause motion or create change.

LESSON 1

ESSENTIAL QUESTION
What Are Some Forms of Energy?

 Engage Your Brain

Find the answer to the following question in this lesson and record it here.

How does this person use energy to ride the river's rapids?

_____

_____

_____

_____

ACTIVE READING

Lesson Vocabulary
List the terms. As you learn about each one, make notes in the Interactive Glossary.

_____   _____

_____   _____

_____   _____

Main Idea and Details
In this lesson, you'll read about different kinds of energy. Active readers look for main ideas before they read to give their reading a purpose. Often, the headings in a lesson state the main ideas. Preview the headings in this lesson to give your reading a purpose.

What Is Energy?

All the lights in your house need energy.
So do the refrigerator and washing machine.
Can you name three other things in your home or
school that use energy?

ACTIVE **READING** As you read these two pages, find and
underline a definition of *energy*. Then circle two sources of energy.

What do you and a car have in common? You both
need energy. Gasoline is the car's source of energy.
This car won't go anywhere if it runs out of gas.

▶ Draw lines to match each item on the left with its source of energy.

Name something that uses electricity as a source of energy.

_____

_____

Making an object move is a change. **Energy** is the ability to cause change in matter. So, everything that moves has energy.

Where does energy come from? You can see some sources of energy on these two pages. What sources of energy have you used today?

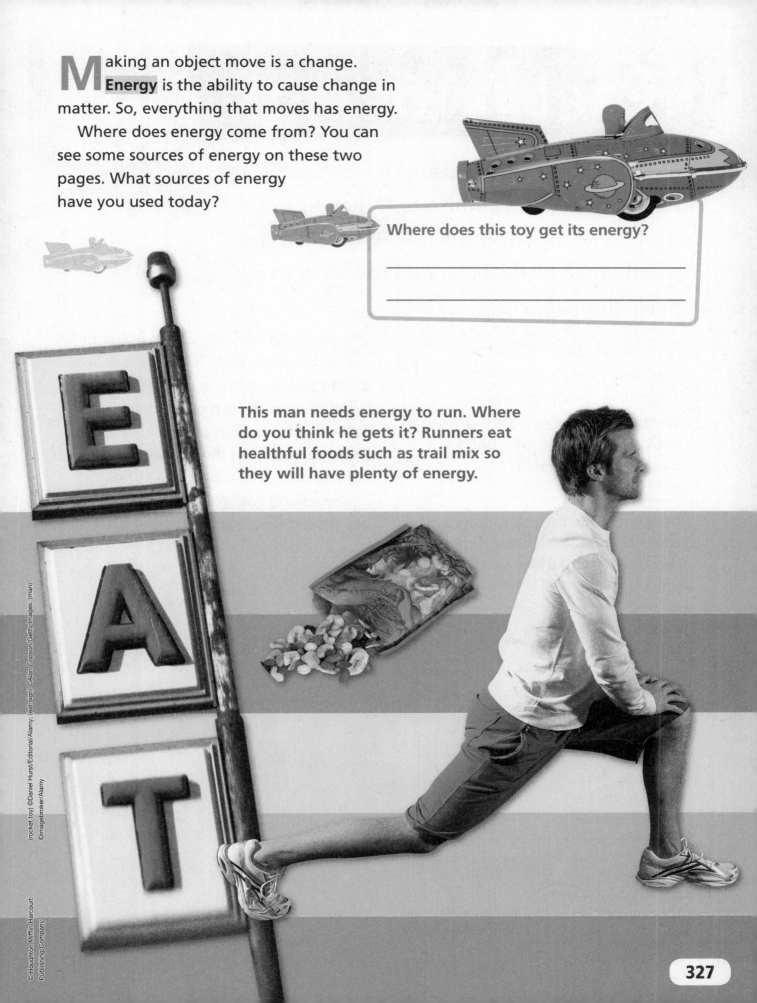

Where does this toy get its energy?

_____

_____

This man needs energy to run. Where do you think he gets it? Runners eat healthful foods such as trail mix so they will have plenty of energy.

Get Moving!

Have you ever been on a roller coaster? When roller coaster cars climb a hill, they seem to stop at the top for just a moment. Then they speed down to the bottom. How does energy make this happen?

ACTIVE READING As you read these two pages, find and underline the definition of *mechanical energy*. Then draw circles around the two parts of mechanical energy.

Something in motion, such as the girl on the pogo stick, has kinetic energy. **Kinetic energy** is the energy of motion. Something at the top of a hill, such as a roller coaster car, has potential energy. **Potential energy** is the energy something has because of its position or condition.

Mechanical energy is the total potential energy and kinetic energy of an object.

▶ **Everything in the left column has potential energy. Tell what happens when the potential energy of each object is changed to kinetic energy.**

A ball sits on top of a hill	
A person stretches back a rubber band	
Someone gets ready to throw a paper airplane	

The girl pushes the pogo stick's spring down. The spring now has potential energy. When the spring spreads out, the pogo stick goes up and has kinetic energy.

As the roller coaster cars climb to the top of a hill, they gain potential energy. The higher the cars go, the more potential energy they have.

As the cars go down a hill, their potential energy decreases because it changes to kinetic energy. The roller coaster cars have more kinetic energy when they move faster. At each point along the ride, the mechanical energy of the cars is the sum of their potential and kinetic energies.

This roller coaster goes fast because of mechanical energy. That's good, because a slow roller coaster isn't much fun!

Flash and Boom!

You see lightning flash across the sky. Then you hear a boom that's so loud, it makes your heart pound. These are two forms of energy.

Light energy is produced and used in different ways. Light is a form of energy that can travel through space. Plants use light from the sun to make food. The same energy from the sun allows us to see. Another source of light energy is electricity. If we couldn't use electricity to produce light energy, it would be difficult to work or play in the evening.

Another form of energy is sound. Sound is made when something moves back and forth. This back-and-forth motion is called vibration. Sound can be described in different ways. For example, pitch describes how high or low a sound is. Loud sounds have more energy than quiet sounds. Can you think of an example of a loud, high-pitched sound?

 DO THE **MATH**

Solve Real-World Problems

How far away was that lightning strike? As soon as you see a flash of lightning, count the seconds until you hear thunder. Then divide the number of seconds by 5. This gives you the approximate distance in miles.

35 seconds _____

20 seconds _____

40 seconds _____

Lightning can be hotter than the surface of the sun. It makes the air around it rapidly expand. This causes the boom of thunder.

► **Describe how each member of this musical group produces sound. Write your answers in the spaces provided.**

Energy Is All Around Us

Do you think you could do without energy for one day? Without chemical energy, you couldn't mow the lawn. Without electrical energy, you couldn't power your MP3 player.

ACTIVE **READING** As you read these two pages, draw a circle around a use of chemical energy. Draw a box around a use of electrical energy.

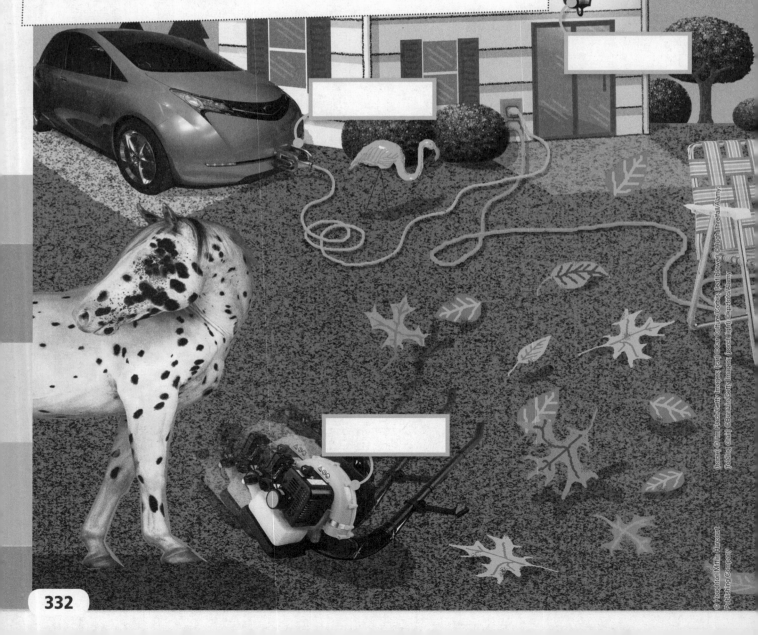

Many things use chemical energy and electrical energy. **Chemical energy** is energy than can be released by a chemical change. Chemical energy from food gives us energy. Most cars run on gasoline, a source of chemical energy. Have you ever warmed yourself by a campfire? Fire is the release of chemical energy.

Electrical energy provides the energy for most of the devices you use, like computers and televisions. **Electrical energy** is energy that comes from electric current. Anything plugged into a wall outlet uses electrical energy.

Where does electricity come from? In most cities, electricity is generated using the chemical energy released during the burning of fossil fuels such as coal and natural gas. The sun and wind can also be used to generate electricity.

▶ **Identify the things in this scene that use chemical energy and those that use electrical energy. Write your answers in the spaces provided.**

Energy Can Change Forms

Can you read by the light of chemical energy? Can you use electrical energy to make something move? You can do both of these things, and more.

ACTIVE READING As you read these two pages, draw a line under two examples of energy changing forms.

Chemical energy changes into light energy in a glow stick.

Energy can change from one form to another. Electrical energy changes to light energy when you turn on a light switch. You may also feel the heat energy given off by some light bulbs. Chemical energy in gasoline changes to mechanical energy when a driver presses the gas pedal to drive.

Glow sticks have a glass tube inside them. The glass tube has chemicals inside it. When you bend the glow stick, the tube breaks. The chemicals in the tube mix with other chemicals in the glow stick. When they mix, light energy is given off.

A remote control sends radio waves to the remote-controlled car. Radio waves are another form of energy, similar to light energy. The radio waves change to electrical energy to tell the motor what to do—start, stop, or go faster. The car also has batteries inside it. The batteries change chemical energy to electrical energy to move the car.

This plant changes light energy from the sun into chemical energy in food.

Changing Energy

Draw a picture that shows another way that energy can change form.

Sum It Up »

Use information in the summary to complete the graphic organizer.

Energy is the ability to cause change in matter. Making an object move is a change. So, everything that moves has energy. Kinetic energy is the energy of motion. Potential energy is the energy something has because of its position. The mechanical energy of an object is the sum of its kinetic and potential energies. Light energy enables plants to make food and helps us see. Sound energy is caused by a vibrating object. Energy can change from one form to another.

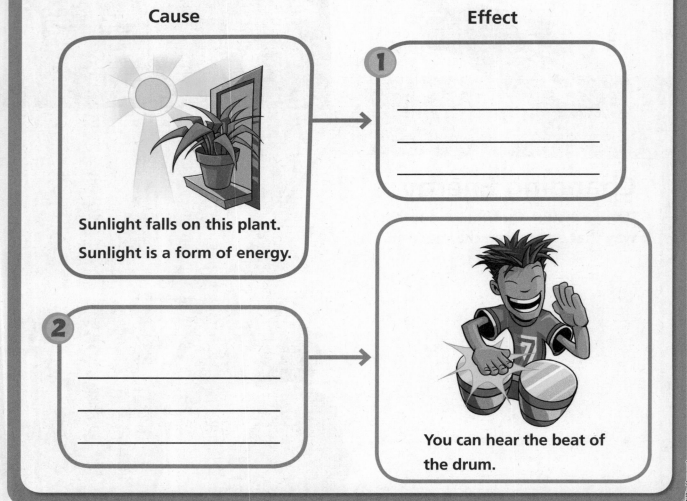

Cause

Sunlight falls on this plant.
Sunlight is a form of energy.

Effect

1 _____
_____
_____

2 _____
_____
_____

You can hear the beat of the drum.

Name _____

Vocabulary Review

1 Choose words from the box to complete the Forms of Energy word web.

Forms of Energy

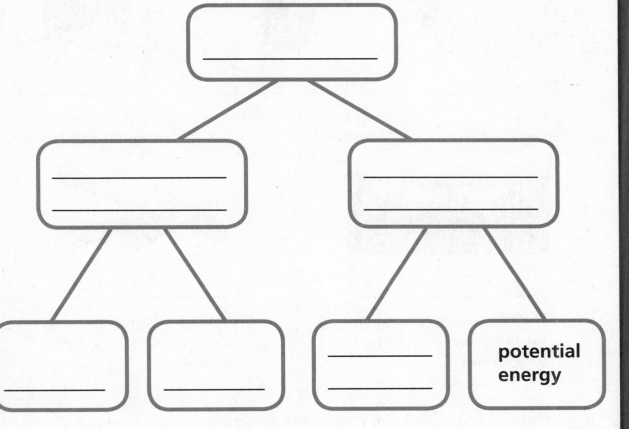

energy*	chemical energy*	mechanical energy*
kinetic energy*	food	gasoline

* Key Lesson Vocabulary

Apply Concepts

2 Use the words from the box to label each picture. Each term will be used once.

chemical energy	kinetic energy	potential energy
sound	light	

_____

This boy has an up-and-down motion.

_____

You can feel the cello's vibrations.

_____

Food gives this bird the energy it needs to live.

_____

The roller coaster cars go to the top of the hill and stop for a moment.

_____

You can carry these glow sticks in the dark so people can see you.

3 A light bulb changes electrical energy into two other forms of energy. What are they?

_____

_____

_____

4 Which of these objects has potential energy? How do you know?

_____

_____

_____

_____

5 Describe how sound energy is produced when you strike the top of a drum.

_____

_____

_____

_____

_____

_____

_____

6 Many forms of energy are around us and within us. Write three paragraphs in the form of an e-mail to a friend or family member describing some ways you use energy in a typical day. Tell your reader where the energy comes from and how it transforms into other forms of energy.

_____

_____

_____

_____

_____

_____

_____

_____

_____

_____

_____

_____

_____

Take It Home!

See *ScienceSaurus*® for more information about energy.

SC.4.N.3.1 Explain that models can be three dimensional, two dimensional, an explanation in your mind, or a computer model.

S.T.E.M.

ENGINEERING & TECHNOLOGY

How It Works:
Piezoelectricity

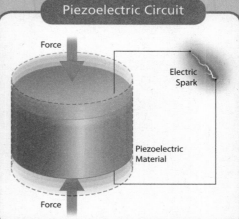

Quartz is a piezoelectric material.

This gas lantern has a tool that changes kinetic energy from an impact into electrical energy. Electrical energy produced this way is called *piezoelectricity*, or electricity from pressure!

Gas Chamber

You don't need a match to light this lantern! It has a piezoelectric igniter. The igniter is a tool made up of a small, spring-loaded bar and a piezoelectric material.

Piezoelectric Igniter

When this red button is pushed, the bar strikes, or impacts, the piezoelectric material.

Piezoelectric Circuit

Force

Electric Spark

Piezoelectric Material

Force

The bar's force squeezes the piezoelectric material, producing electric charges that flow as an electric current. Inside the lantern's gas chamber, the current jumps between two conductors, causing an electric spark. The spark ignites the gas. *Voilà!* Light and heat are produced.

TROUBLESHOOTING

Why might a lantern not light up when a piezo igniter is pushed?

_____

_____

_____

Show How It Works

The gas lantern shows some ways energy changes take place. Kinetic energy changed into electrical energy, which ignited the natural gas. Chemical energy stored in the gas changed into heat and light. Identify different kinds of energy and their sources in your classroom or home. In the space below, draw and describe how energy from one of these sources is transformed.

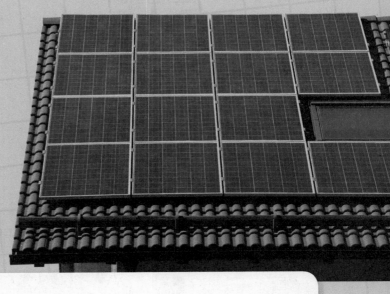

These solar cells transform, or change, solar energy into electrical energy. Electrical energy is changed into heat and light inside the home.

Suppose that popcorn kernels are being cooked over a campfire. Describe the kinds of energy being used and how they are being transformed.

_____

_____

_____

_____

We use heated water to wash our hands and body.

Design It:
Solar Water Heater

The sun is a free source of renewable energy. It makes sense for us to use the sun to meet our energy needs.

In addition to providing natural lighting, sunlight can also be used to heat buildings. Solar water heaters are placed on rooftops to absorb the sun's energy. As the water takes in solar energy, the water temperature rises. The heated water can then be used inside the house.

Suppose you wanted to build a solar water heater. How would you start? What materials would you use? How would you evaluate your design? Try it.

Solar water heaters include storage tanks and solar panels.

These students covered the inside of the shoebox with black construction paper. How do you think it will affect the performance of their solar water heater model?

DESIGN PROCESS STEPS

1 Find a Problem
2 Plan & Build
3 Test & Improve
4 Redesign
5 Communicate

What to Do:

1. Learn about heat and the transfer of energy.

2. Find out about how solar energy can be used to meet our energy needs. Are there any solar water heaters in your community?

3. Use your research to build a solar water heater model. Begin by setting your design criteria.

4. Draw a model.

5. Use available materials to build and test your design.

6. Use a thermometer to measure the effectiveness of your solar water heater model. How can you improve its performance?

7. If needed, redesign your solar water heater model until it meets your design criteria.

8. Keep a record of your work in your Science Notebook.

Name _____

ESSENTIAL QUESTION

Where Does Energy Come From?

Materials

thin wooden dowel
plastic-foam ball
spring
masking tape
tape measure
safety goggles

EXPLORE

In this activity, you and your classmates will explore how energy can cause motion.

Before You Begin—Preview the Steps

① **CAUTION:** Wear safety goggles. With a partner, tape one end of a thin wooden dowel to a tabletop. Half of the dowel should stick out past the edge of the table. Slide a spring onto the dowel.

② Push a plastic-foam ball onto the end of the dowel. Slide the ball back and forth until it can move freely.

③ Push the ball toward the desk until the coils of the spring are squeezed tightly together. Let go of the ball. Measure how far the ball traveled. Repeat this step until you have five distances recorded.

④ Repeat Step 3, but only squeeze the spring halfway. Predict how far the ball will travel. Release the ball. Measure and record the distance it travels five times.

Set a Purpose

What will you learn from this experiment?

_____

_____

_____

State Your Hypothesis

Write your hypothesis, or testable statement.

_____

_____

_____

Think About the Procedure

Why did you repeat Step 3 four times?

_____

_____

_____

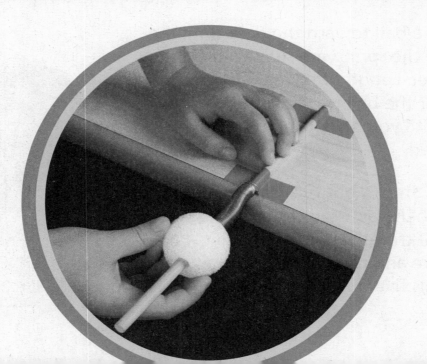

Name _____

Record Your Data

In the space below, make a table in which you record your results.

Draw Conclusions

What did you observe in this investigation?

_____

_____

_____

_____

Claims • Evidence • Reasoning

1. Write a claim about how the distance the ball traveled is related to the spring. Cite evidence that supports the claim and explain your reasoning.

_____

_____

_____

_____

2. When you compressed the spring, it gained potential energy. What was the source of the energy?

_____

_____

3. What happened to the spring's potential energy when you let go of the ball?

_____

_____

4. Why did squeezing the spring halfway affect the distance the ball traveled? Explain your reasoning.

_____

_____

5. Did each group in the class have the same results from the investigation? Why or why not?

_____

_____

_____

SC.4.E.6.5 Investigate how technology and tools help to extend the ability of humans to observe very small things and very large things. SC.4.N.2.1 Explain that science focuses solely on the natural world.

DETOUR

8 Things YOU SHOULD KNOW ABOUT Civil Engineers

1 Civil engineers plan the structures that are built in cities and towns. Roads, buildings, bridges, and dams are some of the things they plan.

2 The projects that civil engineers build need to be safe. They must hold up to daily use and bad weather.

3 Civil engineers improve how we live. They help people get clean drinking water and solve our energy needs.

4 Civil engineers are important to a growing city or town. They look at the need for new buildings, sewers, and transportation.

5 Civil engineers keep cars and trucks moving. They fix roads that are old and no longer safe.

6 Civil engineers make drawings called construction plans. They choose the best materials to use.

7 Civil engineers use tools, such as compasses and rulers. Many engineers use computers to design their plans.

8 Some civil engineers survey, or measure, the surface of the land. They use this data to plan buildings.

Engineering Emergency!

Match the problems that can be solved by a civil engineer with its solution in the illustration. Write the number of the problem in the correct triangle on the picture.

 1 We have an energy shortage! We can harness the river's energy to generate electricity.

 2 The city is getting crowded! More people are moving here. They need more places to live and work.

 3 The streets are always jammed. We have a transportation crisis!

 4 The nearest bridge is too far away. We need a faster and easier way to get across the river.

Think About It!

If you were a civil engineer, what kind of changes would you make where you live?

_____

_____

SC.4.P.10.3 Investigate and explain that sound is produced by vibrating objects and that pitch depends on how fast or slow the object vibrates SC.4.N.1.1 Raise questions... conduct both individual and team investigations... and generate appropriate explanations... SC.4.N.1.4 Attempt reasonable answers to scientific questions and cite evidence... SC.4.N.1.6 Keep records that describe observations made.

INQUIRY
LESSON 3

Name _____

ESSENTIAL QUESTION

What Is Sound?

EXPLORE

In this activity, you and your classmates will explore pitch, which is one of the properties of sound.

Before You Begin—Preview the Steps

(1) **CAUTION:** Put on your safety goggles. Use a pencil to poke a hole in the bottom of the cup.

(2) Thread a thick rubber band onto a paper clip. Put them in the cup, and then pull the rubber band through the hole.

(3) Place the cup upside down on a table. Tape a ruler to the cup (as shown), with the 1-cm mark at the top. Pull the end of the rubber band over the end of the ruler, and tape it to the back.

(4) Pull the rubber band to one side, and then let it go. Observe the sound. Record your observations.

(5) Use one finger to press the rubber band against the 2-cm mark and then the 4-cm mark. Repeat Step 4 each time.

(6) Repeat Steps 2–5, using the thin rubber band.

Set a Purpose

What skills will you learn from this experiment?

_____

_____

_____

Think About the Procedure

What two variables did you test?

_____

_____

_____

_____

Why did you repeat the whole activity with the thin rubber band?

_____

_____

_____

_____

_____

_____

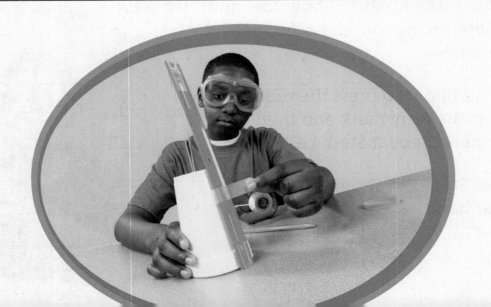

Name _____

Record Your Data

In the space below, make a table in which you record your results.

Draw Conclusions

Compare the sounds you made.

_____

_____

_____

_____

_____

_____

Claims • Evidence • Reasoning

1. In this investigation, did you rely more on observations of your eyes or your ears? Explain your reasoning.

_____

_____

2. Make a claim about how the length of the rubber band affects its pitch.

_____

_____

3. Cite evidence that supports your claim and explain why the evidence supports the claim.

_____

_____

_____

4. How did using numbers on the ruler help you make accurate comparisons?

_____

_____

5. Loudness is also a property of sound. How could you use this rubber band model to test loudness?

_____

_____

6. Think about other questions you would like to ask about sound.

_____

_____

SC.4.P.10.4 Describe how moving water and air are sources of energy and can be used to move things.

LESSON **4**

ESSENTIAL QUESTION

How Do We Use Wind and Water for Energy?

Engage Your Brain

Find the answer to the following question in this lesson and record it here.

How do we use wind to provide us with energy?

_____

_____

_____

_____

📖 ACTIVE **READING**

Lesson Vocabulary

List the terms. As you learn about each one, make notes in the Interactive Glossary.

_____

_____

_____

Main Idea

The main idea of a paragraph is the most important idea. The main idea may be stated in the first sentence, or it may be stated elsewhere. Active readers look for main ideas by asking themselves, What is this paragraph mostly about?

Water Energy

Have you ever stood in the ocean and been knocked down by a wave? Water can have a lot of energy!

ACTIVE READING As you read these two pages, draw a line under the main idea of each paragraph on the next page.

This illustration shows how a dam can be used to change the kinetic energy of falling water into electrical energy. Electricity made in this way is known as **hydroelectric energy**. *Hydro* means "water."

① A river brings water to a dam. The dam holds the water behind it in an artificial lake called a reservoir [REZ• er•vwar].

② Water is released through the dam. The water spins the blades of giant turbines.

③ Each turbine is connected to a generator. The turbine makes the generator spin to produce electricity.

④ The water then flows back into the river.

People have long used water's energy to move people and things. Before boats had engines, ferries and rafts used the motion of rivers to carry people and goods from place to place.

Engineers and scientists have developed new ways to harness the energy of moving water. For example, tidal energy stations use the energy in the regular rise and fall of the ocean's tides to generate electricity.

Mills powered by water have been used for hundreds of years. Water flows over the wheel to turn it. The wheel turns an axle, or shaft, that turns a mill wheel or some other device.

Compare this water wheel to the hydroelectric dam. How are they alike? How are they different?

_____

_____

_____

_____

_____

_____

④

How are these people using the energy of moving water?

_____

_____

Wind Energy

Flying a kite is a good way to experience energy. Sometimes the wind blows with so much force, you have to brace yourself!

ACTIVE **READING** As you read this page, circle two uses of wind energy.

Windmills, like water mills, have been used for hundreds of years. They use wind energy to move. **Wind energy** is energy produced by moving air. Older windmills were often used to grind grain. Today, windmills known as wind turbines are used in some places to produce electricity. The wind's kinetic energy causes the turbine's blades to move. A generator changes this energy of motion into electrical energy.

One wind turbine could make enough electricity to run your school. You could even have enough left over to sell to the local electric company! Wind, like water, is a clean energy source and does not hurt the environment. Both are renewable resources.

Floating windmills take advantage of stronger and steadier winds over the water. Undersea cables carry electricity to the shore.

(bkgd) ©Paul Glendell/Alamy

© Houghton Mifflin Harcourt Publishing Company

Look at the map. Where in the United States could wind energy be used the most? What would you expect the land to look like in those areas?

_____

_____

_____

_____

Little wind
Some wind
Windy

Hang gliders and eagles use wind energy to fly.

Sailors must learn how to use sails to capture the wind.

Renewable Energy
Is Our Future

We may someday run out of fossil fuels like coal, petroleum, and natural gas. If we want to use electricity in the future, we'll have to find ways to use other sources of energy.

Many calculators use solar energy, or energy from sunlight. A solar cell uses energy from the sun or from lights to produce electricity.

Fossil fuels are nonrenewable sources of energy. Once they're gone, they're gone. Water and wind are renewable sources of energy. We'll always have water and wind. *Biofuels*, which are made from living things, are renewable resources too.

Scientists are working hard to increase our use of renewable energy sources. You are already using some of these resources every day.

Many farmers in the Midwest use windmills to make some of the electricity they need to run their farms.

This bus has a tank filled with hydrogen instead of gasoline. The hydrogen goes to a fuel cell, where hydrogen and oxygen produce electricity. The electricity drives the bus's motor. The bus's fuel cell is similar to the one shown here from a hydrogen car.

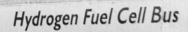

Hydrogen Fuel Cell Bus

DO THE MATH

Solve Real-World Problems

This house just had solar panels added to its roof. Before the solar panels, the homeowners' monthly electric bill was about $250. With the solar panels, their bill dropped to about $175 per month. How much money are the solar panels saving them each month? _____

Sum It Up »

Use information in the summary to complete the graphic organizer.

Wind and water are two important sources of renewable energy. Humans have long used water's energy to move people and things. Windmills were often used to grind grain. Today, we use wind energy and water energy to drive generators. The generators change mechanical energy to electrical energy. Scientists are working hard to increase our use of renewable energy sources.

Main Idea: Wind and water are two important sources of renewable energy.

Detail: Humans have long used water's energy to move people and things.

1

Detail: _____

_____

_____

2

Detail: _____

_____

_____

_____

Name _____

Vocabulary Review

1 Use the clues to help you unscramble the letters that make up each of the terms listed at the bottom of the page. Write each term in the boxes.

A. This is produced by moving water. leehdocictryr geneyr

☐☐☐⊙☐☐☐☐☐☐☐☐   ☐☐☐☐☐☐

B. This has blades that spin and can be connected to a generator. betnuri

☐☐☐☐☐⊙☐

C. This can be used to grind grain. ndiw neeygr

⊙☐☐☐   ⊙☐☐☐☐☐

D. This spins to make electricity. aroegnert

☐⊙☐☐☐⊙☐☐☐

E. This comes from the sun. losra ygeren

☐☐⊙☐☐   ☐⊙☐☐☐

F. This comes from living things. lubifeo

⊙☐☐☐☐☐

Unscramble the circled letters to complete the message.

We need to find more ways

to use __ __ __ __ __ __ __ __ __ energy sources.

generator	solar energy*	wind energy*
biofuel	hydroelectric energy*	**turbine**

* Key Lesson Vocabulary

Apply Concepts

2 In the space below, draw a picture to show one way that water moves an object.

3 Circle the activities that use a clean energy source.

4 Describe why the activities you circled involve a clean energy source.

_____

_____

_____

_____

5 Make a list of six ways you use renewable energy at home or at school.

_____

_____

_____

_____

_____

_____

6 Tell how a dam is used to make electricity.

_____

_____

_____

_____

_____

_____

7 Which of these is a renewable resource? How do you know?

_____

_____

_____

8 What energy source do you think people will use most in the future? Explain your answer.

_____

_____

9 Which of these is a nonrenewable resource? Circle it.

10 Wind and water energy account for less than 3% of the energy used in the United States each year. Use the circle graph to explain in a letter to a lawmaker why using renewable energy sources is important.

_____

_____

_____

_____

_____

_____

_____

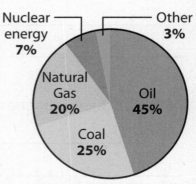

U.S. Energy Sources

Nuclear energy 7%
Other 3%
Natural Gas 20%
Oil 45%
Coal 25%

Take It Home!

Share what you have learned about wind and water uses with your family. With a family member, name uses of water in places in your home and yard.

Name _____

Vocabulary Review

Use the terms in the box to complete the sentences.

> kinetic energy
> sound energy
> potential energy
> mechanical energy

1. The energy of motion is _____.

2. The energy something has because of its position or condition is _____.

3. The type of energy that results from vibrations traveling through air is _____.

4. The total energy of water as it falls from a waterfall is _____.

Science Concepts

Fill in the letter of the choice that best answers the question.

5. Energy can change form. Which picture shows electrical energy becoming heat energy?

   A

   B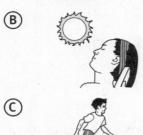

   C

   D

6. Niko jumps on a trampoline. The pictures below show him at different points during jumping.

   At which point does Niko have the most potential energy?

   F point 1   H point 3

   G point 2   I point 4

7. Fossil fuels are a major source of energy. Which material is **not** a fossil fuel?

Ⓐ coal

Ⓒ oil

Ⓑ natural gas

Ⓓ wood

8. Today, three of the most important fuels are wood, coal, and oil. Which of the following is another type of fuel?

Ⓕ natural gas

Ⓗ water

Ⓖ kinetic

Ⓘ wind

9. The energy of falling water can be converted into different forms of usable energy. Which of these can be generated from falling water?

Ⓐ electrical energy

Ⓒ solar energy

Ⓑ fossil fuels

Ⓓ wind energy

10. Isabella is investigating the properties of sound. The picture below shows how far she pulled the rubber bands.

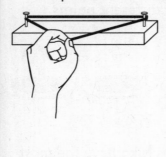 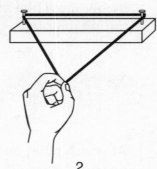

1   2

How would the sound from number 2 compare with the sound from number 1?

Ⓕ higher

Ⓗ lower

Ⓖ louder

Ⓘ softer

11. When you hear sound, it has a pitch. What is the change in pitch most related to?

Ⓐ how loud the vibration is

Ⓑ how long the vibration continues

Ⓒ how soft the vibration is

Ⓓ how fast the vibration moves back and forth

12. Sam's science class is studying motion. During an activity, Sam uses a piece of equipment that can send balls a short distance. The picture below shows the equipment that he used.

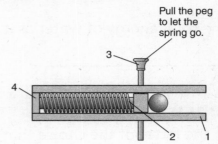

Which part of the equipment has the most potential energy?

Ⓕ 1

Ⓗ 3

Ⓖ 2

Ⓘ 4

13. Which is **true** about energy?

Ⓐ Objects at rest do not have energy.

Ⓑ Most sources of energy are renewable.

Ⓒ Energy can be destroyed when work is done.

Ⓓ Energy can change from one form to another.

Name _____

14. Ang and Jessica put a spring on a dowel. Then they add a foam ball to the dowel. They push on the ball to squeeze the spring and then let the ball go. The potential and kinetic energies of the ball in their investigation are forms of which of the following kinds of energy?

   (F) chemical energy

   (G) electrical energy

   (H) magnetic energy

   (I) mechanical energy

15. A scientist measured how much energy a certain wind turbine produced in locations with different wind speeds. The graph of her results is shown below.

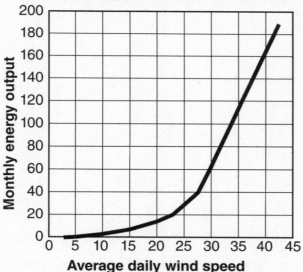

Energy Output from Wind Turbine

Monthly energy output vs *Average daily wind speed*

How much energy does the turbine produce at an average wind speed of 30 km/hr in 1 month?

   (A) about 50 kWh   (C) about 90 kWh

   (B) about 60 kWh   (D) about 110 kWh

16. Look at the image below.

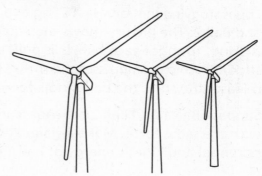

What type of energy is being captured in the figure?

   (F) heat energy

   (G) hydroelectric energy

   (H) light energy

   (I) wind energy

17. Miguel carries an empty bucket to his garden. He fills the bucket with tomatoes. Then he carries the bucket back to his house. Which statement correctly describes the energy used for each trip?

   (A) Miguel used the same amount of energy to carry both the empty bucket and the full bucket.

   (B) Miguel used different sources of energy to move the bucket on each trip.

   (C) Miguel used more energy carrying the full bucket than he did carrying the empty bucket.

   (D) Miguel transferred energy to the bucket the first time and to the tomatoes the second time.

Apply Inquiry and Review the Big Idea

Write the answers to these questions.

18. Luis is studying motion. He is using two balls—Ball 1 and Ball 2. The picture shows the equipment he is using. To shoot each ball, Luis pulls back on the stick (5), which compresses the spring (4). When he releases the stick, the ball shoots forward.

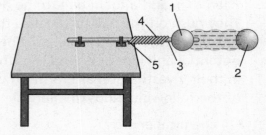

Suppose Ball 1 and Ball 2 are shot from the table with the same force. Make a claim about how the potential and kinetic energy of Ball 1 compare to that of Ball 2. Explain your reasoning.

_____

_____

_____

_____

_____

19. Look at the image below.

Make a claim about the types of energy that enable the greenhouse to keep the plants inside it warm. Cite evidence to support your claim.

_____

_____

_____

_____

Heat

FLORIDA BIG IDEA 11

Energy Transfer and Transformations

Dinner can be cooked on the beach.

I Wonder Why

A cook prepares food over an open flame. What does the flame do to the food? *Turn the page to find out.*

Here's Why

The flame heats the pan and the food. As it becomes warmer, the food cooks so that friends can enjoy it.

Essential Questions and Florida Benchmarks

LESSON 1
What Is Heat? 373
SC.4.P.11.1 Recognize that heat flows from a hot object to a cold object and that heat flow may cause materials to change temperature.

LESSON 2
How Is Heat Produced? 385
SC.4.P.11.1, SC.4.N.1.1, SC.4.N.3.1

LESSON 3
What Are Conductors and Insulators? 389
SC.4.P.11.2 Identify common materials that conduct heat well or poorly.

LESSON 4
Which Materials Are Conductors? 399
SC.4.P.11.1, SC.4.P.11.2, SC.4.N.1.3, SC.4.N.1.4, SC.4.N.1.8

PEOPLE **IN SCIENCE**
Halimaton Hamdan 403
SC.4.E.6.5 Explain how technology and tools help ... humans....
SC.4.P.11.2, SC.4.N.2.1

Unit 8 Benchmark Review 405

Science Notebook

Before you begin each lesson, write your thoughts about the Essential Question.

SC.4.P.11.1 Recognize that heat flows from a hot object to a cold object and that heat flow may cause materials to change temperature.

LESSON **1**

ESSENTIAL QUESTION
What Is Heat?

 Engage Your Brain

Find the answer to the following question in this lesson and record it here.

Most photographs show people and objects as we see them. What do you think this photograph shows?

_____

_____

_____

📖 ACTIVE **READING**

Lesson Vocabulary
List the terms. As you learn about each one, make notes in the Interactive Glossary.

_____

_____

_____

_____

Signal Words: Contrast
Signal words show connections between ideas. Words that signal contrasts include _unlike, different from, but,_ and on _the other hand._ Active readers remember what they read because they are alert to signal words that identify contrasts.

The Energy of Heat

It takes heat to shape glass or to make tea. But what is heat, exactly? Think about it for a moment. How would you define *heat*?

ACTIVE **READING** As you read these two pages, find and underline the definition of *heat*.

Temperature measures how hot or cold something is. Energy moves between objects that have different temperatures. You've already learned about many kinds of energy. **Heat** is the energy that moves between objects of different temperatures. The difference in temperature makes the energy move.

You sense heat as a warming feeling. More precisely, you feel the change in temperature as you gain energy. Heat moves naturally from an object with a high temperature to one with a lower temperature. In other words, heat moves from a warmer object to a cooler object.

Super Hot

You can see and feel heat moving from the flame to the glass. This melted glass is about 1,500 °C/2,732 °F!

Incredibly Cold

This is dry ice—frozen carbon dioxide. It is really cold—about −80 °C/−112 °F.

➕➖✖️➗ DO THE **MATH**

Use Temperature Scales

Temperature is measured in different scales. The two scales on this thermometer are Celsius and Fahrenheit. Write the letter of each picture at the appropriate place on the thermometer.

This girl's clothes trap heat near her body. Her jacket slows down energy transfer to the cold air. This girl stays warm while playing in the snow in temperatures as low as 0 °C/32 °F.

The water coming from this shower head is hotter than the air around it. The average temperature of shower water is 42 °C/108 °F.

Heat moves from the burner to the kettle, from the kettle to the water, and then from the water vapor to the air. Water boils at 100 °C/212 °F.

Ice cubes melt as heat transfers to them from the warm air. The puddle of water is about 20 °C/68 °F.

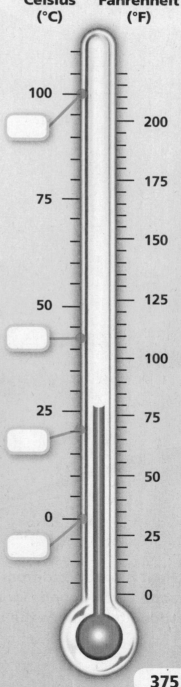

Celsius (°C)   Fahrenheit (°F)

100

75

50

25

0

200

175

150

125

100

75

50

25

0

375

Heat on the Move!

Heat can move in different ways.

ACTIVE READING As you read these two pages, draw a box around each main idea.

Heat is conducted from your hand into the snow. The snow melts. Your hand feels cold.

Conduction

Conduction is the transfer, or movement, of heat between two objects that are touching. It can also occur *within* an object. Heat moves from inside your body to warm your skin. Your feet and hands stay warm because heat moves all around your body.

Heat is conducted from the soup to the spoon. Soon the spoon feels hot to the touch.

1. Heat is conducted from the burner to the pot to the water.

2. Heated water travels up, warming the cooler water above.

3. Cooler water sinks to the bottom, where it gets heated. The cycle repeats. This movement is called a *convection current*.

Convection

Convection is the transfer of heat within a liquid or a gas. Particles in liquids and gases move easily, and they take heat with them. Heat from a campfire warms the air around it by convection. Warmer air is always buoyed upward. In this case, the fire is the source of heat for convection.

Hot air rises above cooler air. That's what keeps a hot-air balloon in flight.

▶ Write the kind of heat transfer that takes place in the following situations.

An eruption of lava on the ocean floor

Winds blowing in from a warmer part of the country

Feet touching a cold floor

_____

_____

_____

Feeling Radiant!

Heat moves by conduction between solids that are touching. Heat moves by convection through gases and liquids. But can heat travel without moving through matter? Find out.

Heat travels from the campfire by convection and radiation.

The third way heat can move is radiation. **Radiation** is the transfer of heat without matter to carry it. Heat simply leaves one object and goes directly to another. Suppose you're standing near a campfire. You can feel the heat from the fire because it warms the air. But you can also feel the heat because it warms you directly through radiation.

In some ways, radiation may be the most important way heat can move. Life on Earth needs heat from the sun. But space is a vacuum. How does heat travel through the emptiness of space? By radiation.

The room is cool and air-conditioned. On the other hand, heat radiating from this light keeps the young chickens warm.

▶ Circle the objects that are radiating heat.

Heat from the sun radiates through space and through the atmosphere before it warms this girl's face.

Sum It Up »

Fill in the missing words to complete the conversation.

Rebecca: Ow! How did my cell phone get so hot?

Abdullah: Well, there are (1) _____ ways that heat could have moved into your phone.

Rebecca: I know. If it had been sitting in sunlight, I'd know it was heated through (2) _____ . But it was in the shade.

Abdullah: Well, there's also convection.

Rebecca: Yeah, but that only happens within (3) _____ and (4) _____ . My phone's a solid.

Abdullah: Then it must have been the third way: (5) _____ .

Rebecca: But that only happens when two things are (6) _____ each other. My phone was sitting by itself.

Abdullah: Where?

Rebecca: On top of my laptop.

Abdullah: In that case, heat traveled into your phone through (7) _____ .

Rebecca: Really? How does it do that?

Abdullah: Heat moves from warm objects to (8) _____ objects. Your laptop was probably much warmer than your cell phone.

Rebecca: Maybe I'll leave it on my wooden desk from now on!

Name _____

Vocabulary Review

1 Unscramble each word and write it in the boxes.

How heat moves from one end of a solid to the other

C C N O T N O I U D

How heat moves from one end of a solid to the other

The topic of this lesson

T H E A

What heat does during convection or conduction

S R T F N R A E S

How heat moves through a liquid

T N E V C O I N C O

Heat moves from this source by convection and radiation

F I R M P A C E

How heat travels through empty space

D O T A I R N I A

Unscramble the letters in the circles to form a word that is related to this lesson.

_____

Apply Concepts

2 A transfer of heat happens between objects of different temperatures. Draw an arrow between each pair of objects to show the direction heat would travel between them.

3 Label each part of the drawing as an example of conduction, convection, or radiation.

A.

_____

B.

_____

C.

_____

4 Label each of the following as examples of conduction, convection, or radiation.

hot water added to bath

_____

space heater

_____

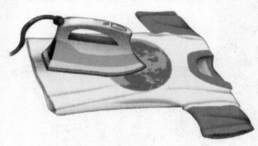

iron-on decal

_____

clothes dryer

_____

sunlight through a window

_____

sandwich press

_____

5 In this pizza restaurant, heat is traveling in different ways. Label the examples of conduction, convection, and radiation in the spaces provided.

Take It Home! See *ScienceSaurus*® for more information about energy.

SC.4.P.11.1 Recognize that heat flows from a hot object to a cold object and that heat flow may cause materials to change temperature SC.4.N.1.1 Raise questions... use appropriate reference materials... conduct both individual and team investigations... and generate appropriate explanations... SC.4.N.3.1 Explain that models can be three dimensional, two dimensional...

i INQUIRY LESSON **2**

Name _____

ESSENTIAL **QUESTION**

How Is Heat Produced?

EXPLORE

You know that heat moves by conduction, convection, and radiation. You can feel it move. In this investigation, your job is to make a model that will allow you to "see" heat move.

Before You Begin—Preview the Steps

(1) CAUTION: Be careful using scissors. Draw a spiral on a sheet of paper. Cut the spiral out.

(2) CAUTION: Wear goggles. Be careful not to poke yourself with the needle! Thread the sewing needle. Tie a knot on the far end of the thread. Then put the thread through the center of the spiral.

(3) Push the needle into the dowel so that the spiral is hanging from the dowel.

(4) Put one of the light bulbs in the base and turn it on. Hold your hand about 30 cm above the bulb. Do NOT touch the bulb. Observe and record. Then hold the spiral 30 cm above the bulb. Observe and record.

(5) Test the other light bulb in the same way. Record your observations.

Materials

lightweight paper
dowel

pencil
safety goggles

scissors
piece of thread, 50 cm long

sewing needle

incandescent light bulb and base

compact fluorescent light bulb and base

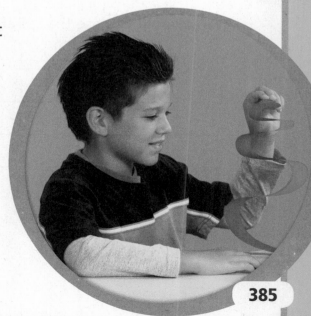

Set a Purpose

What do you think you will learn from this experiment?

_____

_____

_____

State Your Hypothesis

Write your hypothesis, or testable statement.

_____

_____

_____

_____

Think About the Procedure

How does the paper spiral test for the presence of heat?

_____

_____

_____

Why would you use the spiral instead of your hand?

_____

_____

_____

_____

© Houghton Mifflin Harcourt Publishing Company

Name _____

Record Your Data

In the table below, record the data you gathered.

Draw Conclusions

What conclusions can you draw about light sources and heat?

_____

_____

Claims • Evidence • Reasoning

1. Interpret your data. Write a claim about whether your hypothesis was supported. Cite evidence that supports the claim and explain why the evidence supports the claim.

_____

_____

_____

_____

_____

2. Write a claim about the difference between compact fluorescent bulbs and incandescent light bulbs. Cite evidence that supports the claim and explain why the evidence supports the claim.

_____

_____

_____

3. Incandescent light bulbs use more electrical energy than compact fluorescent bulbs do. Why do you think this is so?

_____

_____

4. What other materials could you test in this way to see if they produce heat?

_____

_____

5. What other questions do you have about heat transfer?

_____

_____

SC.4.P.11.2 Identify common materials that conduct heat well or poorly.

LESSON 3

ESSENTIAL **QUESTION**

What Are Conductors and Insulators?

Engage Your Brain

Find the answer to the following question in this lesson and record it here.

How can these dogs stay warm in such cold weather?

_____

_____

_____

_____

_____

ACTIVE READING

Lesson Vocabulary
List the terms. As you learn about each one, make notes in the Interactive Glossary.

_____

_____

_____

_____

Cause and Effect
Some ideas in this lesson are connected by a cause-and-effect relationship. Why something happens is a cause. What happens as a result of something else is an effect. Active readers look for effects by asking themselves, What happened? They look for causes by asking, Why did it happen?

Go with the Flow...of Heat

A pan in the oven gets very hot. But if you pick it up with an oven mitt, your hand stays cool. Why?

ACTIVE READING As you read these two pages, circle lesson vocabulary each time it is used.

Heat moves through some materials very easily. In the example above, heat from the oven moved easily into the pan. But heat from the pan did not pass through the oven mitt. A material that allows heat to move through it easily is called a **conductor**. Many heat conductors also conduct electricity well.

For the most part, solids are better conductors of heat than liquids or gases are. That's because the particles that make up a solid are packed closely together. They vibrate, but don't move apart much. Heat can move quickly from one particle to another.

Glass
Glass does not conduct heat well. If you pour boiling water into a metal bowl, the outside of the bowl quickly gets hot. A glass bowl gets warm more slowly.

Stone
Marble does not conduct heat as well as metals do. But it can still conduct heat away from your body. That's why marble feels cool when you touch it.

Metal
Metals are great heat conductors. Some metals conduct heat better than others do.

390

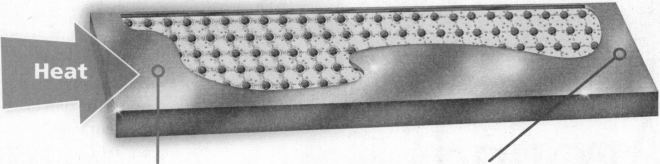

Heat

Getting Hot

This diagram shows the particles of a metal bar. The particles on this end are hot. This end was placed over a flame, but the other end wasn't.

Still Cool

The particles on this end aren't hot yet, but they will be soon. In metals, heat moves from particle to particle very easily.

▶ Imagine you touched the handles of all four spoons. Circle the spoon handle that would be the hottest. Then explain your choice.

_____

_____

_____

wood

metal

porcelain

plastic

Turn the Heat Around

Wearing gloves insulates your hands. The gloves trap heat near your skin.

Not all materials are conductors. Heat does not move easily—or at all—through some materials.

ACTIVE READING As you read these pages, find and underline two effects of insulators.

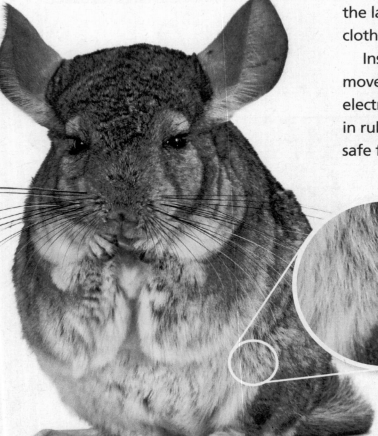

Materials that do not conduct heat well are called **insulators**. Oven mitts are insulators. They are made of materials that are poor conductors of heat. When you remove a pan of cookies from the oven, your hands don't get burned.

Gases can be good insulators. A thin layer of trapped air is an excellent insulator. In cold weather, layers of clothing trap your body heat near you. There's air between the layers of clothing. Along with the clothing, the air insulates your body.

Insulators can be used to slow down the movement of heat. Metal wires conduct electricity and heat. Most wires are covered in rubber to insulate them and keep people safe from the electricity and heat.

Hair as an Insulator

Most furry animals stay warm in cold weather. Fur is made of thick hairs. Around each hair is air. The air and the fur act as insulators, keeping the animal warm.

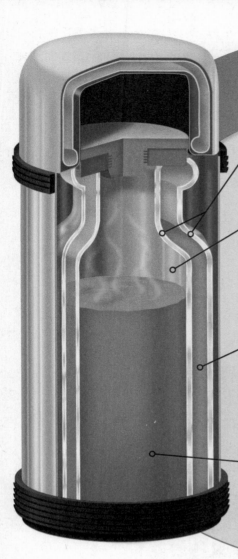

Why Does a Thermos Work?

Glass lining
A layer of glass holds the tea. Glass does not conduct heat very well.

Reflection
Even in a vacuum, radiation can move energy. The facing sides of the layers are coated in silver, which act like a mirror. It reflects some heat back.

Vacuum
There is a vacuum between the inner and outer glass layers of the bottle. The vacuum keeps conduction or convection from taking place.

Still Hot
With the conduction, convection, and radiation slowed down, the tea stays hot for a long time!

▶ Although the straw house is not the sturdiest, a straw house can be well insulated. Why?

_____

_____

Heat Proofing a Home

All across the United States, people are trying to conserve, or save, energy. It's good for the environment, and it saves money. Heat proofing a home is one way that people can conserve energy.

When the weather is hot, you want to keep heat from coming into your home. When the weather is cold, you want to keep heat from leaving your home. It costs money to cool and heat a home!

There are different ways to slow the flow of heat into or out of a house. Some things need to be done while the house is being built. Others can be done to an existing home. Insulating a home saves money. It also helps conserve energy.

1 Insulation

Insulation is blown inside the walls of a house. Insulation keeps heat from traveling through to the attic.

2 glass panes

2 Windows

These windows have two panes of glass to limit conduction. They also have a coating that limits heat radiation.

3 Pipes

Hot pipes radiate heat from water into the air. Wrapping them keeps the heat from escaping.

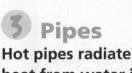

4 Soil

Soil is a great insulator. Basements are usually cool, even in the summer.

DO THE MATH

Solve Real-World Problems

The Ogburn family wants to heat proof their house. They can save about $800 a year by adding insulation. Wrapping the water pipes will save an additional $5 each month. Buying new, energy-efficient windows will save them about $2,000 every year.

1. How much money will wrapping the water pipes save the Ogburns in a year?

_____

2. About how much more money will replacing the windows save each year than wrapping the water pipes?

_____

3. Write an equation to calculate how much all three things will save the Ogburns in a year.

_____

Bonus!

If new windows cost $10,500, pipe insulation costs $100, and adding insulation costs $400, in how many years will the savings pay for the cost of these home improvements?

_____

_____

_____

Sum It Up »

Write the vocabulary term that describes each material.

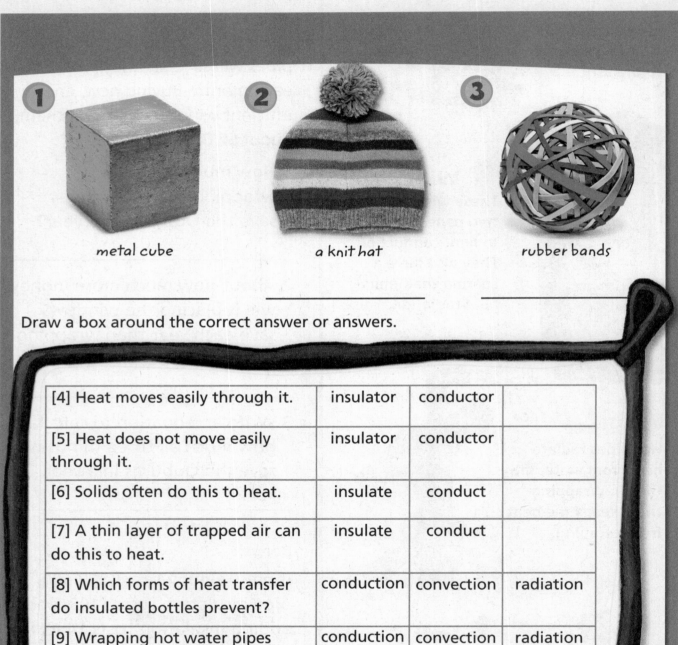

1 metal cube

2 a knit hat

3 rubber bands

_____ _____ _____

Draw a box around the correct answer or answers.

[4] Heat moves easily through it.	insulator	conductor	
[5] Heat does not move easily through it.	insulator	conductor	
[6] Solids often do this to heat.	insulate	conduct	
[7] A thin layer of trapped air can do this to heat.	insulate	conduct	
[8] Which forms of heat transfer do insulated bottles prevent?	conduction	convection	radiation
[9] Wrapping hot water pipes prevents which form of heat transfer?	conduction	convection	radiation

Name _____

Vocabulary Review

1 Use the clues to help you write the correct word in each row. Some boxes have been filled in for you.

A. | | I | N | | | | |
B. | | I | N | | | | | |
C. | | I | N | | | | |
D. | | | | | | C | |
E. | | | | | | C | |
F. | | | | M | | |
G. | | | | M | | |
H. | | | | M | | |
I. | | | | | M | |

A. Some of them have two panes of glass.

B. It can be blown inside walls.

C. It slows the transfer of heat.

D. It's the opposite of answer C.

E. The silver layer of an insulated bottle does this to radiated heat.

F. Because of natural insulation, it's often the coolest part of a house.

G. It's an excellent conductor.

H. It does not conduct as well as metals do.

I. It makes conduction and convection impossible.

Apply Concepts

2 You are going to make a kitchen spoon. It will be used to stir hot liquids. Circle the material that will be warmest when you touch its handle.

cotton

metal

plastic

wood

3 Many people are building "green" houses, which use very little energy. Some of these houses are partially or completely underground. Why?

_____

_____

_____

4 How would you design a lunchbox that could keep hot food hot or cold food cold? Sketch a diagram of the box.

Take It Home!

Look around your kitchen with your family. Find two things that conduct heat and two things that are heat insulators.

SC.4.N.1.3 Explain that science does not always follow a rigidly defined method...
SC.4.N.1.4 Attempt reasonable answers to scientific questions and cite evidence in support.
SC.4.N.1.8 Recognize that science involves creativity in designing experiments. **SC.4.P.11.1** Recognize that heat flows from a hot object to a cold object and that heat flow may cause materials to change temperature. **SC.4.P.11.2** Identify common materials that conduct heat well or poorly.

Name _____

ESSENTIAL QUESTION

Which Materials Are Conductors?

Materials

metal knife
butter
plastic knife
marker
2 clear plastic cups
hot water
stopwatch or clock

EXPLORE

You and your classmates will explore which materials conduct heat well. And the best part is that you get to use butter!

Before You Begin—Preview the Steps

(1) **CAUTION:** Be careful when using knives! Cut four equal-size pieces of butter.

(2) Put one piece of butter on the tip of each knife, and one halfway down the blade of each knife.

(3) Put one knife, handle first, in each cup. Mark each cup at the level of the lower piece of butter. Then remove the knives.

(4) Your teacher will fill each cup to just below the mark with hot water. Put the knives back in their cups, handle first. Observe the butter for 10 minutes. Record your observations.

Set a Purpose

What do you think you will learn from this experiment?

_____

_____

State Your Hypothesis

Write your hypothesis, or testable statement.

_____

_____

_____

Think About the Procedure

What is the tested variable?

_____

_____

What things must be the same in each setup?

_____

_____

_____

_____

© Houghton Mifflin Harcourt Publishing Company

Name _____

Record Your Data

Make a chart in the space below to record your observations.

Draw Conclusions

Which material did heat move through more quickly?

_____

Claims • Evidence • Reasoning

1. Interpret your data. Write a claim about which material is a conductor and which is an insulator.

_____

_____

2. Cite evidence that supports your claim and explain why the evidence supports the claim.

_____

_____

_____

3. On which knife did the butter melt faster? On that knife, which pat of butter melted faster?

_____

_____

4. Write a claim about which knife would lose heat faster. Then, plan an experiment to gather evidence to support your claim.

_____

_____

_____

5. What other materials could you test this way?

_____

_____

6. What other questions would you like to ask about conductors and insulators?

_____

_____

◯PEOPLE **IN SCIENCE**

Ask Halimaton Hamdan

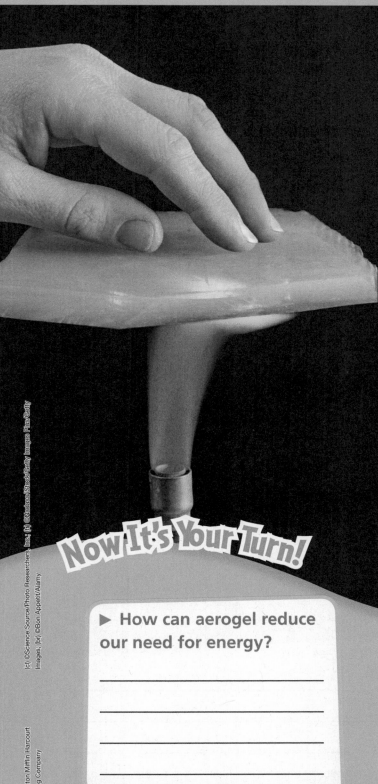

Q. What scientific discovery did you make?

A. I discovered a way to make aerogel from the husks that cover grains of rice. I come from a rice-growing country called Malaysia. I named my aerogel Maerogel in honor of my home country.

Q. What is aerogel?

A. *Aerogel* is the lightest solid on Earth. It is made mostly of air, yet it is very strong. Aerogel is the best insulator. It protects things from heat, electricity, and sound. Aerogel can be used in windows, on walls, in aircraft, and even in clothing.

Q. Why is your discovery important?

A. Aerogel has been around since 1931, but it costs a lot to make. Because it costs a lot, aerogel is not used often. It costs much less to make Maerogel. I am still studying Maerogel, but I hope that someday it will be used by many people.

Now It's Your Turn!

▶ **How can aerogel reduce our need for energy?**

_____

_____

_____

_____

This Leads to That

There are many possible uses for Hamdan's low-cost aerogel.

▶ Write its possible uses for the objects below. The first one has been done for you.

Low-Cost Aerogel

Aerogel can be used to make tennis rackets stronger, while keeping the racket light.

_____
_____
_____
_____
_____
_____

_____
_____
_____
_____
_____
_____

Think About It!

▶ **How would you use aerogel?**

_____
_____
_____

Name _____

Vocabulary Review

Use the terms in the box to complete the sentence.

| conduction |
| conductor |
| convection |
| heat |
| insulator |
| radiation |

1. The energy that moves between objects of different

    temperatures is _____.

2. The transfer or movement of heat between two objects

    that are touching is _____.

3. The transfer of heat within a liquid or a gas is _____.

4. The movement of heat without matter to carry it is _____.

5. A material that allows heat to move through it easily is a(n) _____.

6. A material that does not let heat move through it easily is a(n) _____.

Science Concepts

Fill in the letter of the choice that best answers the question.

7. Rachel tests how quickly different
    materials change temperature when
    they are heated. All materials start at the
    same temperature. She then heats them
    at the same time. The table shows the
    temperatures after 5 min.

	Starting temperature (°C)	Temperature after 5 min (°C)
Material 1	19	37
Material 2	19	48
Material 3	19	31
Material 4	19	42

    Which is the **best** insulator?

    Ⓐ Material 1   Ⓒ Material 3

    Ⓑ Material 2   Ⓓ Material 4

8. The picture shows a pot of water heating
    on a stove top.

    Which statement explains what happens
    to the water in the pot?

    Ⓕ The water temperature decreases.

    Ⓖ The water will freeze over time.

    Ⓗ Heat energy travels from the water in
    the pot to the burner.

    Ⓘ Heat energy travels from the burner
    to the pot and the water.

9. Russell is on a camping trip with his family. To warm their food, they put it in a bowl and place the bowl on a rack near the fire. Which material should the bowl be made from to allow the heat of the fire to warm the food most easily?

Ⓐ aluminum   Ⓒ rubber

Ⓑ plastic   Ⓓ wood

10. Rondell knows that radiation is one form of heat transfer. Which example describes a transfer of heat through radiation?

Ⓕ a hand holds a cold glass of milk

Ⓖ a flame warms air in a hot-air balloon

Ⓗ a puddle of water warms in the sun

Ⓘ a pot of boiling water sits on a gas burner

Apply Inquiry and Review the Big Idea

Write the answers to these questions.

11. Paula stands by a campfire. Make a claim about all methods of heat transfer taking place as she warms her hands. Explain your reasoning.

_____

_____

_____

12. Misa puts thermometers in four identical boxes, covers each box, and leaves them outside on a hot, sunny day. Make a claim about which thermometer should show the highest temperature after two hours. Cite evidence to support your claim.

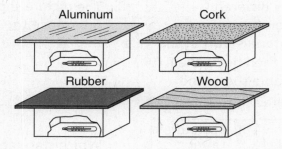

Aluminum   Cork

Rubber   Wood

_____

_____

_____

Forces and Motion

FLORIDA BIG IDEA 12

Motion of Objects

I Wonder Why

Rides at a boardwalk move in many different directions and at many different speeds. Why is this so? *Turn the page to find out.*

Here's Why

Forces make objects move in straight lines, in curves, or back and forth. A force can change the speed or direction of an object.

Essential Questions and Florida Benchmarks

LESSON **1**

What Is Motion? 409
SC.4.P.12.1 Recognize that an object in motion always changes its position and may change its direction.
SC.4.P.12.2 Investigate and describe that the speed of an object is determined by the distance it travels in a unit of time and that objects can move at different speeds.

ⓘ LESSON **2**

What Is Speed? 425
SC.4.P.12.2, SC.4.N.1.1, SC.4.N.1.5

CAREERS **IN SCIENCE**
Biomechanist 429
SC.4.E.6.5 Explain how technology and tools help ... humans....
SC.4.N.2.1

S.T.E.M. **Engineering and Technology**
How It Works: Gyroscopes/Improvise It: A Game of Skill and Motion 431
SC.4.N.1.8

Unit 9 Benchmark Review 435

Science Notebook

Before you begin each lesson, write your thoughts about the Essential Question.

80 meters

100 meters

| 50 | 55 | 60 | 65 | 70 | 75 | 80 | 85 | 90 | 95 | 100 |

➕➖✖️➗ DO THE **MATH**

Calculate Speed

1. What is the speed of the rabbit during the race?

_____

2. What is the speed of the turtle during the race?

_____

3. A chicken joins the race and runs at 4 m/sec. On the distance line, draw the chicken where it would be after 10 seconds.

_____

_____

_____

_____

Pushes and Pulls

Gravity

Gravity pulls down with a force that keeps the truck on the road.

Sand

What causes objects to start moving? What causes objects to stop moving once they are in motion?

ACTIVE READING As you read these two pages, draw circles around two words that name types of forces.

What have you pushed or pulled today? Maybe you pushed open a door or pulled on your shoes. A push or a pull is a **force**. Suppose you want to change the way something is moving. A force can change an object's speed or direction.

Many forces act on you. *Gravity* is a force that pulls objects down to Earth. Gravity keeps you on the ground or on a chair.

Friction is a force that acts directly against the direction of motion. Friction can slow things down or make them stop.

416

▶ Why do you think workers spread sand on icy, snow-covered roads?

_____

_____

Force

The force of the road on the truck pushes the truck forward.

Friction

The snow exerts a force of friction that pushes backward against the truck and slows it down.

▶ Look at the girl on the sled. Draw arrows and label *gravity*, *force*, and *friction*.

(b) ©Getty Images/PhotoDisc

© Houghton Mifflin Harcourt Publishing Company

Changing It Up

The gas pedal on a car is called an accelerator. Did you know that the brakes and steering wheel are also accelerators?

ACTIVE READING As you read these pages, circle three phrases that tell how an object can accelerate.

You may hear people say that a car is accelerating when it speeds up. That's only partly correct. **Acceleration** is any change in velocity. Remember that velocity tells both the speed and the direction of motion. So matter accelerates if it speeds up, slows down, or changes direction.

Acceleration of any kind is caused by forces. Forces can push and pull on matter from all directions. If a force pushing against an object in one direction is greater than a force pushing in the opposite direction, the object will accelerate.

Turn and Speed Up

In this section, the fly accelerates because it changes both its direction and its speed.

Look at the path of the fly. The fly accelerates each time it changes either its speed or its direction. Sometimes it changes both its speed and its direction at the same time!

Slow Down

Here, the fly is traveling in a straight line while slowing down. This is also acceleration.

Speed Up

In this section of its path, the fly travels in a straight line. It accelerates because it is speeding up.

Name _____

Vocabulary Review

1 Important words from this lesson are scrambled in the following box.
Unscramble the words. Place each word in a set of squares.

| lcaoeciranet | despe | eerrfcnee | oitmon |
| hups | crefo | vatgiyr | ovltyiec |

| | | | c | |

| | r | | | | |

| | | | o | |

| | c | | | | | | | | |

| | | s | |

| | | | r | | | |

| | | | d | |

| | | o | | | |

Rearrange the letters in the colored boxes to form
a word that describes the location of an object.

| | | | | | | | | | |

Put a star next to two words that describe
how fast something moves.

Apply Concepts

2 Describe the motion and path of the diver. Use the words
position, speed, velocity, and *acceleration* in your description.

_____

_____

_____

_____

_____

_____

_____

_____

_____

_____

_____

_____

3 You are riding in a bus. Your friend is standing on the street corner as the bus
goes by. How would you describe the way your friend seems to move? How
would your friend describe your motion? Why do the descriptions differ?

_____

_____

_____

_____

_____

_____

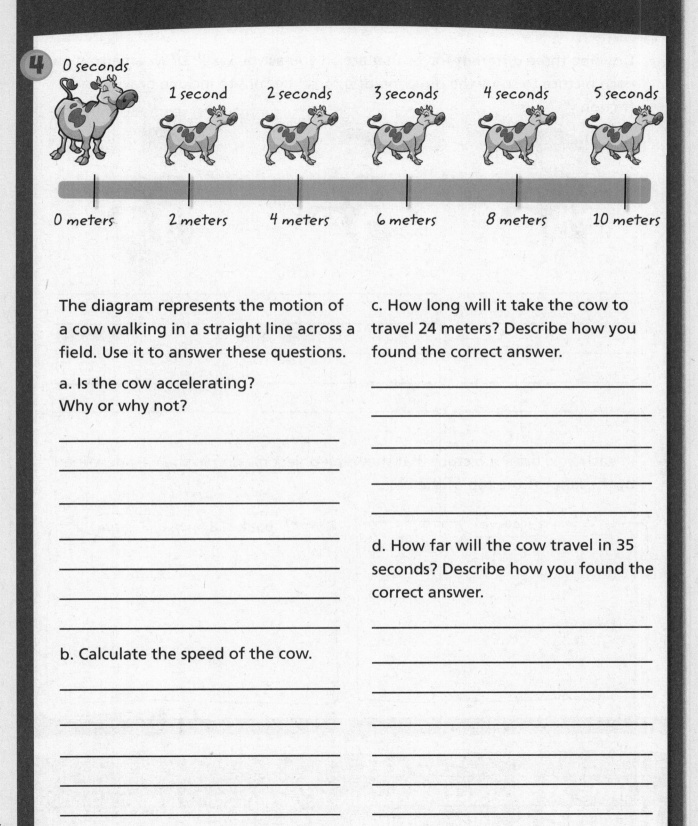

4 0 seconds   1 second   2 seconds   3 seconds   4 seconds   5 seconds

0 meters   2 meters   4 meters   6 meters   8 meters   10 meters

The diagram represents the motion of a cow walking in a straight line across a field. Use it to answer these questions.

a. Is the cow accelerating? Why or why not?

_____

_____

_____

_____

_____

b. Calculate the speed of the cow.

_____

_____

_____

_____

c. How long will it take the cow to travel 24 meters? Describe how you found the correct answer.

_____

_____

_____

_____

_____

d. How far will the cow travel in 35 seconds? Describe how you found the correct answer.

_____

_____

_____

_____

_____

5 Describe three different forces that act on you as you walk. Draw an arrow on each picture to show the direction of a force. Be sure to include gravity and friction.

_____   _____   _____

_____   _____   _____

_____   _____   _____

_____   _____   _____

_____   _____   _____

6 In each box, draw a picture that shows an object moving in the way described by the label at the top of the box.

curve

back and forth and curve

Take It Home! See *ScienceSaurus*® for more information about forces and motion.

SC.4.P.12.2 Investigate and describe that the speed of an object is determined by the distance it travels in a unit of time and that objects can move at different speeds. SC.4.N.1.1 Raise questions… use appropriate reference materials… conduct both individual and team investigations… and generate appropriate explanations… SC.4.N.1.5 Compare the methods and results… done by other classmates.

INQUIRY
LESSON 2

Name _____

ESSENTIAL QUESTION
What Is Speed?

Materials

meterstick
masking tape
stopwatch
large rubber band
ball
chair

EXPLORE

In this activity, you will measure the speed of a ball as different forces act on it.

Before You Begin—Preview the Steps

1. Use a meter stick and masking tape to mark off a distance of 10 m. Then place the meter stick so that the 0 on the meter stick is on the end of the tape.

2. Wrap a large rubber band around the leg of a chair. Place the chair so that the rubber band is stretched across the 0 on the meter stick.

3. Place the ball in front of the rubber band at the 0 mark on the meter stick. Pull back the ball and rubber band to the 10 cm mark.

4. Release the ball and start the stopwatch. Stop the stopwatch when the ball crosses the 10 m mark on the masking tape.

5. Repeat Steps 3 and 4 four more times. Each time, increase the distance you pull back the ball.

Set a Purpose

What do you think you will you learn from this experiment?

_____

_____

_____

State Your Hypothesis

Write your hypothesis, or testable statement.

_____

_____

_____

_____

Think About the Procedure

How can you figure out the speed at which the ball is moving?

_____

_____

_____

As you pull the ball back farther each time, what happens to the force with which the ball is launched?

_____

_____

_____

Name _____

Record Your Data

In the space below, draw a table in which to record your observations.

Draw Conclusions

What is the relationship between the times you recorded and the speed of the object?

_____

_____

_____

_____

Claims • Evidence • Reasoning

1. Interpret your data. Write a claim about whether your hypothesis was correct. Cite evidence that supports your claim and explain why the evidence supports the claim.

_____

_____

_____

2. Write a claim about how the same object can move at different speeds. Cite evidence that supports your claim and explain why the evidence supports the claim.

_____

_____

_____

_____

3. What other factors might have affected the speed at which the ball moved?

_____

_____

4. Are there limits to how much force you could apply to the ball in this inquiry? If so, what are they?

_____

_____

_____

_____

5. What would you expect to happen if you were to use a larger rubber band? Explain your reasoning.

_____

_____

SC.4.E.6.5 Investigate how technology and tools help to extend the ability of humans to observe very small things and very large things. SC.4.N.2.1 Explain that science focuses solely on the natural world.

CAREERS IN SCIENCE

8 THINGS YOU SHOULD KNOW ABOUT Sports Biomechanists

1 Sports biomechanists use science to help athletes perform better.

2 Sports biomechanists study the forces that act on the body as it moves.

3 Sports biomechanists use different tools. High-speed cameras and sensors record an athlete's motions. A computer is used to study the data.

4 When seconds count, sports biomechanists can increase an athlete's speed. They can help a runner move faster to win the race.

5 Sports biomechanists show athletes the right way to move so that they don't hurt their bodies.

6 Sports biomechanists study Olympic swimmers using a small pool called a flume.

7 In a wind tunnel, a giant fan moves air over a bicycle and its rider. A sports biomechanist uses this machine to measure how the wind flows past the rider's body.

8 Strong bands called resistance cords are put on an athlete's arms and legs. They can help improve a runner's speed and acceleration.

Be a Sports Biomechanist!

▶ **Answer the questions to get to the finish line!**

1 What do we call a person trained in a sport? _____

2 Sports biomechanists study the _____ that act on a person's body as it moves.

3 Name a tool that sports biomechanists use.

_____

4 What machine is used by swimmers at an Olympic training center?

_____

5 Draw a picture of yourself playing your favorite sport.

Think About It

▶ Why would athletes want to see slow-motion videos of themselves playing their sport? _____

S.T.E.M.

ENGINEERING & TECHNOLOGY

How It Works:

Gyroscopes

Have you ever played with a top? A top can balance on a point as it spins around its axis. The spinning motion keeps the top standing up. When the top begins to slow down, gravity makes it wobble and fall over. A gyroscope behaves like a top.

When a force acts on the gyroscope, the disk's spinning motion makes the central ring resist changing position. The rest of the gyroscope turns around the fixed central ring.

Central ring

Disk and Axle

Gimbal

This gyroscope has a disk and axle and a central ring that swivels on an outer ring, or gimbal.

The axle is attached to the central ring. There is little friction where these parts connect, so the disk spins rapidly on the axle.

TROUBLESHOOTING

Suppose that the disk of a gyroscope spins for a very short time before coming to a quick stop. What could be wrong? How would you fix it?

_____

_____

_____

S.T.E.M. continued

Show How It Works

Gyroscopes are used in airplanes, boats, and spacecraft. Electronic sensors around a gyroscope tell how the vehicle has moved. Think about how data from a gyroscope might help keep a spacecraft from veering off course.

On Earth, a magnetic compass tells us which direction we are facing. A space telescope cannot use a magnetic compass. These compasses do not work in space. So, the Hubble Space Telescope uses gyroscopes to maintain direction.

In the space below, make a list of the vehicle's systems that may use data from the gyroscope.

_____

_____

_____

Design a toy, tool, or any device that uses a built-in gyroscope. Draw a picture of your device. Then, answer the questions.

Explain what your toy, tool, or device does and how it works.

_____

_____

_____

Why does your invention need a gyroscope?

_____

_____

_____

_____

_____

_____

_____

(t) ©STCI/NASA 2009

Improvise It:
A Game of Skill and Motion

Amusement parks can be fun! You can go on rides as well as play different games of skill.

Have you ever wanted to design your own amusement park game? Here is your chance. You'll use what you know about motion and energy to build a game that your classmates will play.

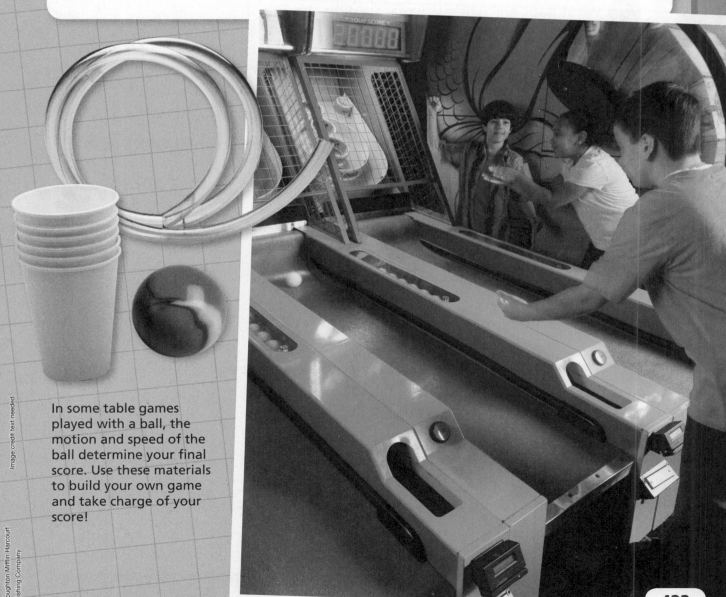

In some table games played with a ball, the motion and speed of the ball determine your final score. Use these materials to build your own game and take charge of your score!

S.T.E.M. continued

DESIGN PROCESS STEPS

1 Find a Problem
2 Plan & Build
3 Test & Improve
4 Redesign
5 Communicate

What to Do:

1 Research games that depend upon motion and skill.

2 Explore how a marble travels through a plastic tube. How does the angle of the tube affect the marble's motion?

3 What happens when the marble exits the tube?

4 Can you get the marble to fly through the air?

5 Design a game using the plastic tube, the marble, and other available materials.

6 Identify your game's design criteria.

7 Build and test it.

8 Improve your game design until it meets your design criteria.

9 Have your classmates play your game.

10 Keep a record of your work in your Science Notebook.

Life Cycles and Growth

FLORIDA BIG IDEA 16

Heredity and Reproduction

Florida panthers have a whorl of hair in the middle of their back.

I Wonder Why

This panther looks like he just rolled out of bed. Why does he have such strange fur? *Turn the page to find out.*

Here's Why

The panthers are all descended from panthers that have a black "cowlick" on their backs. Their parents passed the trait on to their offspring.

Essential Questions and Florida Benchmarks

LESSON 1

How Do Plants Reproduce?..................441
SC.4.L.16.1 Identify processes of sexual reproduction in flowering plants ....
SC.4.L.16.4 Compare ... stages in the life cycles of Florida plants and animals ....

LESSON 2

What Factors Affect Germination Rate?..............457
SC.4.L.16.1, SC.4.N.1.4

S.T.E.M. Engineering and Technology
How It Works: Water Irrigation System/
Make a Process: Planting and Caring for a Garden **461**
SC.4.N.1.6

LESSON 3

How Do Animals Reproduce? 465
SC.4.L.16.4

LESSON 4

What Are Heredity, Instincts and Learned Behaviors? 479
SC.4.L.16.2 Explain that ... characteristics can be affected by the environment.
SC.4.L.16.3 Recognize that animal behaviors may be shaped ....

CAREERS IN SCIENCE
Animal Behaviorist 493
SC.4.N.2.1

Unit 10 Benchmark Review...................495

Science Notebook

Before you begin each lesson, write your thoughts about the Essential Question.

SC.4.L.16.1 Identify processes of sexual reproduction in flowering plants, including pollination, fertilization (seed production), seed dispersal, and germination. SC.4.L.16.4 Compare and contrast the major stages in the life cycles of Florida plants and animals, such as those that undergo incomplete and complete metamorphosis, and flowering and nonflowering seed-bearing plants.

LESSON **1**

ESSENTIAL **QUESTION**

How Do Plants Reproduce?

Engage Your Brain

Find the answer to the following question in this lesson and record it here.

Bees need flowers for food. How do flowers need bees?

_____

_____

_____

_____

_____

📖 ACTIVE **READING**

Lesson Vocabulary

List the terms. As you learn about each one, make notes in the Interactive Glossary.

_____   _____

_____   _____

_____   _____

Signal Words

In this lesson, you will read about the sequence of stages in a plant's life cycle. Words that signal sequence include *now, before, after, first, next, start,* and *then.* Active readers look for signal words that identify sequence to help them remember what they read.

How Does a
Garden Grow?

Think of some of the plants you saw on your
way to school today. You might have seen trees,
grasses, flowers, or even weeds. Where did all of
these plants come from?

ACTIVE READING As you read the next page, circle the
signal words that show the sequence in which a plant grows.

Radish Life Cycle

A seed, such as this radish
seed, contains the embryo of
a plant.

When a seed sprouts
during a process known
as germination, the
embryo in the seed
begins to grow.

When a plant grows to
its full size, it reaches
maturity. Mature plants
make seeds that can
grow into new plants.

As the plant continues to
grow, it gets larger. It also
gets more roots.

When a plant grows, it goes through a series of set stages. The series of stages that a living thing goes through as it develops is called a *life cycle*. It is important for people to understand plant life cycles, because most of the food we eat comes from plants.

Most plants grow from seeds. First, a seed is placed in soil, so it can sprout. Next, the plant grows until it reaches maturity. A mature plant may grow flowers or cones. Then these structures make more seeds. You will learn about flowers and cones on the next pages.

Lima Bean Life Cycle

Place the pictures in the correct sequence to show the life cycle of a lima bean plant. Write a number next to each picture. Start with the seed.

Flowers and Cones

There are about 310,000 types of plants. Almost 90% of them produce seeds. How do plants produce seeds?

ACTIVE READING As you read this page, underline the names of male plant parts and circle the names of female plant parts.

Flowers and cones are reproductive structures that make seeds. They produce sex cells. Sex cells are used during *sexual reproduction*. Male sex cells are called sperm, and female sex cells are called eggs. **Fertilization** is the process of a sperm and an egg cell joining together. A fertilized egg grows into an embryo inside a seed.

About 1,000 types of plants produce seeds in cones. In plants with cones, sperm are made in male cones and eggs are made in female cones.

Most plants produce seeds in structures called flowers. In plants with flowers, grains of pollen, produced in parts called anthers, contain the sperm. Eggs are made in a structure called a pistil. Many flowers have both anthers and a pistil. As you can see in the picture, flowers have many other parts as well.

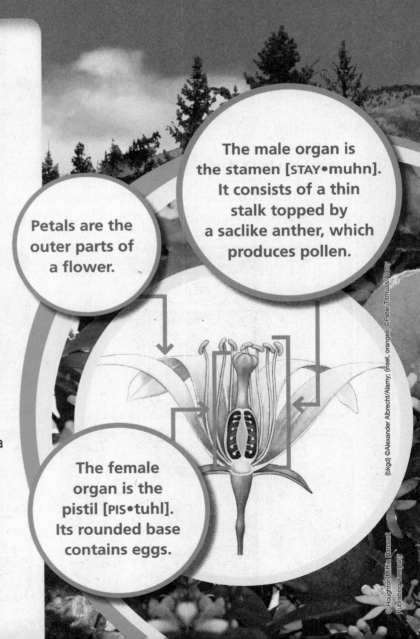

Petals are the outer parts of a flower.

The male organ is the stamen [STAY•muhn]. It consists of a thin stalk topped by a saclike anther, which produces pollen.

The female organ is the pistil [PIS•tuhl]. Its rounded base contains eggs.

Most cone-bearing plants are trees. Pines, spruces, and cycads [SY•kadz] are all cone-bearing plants.

A female pine cone makes egg cells.

A male pine cone makes sperm cells.

Plant Parts

Add labels to the flower.

stigma

anther

petal

filament

stem

The Power of Pollen

In order for plant eggs to be fertilized, pollen has to move from the male parts to the female parts. How does the pollen get there?

ACTIVE READING Underline ways plants can be pollinated.

Plants reproduce through pollination. **Pollination** is the process of pollen moving from a male plant part to a female plant part. There are several ways this can happen. Sometimes wind can blow the pollen from one plant to another, which is how many grasses and trees are pollinated.

Other plants are pollinated by *pollinators*. Some bees, birds, butterflies, and other animals are pollinators. For example, a butterfly goes from flower to flower drinking nectar. At each flower, the pollen on the stamens rubs off on the butterfly. When the butterfly visits the next flower, the pollen may drop off and fall on the pistil. As a result, the flower will be pollinated.

Brightly colored flower petals attract pollinators.

© Houghton Mifflin Harcourt Publishing Company

Some water plants are pollinated by water. Flowing water carries the pollen from plant to plant.

Pollen Cloud

DO THE MATH

Work with Fractions

Animals pollinate $\frac{3}{4}$ of seed-making plants. Wind and water pollinate the other $\frac{1}{4}$ of plants. Use this information to label the parts of the circle.

Wind blows pollen from male cones. The wind may carry the pollen to a female cone.

Seeds on the Move

Unlike most animals, plants cannot move around in their environment. So how can a plant's seeds be spread from place to place?

ACTIVE READING As you read, underline three things that help seeds move from place to place.

Animals play a big role in moving plant seeds. The base of the pistil of flowers grows into a fruit that contains the flower's seeds. Think of the seeds in an apple or in a blackberry. When an animal eats these fruits, the seeds pass through the animal's body before being deposited elsewhere.

Other animals will find and bury seeds. Think of squirrels. Squirrels bury acorns so that they will have food in the winter. The squirrels will dig up and eat most of the acorns, but they may forget a few. These acorns will grow into new oak trees.

Seeds, such as burs, can also travel on an animal's body. Other kinds of seeds are very light. They can be carried by the wind. Still other seeds, including coconuts, float in water.

Some seeds are very light. They can be blown around by the wind.

Some seeds are covered in little hooks. These seeds are called burs. They can easily attach to fur or even to your socks!

▶ How are each of these seeds most likely spread from place to place?

_____

_____

_____

_____

Many animals eat fruit. This helps spread the seeds contained in fruit.

Other Ways Plants Grow

Pine trees, beans, and sunflowers all grow from seeds. Other plants do not grow from seeds. These plants grow from structures called spores.

ACTIVE **READING** As you read this page, draw one line under a cause. Draw two lines under its effect.

Have you ever looked at the underside of a fern leaf? You may have seen black or brown spots, like the ones in this picture. These spots are made up of pockets filled with spores.

A **spore** is a cell that can grow into a new plant when the conditions are right. Some plants, such as mosses and ferns, grow from spores instead of seeds. Plants that grow from spores have two distinct forms in their life cycles.

Spores are released when the structures that hold them break open. Wind carries the spores to new places. If a spore lands in a good spot, it will grow into a plant.

Spores are very tiny. They can be carried long distances by the wind.

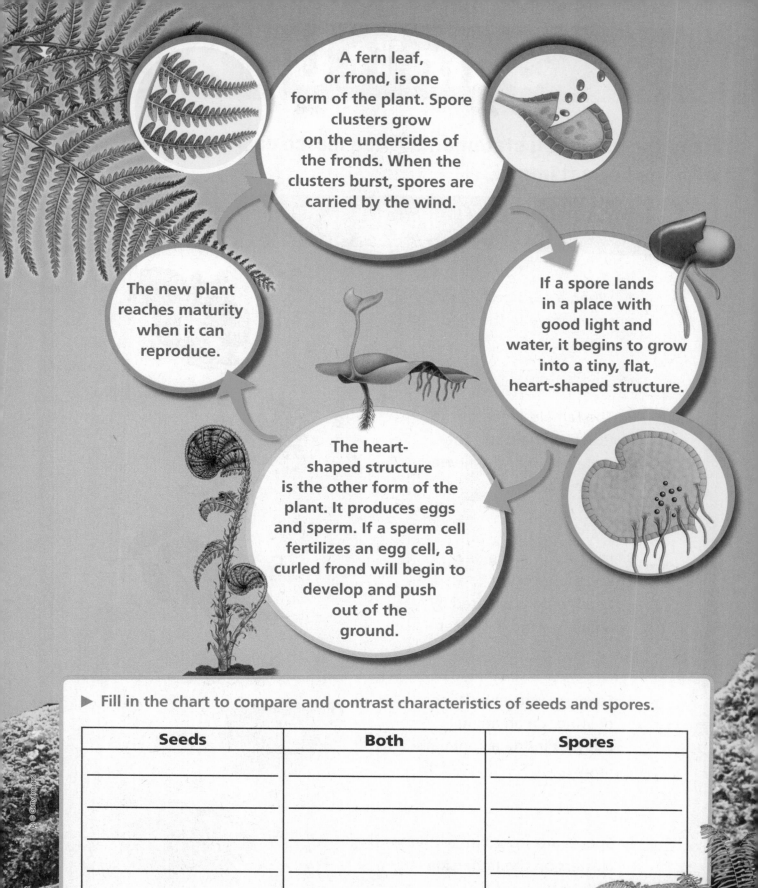

A fern leaf, or frond, is one form of the plant. Spore clusters grow on the undersides of the fronds. When the clusters burst, spores are carried by the wind.

If a spore lands in a place with good light and water, it begins to grow into a tiny, flat, heart-shaped structure.

The heart-shaped structure is the other form of the plant. It produces eggs and sperm. If a sperm cell fertilizes an egg cell, a curled frond will begin to develop and push out of the ground.

The new plant reaches maturity when it can reproduce.

▶ Fill in the chart to compare and contrast characteristics of seeds and spores.

Seeds	Both	Spores

Sum It Up »

Read the summary statements. Then match each statement with the correct image.

_____ 1. When a seed germinates, the embryo in the seed grows.

A

_____ 2. The female organ of the flower is the pistil. The male organ of the flower is the stamen.

B

_____ 3. In order to make new seeds, flowers or cones need to be pollinated by animals, wind, or water.

C

_____ 4. Seeds can travel by water or wind, on an animal's body, or inside an animal's body.

D

_____ 5. Spores are stored in clusters on the underside of fern leaves.

E

Name _____

Vocabulary Review

Use the words in the box to complete each sentence.

cone
cycle
fertilization*
germination*
maturity*
pollen
pollination*
seed
spore*
* Key Lesson Vocabulary

1. The process that happens when a sperm joins with an egg is called _____.

2. _____ is the stage in a plant's life cycle when it has grown enough to reproduce.

3. When an egg within a pistil is fertilized, a _____ forms.

4. All of the stages a plant goes through as it develops is called its life _____.

5. _____ is when pollen falls on a flower's pistil.

6. The process of a small root and stem beginning to grow out of a seed is called _____.

7. _____ contains the male sex cells in seed-forming plants.

8. A _____ is the structure that pine trees and spruce trees use to reproduce.

9. A _____ is a cell that can grow into a new plant when conditions are right.

Apply Concepts

2 Draw the life cycle of a flowering plant.

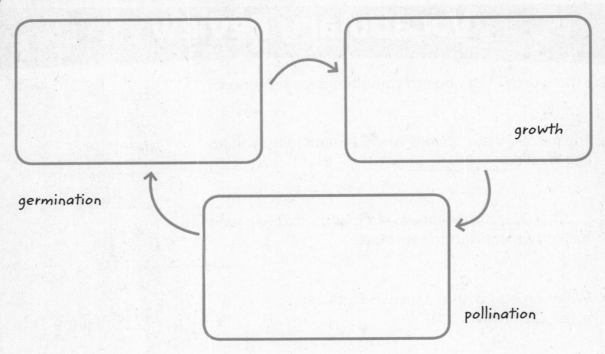

germination

growth

pollination

3 Circle the structure(s) that plants use to reproduce.

4 List three ways a seed-forming plant can be pollinated.

1._____

_____

2._____

_____

3._____

_____

_____

5 Look at the seed shown here. How do you think this seed is spread? Explain your answer.

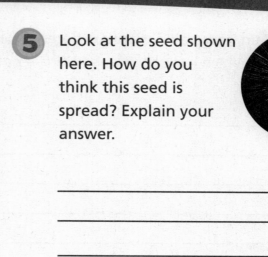

_____

_____

_____

_____

_____

6 Draw a picture of a flower and label its parts.

7 Explain how pollination is different from fertilization in flowers. (Hint: Which needs to happen first—pollination or fertilization?)

_____

_____

_____

_____

_____

8 Circle the pollinator(s) below.

Take It Home!

See *ScienceSaurus®* for more information about characteristics of living things.

SC.4.L.16.1 Identify processes of sexual reproduction in flowering plants, including pollination, fertilization (seed production), seed dispersal, and germination. **SC.4.N.1.4** Attempt reasonable answers to scientific questions and cite evidence in support.

INQUIRY LESSON 2

Name _____

ESSENTIAL QUESTION

What Factors Affect Germination Rate?

Materials

5 plastic cups
potting soil
plastic gloves
graduated cylinder
shoe box
bean seeds
water
ruler

EXPLORE

Every type of plant grows best in certain conditions. In this experiment, you will find out how light and water affect the germination of bean seeds.

Before You Begin—Preview the Steps

(1) CAUTION: Wear plastic gloves when handling potting soil. Place 8 cm of potting soil in each plastic cup.

(2) Place three or four bean seeds on top of the soil in each cup. Then sprinkle 3 cm of soil on top of the seeds.

(3) Place one cup under a shoe box. Label this cup *A*. Place another cup in a lit area. Label this cup *B*. Every day, add about 60 mL of water to both cups.

(4) Place the other cups in a lit area. Label the cups *C*, *D*, and *E*. Do not add water to cup *C*. Every day, add about 40 mL of water to cup *D* and 80 mL of water to cup *E*.

(5) Observe the cups daily. Record any changes you see.

Set a Purpose

Why is it important to know the factors that affect germination?

_____

_____

_____

Think About the Procedure

Which two factors are you testing in this activity?

_____

_____

_____

Name _____

Record Your Data

In the space below, make a table to record your observations.

Draw Conclusions

Which plants grew the most? Which plants grew the least?

_____

_____

Claims • Evidence • Reasoning

1. Interpret your data. Write a claim about how light affects seed germination. Cite evidence to support your claim and explain why it supports the claim.

_____

_____

_____

2. Interpret your data. Write a claim about how water affects seed germination. Cite evidence to support your claim and explain why it supports the claim.

_____

_____

_____

_____

3. What other factors do you think might affect germination?

_____

_____

_____

4. How could you test these factors?

_____

_____

_____

5. Choose one factor you named in question 3 and investigate it. Write a summary of your investigation.

_____

_____

SC.4.N.1.6 Keep records that describe observations made, carefully distinguishing actual observations from ideas and inferences about the observations.

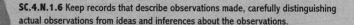

S.T.E.M.
ENGINEERING & TECHNOLOGY

How It Works:
Water Irrigation System

A water irrigation system moves water to where it is needed. This water may come from rivers, lakes, or wells. Pumps and valves control the movement of water into and through the system. Farmers use a control panel to determine how much and how quickly water moves through a field.

pipe and drip pipes

center pivot gear

system control panel

"A" frame

pump and check valve

wheel

CRITICAL THINKING

Find and circle the pump on the diagram. What would happen to the irrigation system if the pump stopped working?

_____

_____

_____

Show How It Works

People use irrigation systems to water their vegetable gardens at home. Look at the picture of a backyard irrigation system. Label its parts. Then answer the questions.

Name some parts of the irrigation system not shown in the diagram.

_____

_____

Identify some problems with this irrigation system. Then, describe how you would solve them.

_____

_____

_____

_____

_____

Make a Process:
Planting and Caring for a Garden

Planning is important to any project. It is especially true when planting a garden. Before the first seed is planted, you need to think ahead.

All plants share some basic needs, but their seeds might germinate under different conditions. To plan a garden, you need to learn about seeds, plant care, and what will grow in your local environment.

It is important to think about your design and know what to expect. As you do this research, you will come up with a process to help you design your garden.

DESIGN PROCESS STEPS

1 Find a Problem
2 Plan & Build
3 Test & Improve
4 Redesign
5 Communicate

What to Do:

1 Research types of gardens. Pick one garden type and decide where to plant it.

2 Find out which types of seeds would be best to plant in your local environment.

3 Make a diagram of your garden's layout.

4 Write a process that describes how you will care for the different seeds, seedlings, and plants that will grow in your garden. What types of resources will you need? How will you get these resources?

5 Make up a schedule to care for your garden. Include daily, weekly, and monthly tasks.

6 Keep a record of your work in your Science Notebook.

SC.4.L.16.4 Compare and contrast the major stages in the life cycles of Florida plants and animals, such as those that undergo incomplete and complete metamorphosis, and flowering and nonflowering seed-bearing plants.

LESSON **3**

ESSENTIAL**QUESTION**

How Do Animals Reproduce?

Engage Your Brain

Find the answer to the following question in this lesson and record it here.

How do you think these young egrets will change as they grow up?

_____

_____

_____

_____

ACTIVE **READING**

Lesson Vocabulary

List the terms. As you learn about each one, make notes in the Interactive Glossary.

_____

_____

_____

_____

Sequence

Many ideas in this lesson are in a sequence, or order, that describes the steps in a process. Active readers stay focused on sequence when they go from one stage or step in a process to another.

465

Life in Full Circle

Like plants, animals have life cycles. Animals are born and then begin to grow up. When animals become adults, they may have young of their own. In this way, life continues to renew itself.

ACTIVE **READING** As you read the next page, underline the description of each stage of an animal's life, and number the stages in the correct order.

When a bird reaches adulthood, it mates with another bird.

Over time, the bird grows. Soon it can live on its own.

After the eggs hatch, the parents feed the young birds.

After mating, a female bird lays eggs. Birds hatch from eggs.

Matching Game

Use the terms on the right to identify the correct life stages in each series of pictures.

Adult
Newborn
Youth

[   ]

[   ]

[   ]

[   ]

[   ]

[   ]

Most animals reproduce sexually. During sexual reproduction, sperm from a male joins an egg from a female. The fertilized egg can then develop into a new animal.

In some animals, such as many kinds of fish, eggs are fertilized outside of the female's body. In other animals, such as birds, eggs are fertilized inside the female's body. After the eggs are fertilized, birds lay the eggs. Bird parents then protect the eggs until they have hatched.

After the young are born, they begin to grow and change. Over time, newborns develop into youths. Youths continue to develop until they grow into adults. Adult animals mate with one another to produce offspring. An animal's life cycle ends when the animal dies. However, the animal's offspring will likely have offspring of their own. In this way, the life cycle repeats again and again.

Bringing Up Baby

Like birds, many other animals hatch out of eggs.
For example, most fish, reptiles, and spiders hatch
from eggs. Other animals give birth to live young.
Dogs, horses, and mice are all born this way.

ACTIVE **READING** As you read these pages, draw a star
next to the names of animals that hatch from eggs and a check
mark next to the names of animals that are born live.

What happens after an animal is born? Some animals, such as turtles, are on their own as soon as they hatch from their eggs. Their parents do not help them. Other animals, such as penguins, give their young a great deal of care. They keep their young warm and fed until the young grow strong enough to take care of themselves.

Animals such as deer, bears, and rabbits take care of their young by feeding them milk. These animals may stay with their parents for months or years until they are able to live on their own.

Birds' eggshells are hard, but alligators and other reptiles have soft, leathery shells.

▶ What are young kangaroos called?

_____

Cats give birth to live young.
Young cats drink their mother's milk.

 ## DO THE **MATH**

Solve a Problem

Raccoons usually give birth to 3 to 5 young at one time. Raccoons give birth only once a year. Suppose a female raccoon lives 10 years. She is able to give birth for 9 of those years. How many offspring will she have?

_____

_____

When kangaroos are born, they are about the size of a dime. They then develop in their mother's pouch.

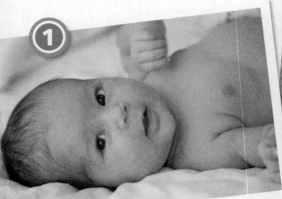

① When babies are born, they drink their mother's milk. They have no teeth, and they are not able to walk on their own.

② Babies grow into toddlers. Toddlers learn how to walk. They also start learning how to speak. Humans get their first set of teeth when they are toddlers.

Growing Up

Just like other animals, humans go through stages of development. After a human egg is fertilized, it grows inside the mother. After nine months, the baby is born. It takes many years for a human baby to grow into an adult. Study these pages to see all of the growth stages humans go through.

ACTIVE **READING** Put a star next to the life stage that you are currently in.

③ As a child develops, the first set of teeth is replaced by permanent teeth. The child grows and develops many physical and mental skills.

Growth Chart

At age 2, children are about 2 ft 10 in. tall. By age 5, children are about 3 ft 6 in. tall. Place these measurements into the chart. Then, measure yourself and an adult. Place those measurements in the chart.

How do you change as you get older?

_____

Age	Height
2	
5	
You	
Adult	

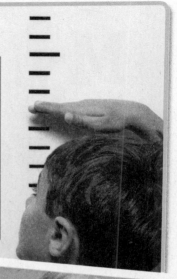

4

During the teenage years, boys and girls start looking more like adults. For example, boys start growing facial hair.

6 As an adult ages, they lose some of their physical abilities. The body changes in other ways, as well. For example, the hair turns gray.

5 During adulthood, people reach maturity. Often, adults marry and have children of their own.

471

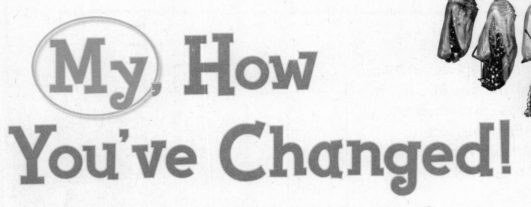

My, How You've Changed!

A young frog, or tadpole, has a long tail and no legs. As it grows, its tail becomes shorter, and it begins to grow legs. An adult frog has no tail, but has legs. The young go through a series of changes known as *metamorphosis*.

ACTIVE READING As you read the next page, underline the sentences that contain vocabulary terms.

▶ Write a caption for this photo of a butterfly breaking out of its chrysalis.

_____

_____

_____

_____

Complete Metamorphosis

Egg

Larva

Pupa

Adult

Butterflies go through complete metamorphosis. The larva of a butterfly is also called a caterpillar. The caterpillar grows into a pupa. Inside a chrysalis [kris•uh•lis], the pupa becomes an adult butterfly.

Incomplete Metamorphosis

Adult

Grasshoppers will molt five times before they reach the adult stage.

Grasshoppers go through incomplete metamorphosis. Young grasshoppers hatch as nymphs. A nymph grows and molts.

Nymph

The female grasshopper lays eggs in the soil.

Eggs

In many animals, the young look similar to the adults. But in other animals, the young look very different. In **complete metamorphosis** [met•uh•MAWR•fuh•sis], an animal goes through four different stages in its life cycle. The egg hatches into a *larva*. The larvae [LAR•vee] of many insects look like worms. A larva develops into a *pupa* [PYOO•puh]. The pupa of a moth is enclosed in a cocoon. While in the cocoon, the pupa develops into an adult moth. The adult splits its cocoon and flies out.

Some insects, such as dragonflies and termites, go through a different series of changes. In **incomplete metamorphosis**, an animal goes through three different stages in its life cycle. First, the animal hatches from the egg as a **nymph** [NIMF]. Nymphs look like tiny adults, but they don't have wings. As the nymph grows larger, it molts. Molting happens when an insect sheds its hard outer skeleton. After several moltings, the insect, which now has wings, reaches its adult stage.

Saving (the) Sea Turtles

Some kinds of animals are endangered. That means there are not many of them left. Scientists study the life cycles of endangered animals to try to save them and help them increase their numbers.

Sea turtles are one example of an endangered animal. Hunting, pollution, and beach erosion have caused the number of sea turtles to go down. To help sea turtles, people have learned about the sea turtle's life cycle. They have used what they learned to rear sea turtles. The turtles are then released into the wild. Over time, scientists hope this will help increase the number of sea turtles.

To rear sea turtles, eggs are collected.

(bl) ©Adi Weda/epa/Corbis

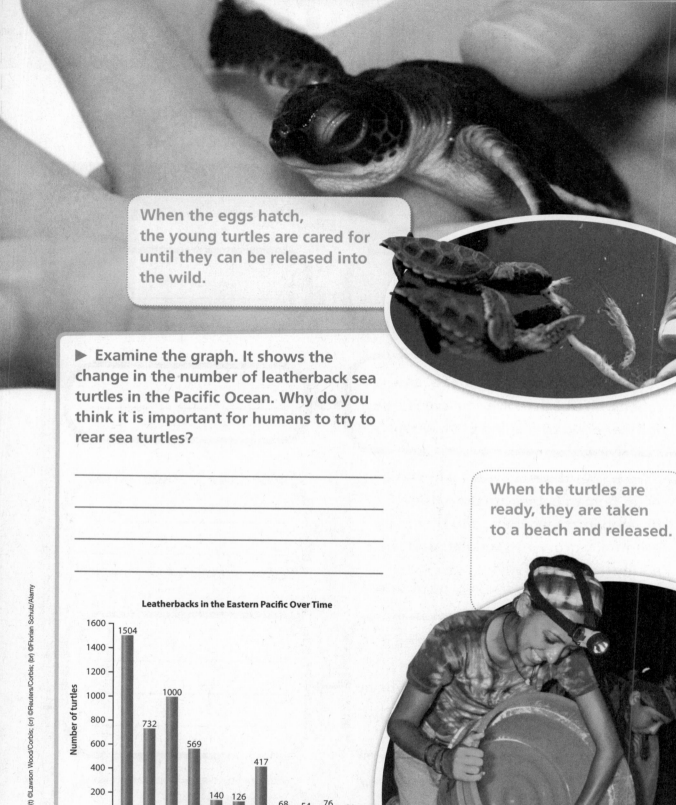

When the eggs hatch, the young turtles are cared for until they can be released into the wild.

▶ Examine the graph. It shows the change in the number of leatherback sea turtles in the Pacific Ocean. Why do you think it is important for humans to try to rear sea turtles?

_____

_____

_____

_____

When the turtles are ready, they are taken to a beach and released.

Leatherbacks in the Eastern Pacific Over Time

Number of turtles

Season	Number of turtles
88/89	1504
90/91	732
92/93	1000
94/95	569
96/97	140
98/99	126
00/01	417
02/03	68
04/05	54
06/07	76
08/09	32

Sum It Up »

Read the summary statements below. Each one is incorrect.
Change the part of the summary in blue to make it correct.

1 Most animals grow from a fertilized sperm cell.

→ _____

2 Some animals, such as cows, cats, and rabbits, give birth to live young and care for the young by feeding them worms.

→ _____

3 After human babies are born, they develop into teenagers, and then they eventually grow into toddlers and then adults.

→ _____
_____

4 Animals that have a larva stage and a pupa stage undergo incomplete metamorphosis, while animals that have a nymph stage undergo complete metamorphosis.

→ _____
_____
_____

5 Humans can try to help endangered animals by rearing them and releasing them into cities.

→ _____

Brain Check

Name _____

Vocabulary Review

1 Match the words to the correct picture.

_____ 1. metamorphosis

_____ 2. incomplete metamorphosis

_____ 3. larva

_____ 4. nymph

_____ 5. molt

_____ 6. pupa

Apply Concepts

2 Circle the animals that hatch from eggs.

3 Draw the life cycle of an eagle.

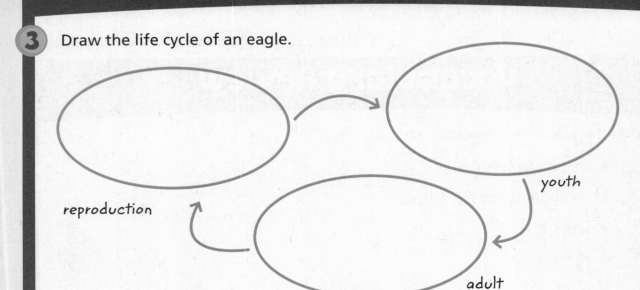

reproduction

youth

adult

4 Use the Venn diagram below to compare complete metamorphosis and incomplete metamorphosis.

5 Circle the one that undergoes incomplete metamorphosis.

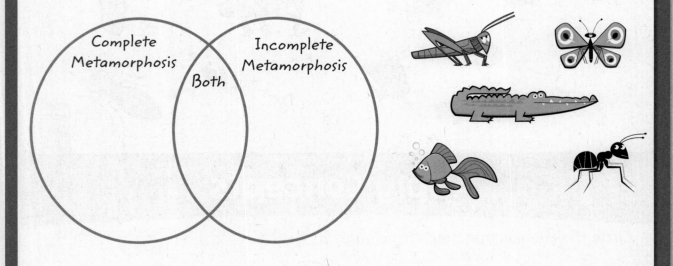

Complete Metamorphosis

Both

Incomplete Metamorphosis

Take It Home!

Ask to see childhood photographs of adult family members. How did your family members change as they grew and developed?

SC.4.L.16.2 Explain that although characteristics of plants and animals are inherited, some characteristics can be affected by the environment. SC.4.L.16.3 Recognize that animal behaviors may be shaped by heredity and learning.

LESSON 4

ESSENTIAL QUESTION

What Are Heredity, Instincts, and Learned Behaviors?

Engage Your Brain

Find the answer to the following question in this lesson and record it here.

How did this whale learn to hunt?

_____

_____

_____

_____

📖 ACTIVE READING

Lesson Vocabulary

List the terms. As you learn about each one, make notes in the Interactive Glossary.

_____

_____

_____

_____

Main Idea

The main idea of a paragraph is the most important idea. The main idea may be stated in the first sentence, or it may be stated elsewhere. Active readers look for main ideas by asking themselves, What is this paragraph mostly about?

Like Mother, Like Daughter

Have you ever noticed how children often look a lot like their parents? This happens because of a process known as heredity.

ACTIVE READING As you read these two pages, circle the inherited traits.

▶ Read about this girl's traits. Then, fill in your own traits.

This girl's hair is brown.
Your hair color:
_____

This girl's eyes are blue.
Your eye color:
_____

This girl's ears have attached lobes.
Your ear lobes:
_____

This girl's chin has no cleft.
Your chin:
_____

Snapdragon Family Tree

Traits, such as flower color and shape, are passed down from one generation to the next.

The passing of traits from parents to offspring is **heredity**. A *trait* is a feature of an individual, such as brown eyes.

All of the features you see when you look in the mirror are traits. Most of these traits came from your parents. For example, suppose you have a friend with blue eyes. Most likely, one or both of your friend's parents also have blue eyes. Your friend inherited her eye color from her parents.

Heredity happens in other living things as well. As you can see on this page, flowers inherit their petal color from their parents. Birds inherit their beak shape. And giraffes inherit their long necks. This is why family members look similar to one other.

It's in the Genes

What controls the traits you inherit? Every living thing contains chemical instructions for traits. These instructions are known as genes.

ACTIVE READING Underline the main idea as you read each paragraph below.

Half of your genes came from your mother. The other half came from your father. Because of this, you have a mixture of traits from both of your parents.

Remember that a sperm is a male sex cell. It contains genes from the father. An egg is a female sex cell. It has genes from the mother. When the two sex cells join, the resulting cell has genes from both parents.

Genes [JEENZ] are found inside cells. When sex cells unite, the new cell has genes from both the sperm and the egg. This chicken's feather color is inherited.

► What do you think are three possible benefits of genetic engineering? What are three possible problems? Record your answers in the chart.

Benefits	Problems

The genes of these carrots have been changed so the carrots are different colors.

Genetic Engineering

Scientists have learned a lot about how genes control traits. Today, scientists can take genes from one living thing and put them in another. This is called genetic engineering. Scientists use genetic engineering to change a living thing's traits. For example, they can make a potato plant poisonous to caterpillars. Scientists can also make goat milk with medicine in it. This technology is very new. Because of this, nobody knows what the effects will be.

Mom?! Why are my carrots **purple?**

483

Genes + Environment = You

Your genes alone do not control all of your traits. The environment you live in affects your traits, too!

ACTIVE **READING** As you read this page and the next one, put a star next to a main idea, and circle a supporting detail.

Skin color can be changed by the environment. Staying in the sun can make your skin darker. Too much sun is dangerous. Be sure to always wear sunblock.

The flower color of this hydrangea [hy•DRAYN•juh] is affected by the soil. Sometimes, the flowers are pink. If the soil becomes acidic, the flowers turn blue.

Some traits are caused when your genes and environment interact. For example, your height is controlled by genes. But it also is controlled by the kinds of foods you eat. If you did not eat nutritious food, you would not grow as tall as you could on a healthy diet.

Can you think of other traits you have that are affected by the environment?

Like you, other living things have traits caused by a mix of genes and other factors. For example, plants grow towards light. If you leave a houseplant near a window, it will grow towards the window. No matter where you move the plant, it will start to grow towards the strongest light.

The environment can change living things in other ways, as well. For example, a tadpole is a frog larva that swims in water. If the pond tadpoles live in starts to dry up, they will undergo metamorphosis at a faster rate. They will become adult frogs faster than tadpoles left in deep ponds.

DO THE MATH

Make a Number Line

The sex of alligators is affected by temperature. If an alligator egg develops at 30 °C or less, it will be a female. If it develops at 34 °C or more, it will be a male. Use this information to label the temperature line below.

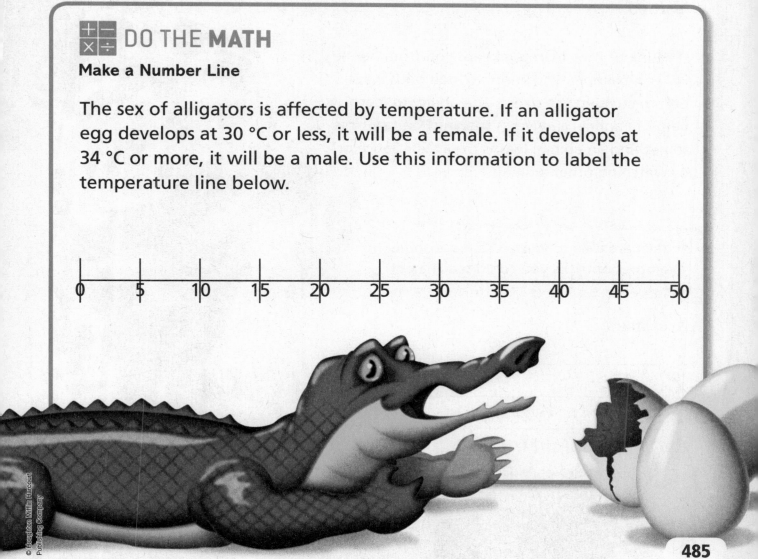

Learning Your Lesson

You know a lot of things. You may know how to tie your shoes, how to read a clock, and how to add numbers. You were not born knowing these things. Instead, you learned them.

ACTIVE READING As you read this page and the next, underline the examples of the skills you've learned.

Think of how learning keeps you from harm. For example, you know to look both ways before crossing the street. The ability to learn helps an animal survive. A **learned behavior** is something an animal learns from experience or by watching other animals.

▶ Pets are able to learn. What are some examples of tricks you could teach a pet?

• To sit

• To stay

• _____

• _____

• _____

This chimpanzee is using a tool to get ants to eat. It probably learned to do this by watching other chimpanzees.

Playing baseball is a learned behavior. You have to learn the rules of the game. You also have to learn how to hit the ball with the bat.

Many animals are able to learn things. Have you ever seen baby ducks following their mother? When the ducks first hatch, they learn to recognize their mother. After this, everywhere the mother goes, the babies follow. This helps keep the baby ducks safe.

Animals can also learn more complex behavior. Some chimpanzees learn how to make a tool for gathering termites to eat. They learn this by watching older chimpanzees make the tool from a branch. Without watching another chimpanzee do this, a young chimpanzee will not know how to make the tool.

Can you think of other examples of learned behavior? If you have a pet, think of things you have taught your pet to do. Also think about behaviors of working animals, such as horses and rescue dogs.

Insight into Instincts

Not all behaviors are learned. Animals are born knowing how to do some kinds of things.

ACTIVE **READING** As you read the text below, draw a circle around all the examples of instinctive behaviors.

Behaviors that an animal is born knowing how to do are called **instincts**. Human babies have an instinct to start crying when they are hungry. Birds build nests because of instincts. Earthworms have an instinct to burrow in the ground. Like learned behaviors, instincts help an animal survive.

So how can you tell the difference between learned behaviors and instincts? Sometimes it is difficult. For example, humans have an instinct to speak a language. However, humans must learn to speak a particular language, such as English or Spanish. In this way, many behaviors are a mix of learning and instincts.

Other behaviors may be instinct alone. For example, very soon after a baby horse is born, it is able to stand up. Within a few hours, the baby horse can walk and run. The horse does not need to learn any part of this behavior. It is all instinctive.

Calves are born with an instinct to nurse by drinking milk from their mother.

Spiders have an instinct to spin webs.

Geese have an instinct to migrate south in the winter.

▶ Look at the behaviors below. Which are learned and which are instincts?

	Learned	Instinct
A parrot saying, "Hello"	○	○
A fish swimming	○	○
A racehorse running down a racetrack	○	○
A ground squirrel hibernating in the winter	○	○
A bee building a hive	○	○

Sum It Up »

Use the information in the summary to complete the graphic organizer.

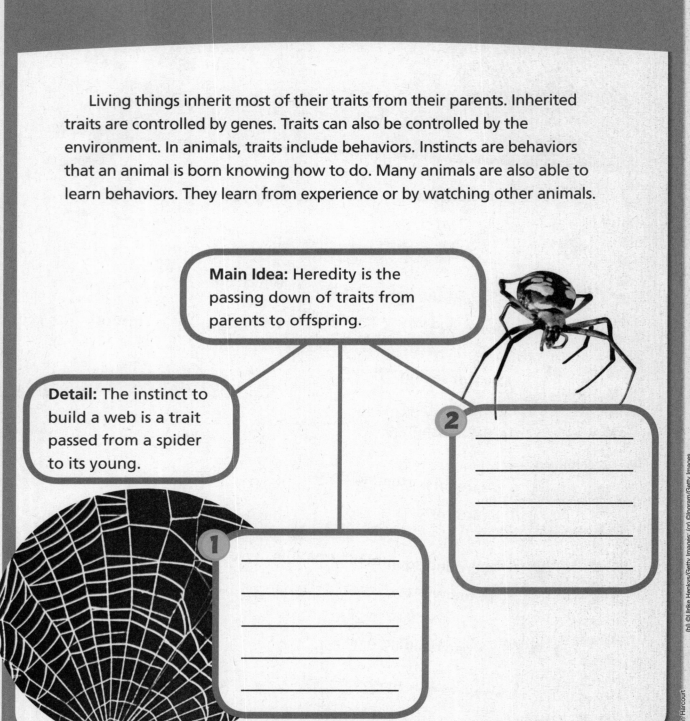

Living things inherit most of their traits from their parents. Inherited traits are controlled by genes. Traits can also be controlled by the environment. In animals, traits include behaviors. Instincts are behaviors that an animal is born knowing how to do. Many animals are also able to learn behaviors. They learn from experience or by watching other animals.

Main Idea: Heredity is the passing down of traits from parents to offspring.

Detail: The instinct to build a web is a trait passed from a spider to its young.

1 _____
_____
_____

2 _____
_____
_____
_____

Brain Check

LESSON 4

Name ________________

Vocabulary Review

1 Use the words in the box to complete each sentence. Then use the circled letters to answer the question below.

gene	heredity*	instinct*
learned behavior*	offspring	traits

*Key Lesson Vocabulary

The passing of characteristics from parents to their young is known as ◯ _ _ _ _ ◯ _ _ .

An example of a _ _ _ _ _ _ _ ◯ ◯ _ _ _ _ _ ◯ is a child learning to read.

A chemical instruction for a trait is known as a _ _ ◯ _ .

Green eyes and red hair are examples of _ _ ◯ _ ◯ _ .

A bird chirping is an example of an ◯ _ _ _ _ _ _ _ .

A living thing's children are also known as its ◯ _ _ _ _ _ _ _ ◯ _ .

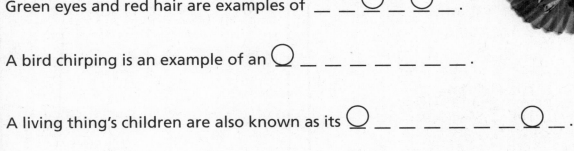

Question:

Mice, ground squirrels, and other animals become inactive during the winter. What is the name of this instinctive behavior?

_ _ _ _ _ _ _ _ _ _ _

©Getty Images/PhotoDisc

Apply Concepts

2 Explain how living things inherit traits.

_____

_____

_____

_____

_____

_____

_____

_____

3 List three examples of physical traits affected by the environment.

_____

_____

_____

_____

_____

_____

_____

4 Draw and label a picture showing a learned behavior and a picture showing an instinctive behavior.

Learned Behavior	Instinct

You perform many different learned behaviors daily. Keep a journal of some of the things you do in a week. Write down how you learned that behavior. For example, if you play tennis, record who taught you to play.

Ask an Animal Behaviorist

Q. What is an animal behaviorist?

A. An animal behaviorist is a scientist. I study an animal's behavior, or how it responds to its environment. In other words, I research how animals act.

Q. Why do animals act the way they do?

A. Animals are born with some behaviors. These behaviors are called *instincts*. Birds migrate, or travel, when the seasons change. Ground squirrels hibernate during cold weather. Animals communicate using sounds or movements. These are all instincts.

Q. Do animal behaviors change as the animal grows?

A. Some animal behaviors are learned. These behaviors change with experience. In the wild, mothers teach their young to hunt. People train animals as pets, as performers, and as companions. Training animals takes time.

Now It's Your Turn!

▶ What are some ways that animals communicate?

_____

_____

_____

_____

Be an Animal Behaviorist

Animals do not talk in words. An animal behaviorist finds other ways to *communicate,* or share information. Find a partner and communicate without using words. Follow the steps below.

My object is a _____.

1 THINK of an object in the classroom.

2 PLAN how you will communicate the object to your partner. Write your plan.

3 Taking turns, COMMUNICATE the object to your partner.

4 DRAW what your partner communicated.

Think About It!

After seeing your partner's drawing, how can you change your plan to better communicate which object you picked?

_____

_____

Name _____

Vocabulary Review

Use the terms in the box to complete the sentences.

> fertilization
> incomplete
>   metamorphosis
> pollination

1. Animals that have three stages in their life cycles go

   through _____.

2. The process by which a sperm cell joins with an egg cell

   is called _____.

3. The movement of sperm cells from the male part of a flower to the female part occurs through the process

   of _____.

Science Concepts

Fill in the letter of the choice that best answers the question.

4. The cones produced by the bristlecone pine tree are either male or female. In contrast, the flowers of the fish poison tree contain both male and female parts. What does this reveal about these two trees?

   Ⓐ Both trees carry out sexual reproduction.

   Ⓑ Both trees have incredibly long life cycles.

   Ⓒ Both trees can disperse their seeds very far.

   Ⓓ Both trees need insects to carry out pollination.

5. The pictures below show animal behaviors. Which one is a learned behavior?

   Ⓕ

   Ⓖ

   Ⓗ

   Ⓘ

6. The ruby-throated hummingbird lives in Florida. It uses its long beak to get nectar from flowers. What term identifies this type of hummingbird's long beak?

(A) a gene

(B) a trait

(C) a learned behavior

(D) a characteristic

7. Suppose Ada could play the clarinet by instinct. Which sentence describes what Ada would do?

(F) Ada would have to practice a lot.

(G) Ada would need a clarinet teacher.

(H) Ada would know how to play the drums.

(I) Ada would play well the first time she tried.

8. Parents pass on traits to their children. What are traits?

(A) genes

(B) instincts

(C) learned behavior

(D) physical features

9. LeeAnn notices a small insect in a pond near her home. The insect looked like a very small dragonfly. Her brother explained that it was a young dragonfly. In what stage of metamorphosis is the insect?

(F) adult   (H) nymph

(G) egg   (I) pupa

10. Sarai visits the local nature center. She sees a number of young animals. Which of the animals hatches from an egg?

(A)

(B)

(C)

(D)

11. The caterpillar is in its second stage of life where it eats a lot.

What is this stage called?

(F) egg   (H) pupa

(G) larva   (I) adult

Name _____

12. People who enjoy fly-fishing use insects as lures to attract fish to the hook. A favorite lure is a model of the caddis fly. This amazing insect can live in streams for months. When the fly's body is more like a worm, it builds an underwater house out of pebbles to protect itself from predators. What stage of metamorphosis is the fly in at this point?

(A) adult   (C) larva

(B) egg   (D) pupa

13. There are different types of metamorphosis. Some animals go through three stages, which is incomplete metamorphosis. Others go through four stages, which is complete metamorphosis. What stage is part of incomplete metamorphosis, but not complete metamorphosis?

(F) adult   (H) nymph

(G) egg   (I) pupa

14. Monarch butterflies migrate to warm places every winter. What causes this?

(A) trait

(B) instinct

(C) characteristic

(D) learned behavior

15. The bald cypress tree produces seeds that are protected within cones. This tree is found in Florida swamps where heavy rains create floods. The floodwaters spread the cones throughout the swamps. What role do the floodwaters play in the life cycle of the bald cypress?

(F) pollination

(G) fertilization

(H) seed dispersal

(I) removal of dead leaves

16. The mahogany tree that grows in southern Florida produces seeds that look like this.

Fan-like blades

Notice the blades on the surface of the seed. What role do these blades play in the life cycle of the mahogany tree?

(A) protect the seed

(B) ends the plant's life cycle

(C) store food for the seedling

(D) produce pollen for sexual reproduction

17. A beetle grows by the process of complete metamorphosis. How many stages are in complete metamorphosis?

(F) 2   (H) 4

(G) 3   (I) 5

Apply Inquiry and Review the Big Idea

Write the answers to these questions.

18. Manuel's science fair project was on seed germination. Here is what he did:

    Step 1: Place equal amounts of moist soil into two 1-gal glass jars.

    Step 2: Plant 10 radish seeds in each jar.

    Step 3: Unroll a strip of steel wool, moisten it, and use string to suspend it inside one of the jars. The moist steel wool should take up most of the oxygen inside this jar.

    Step 4: Cover both jars.

    Step 5: Keep both jars under the same conditions of light and temperature.

    Step 6: Observe both jars at the same time every day. Take notes of any differences in the germination of the seeds.

    Make a claim that identifies the purpose of Manuel's project. Use evidence to support your claim.

    _____

    _____

    _____

19. There are many ways that animals help disperse seeds. For example, a box turtle eats the fruits and seeds of many plants. The turtle digests the fruit. Eventually, the turtle drops the seeds with its waste matter. The table shows how long it takes for a box turtle to digest different types of seeds.

Seed type	Number of days
Q	20
R	2
S	12
T	5

    Make a claim about which seed the box turtle could disperse the **greatest** distance from the parent tree. Cite evidence to support your claim.

    _____

    _____

Organisms and Their Environment

A pod of dolphins swims through the ocean.

FLORIDA **BIG IDEA** 17

Interdependence

I Wonder Why

Why are these living things able to move and grow? How do they get their energy? *Turn the page to find out.*

Here's Why

Living things get the energy they need to move and grow from food. Plants make their own food. Animals eat plants or other animals.

Essential Questions and Florida Benchmarks

LESSON 1 **How Do Organisms Change with the Seasons?** 501
SC.4.L.17.1 Compare the seasonal changes in Florida plants and animals to those in other regions of the country.

LESSON 2 **How Do Organisms Obtain and Use Food?** 515
SC.4.L.17.2 Explain that ... when animals eat ... the energy stored in the food source is passed to them.

LESSON 3 **What Are Food Chains?** 527
SC.4.L.17.3 Trace the flow of energy from the Sun as it is transferred along the food chain through the producers to the consumers.

LESSON 4 **How Do Organisms Affect Their Environment?** 543
SC.4.L.17.4 Recognize ways plants and animals ... impact the environment.

ⓘ **LESSON 5** **How Do People Affect Their Environment?** 555
SC.4.L.17.4, SC.4.N.1.2

PEOPLE IN SCIENCE
Willie Smits/Wangari Maathai 559
SC.4.N.2.1

S.T.E.M. Engineering and Technology
Underwater Exploration/Solve It: Getting Around a Dam 561
SC.4.N.3.1

Unit 11 Benchmark Review 565

Science Notebook

Before you begin each lesson, write your thoughts about the Essential Question.

SC.4.L.17.1 Compare the seasonal changes in Florida plants and animals to those in other regions of the country.

LESSON **1**

ESSENTIAL **QUESTION**

How Do Organisms Change with the Seasons?

 Engage Your Brain

Find the answer to the following question in this lesson and record it here.

Which season are these trees experiencing? How do you know?

_____

_____

_____

_____

📖 ACTIVE **READING**

Lesson Vocabulary

List the terms. As you learn about each one, makes notes in the Interactive Glossary.

_____

_____

_____

Using Headings

Active readers preview headings and use them to ask questions. The questions help set a purpose for reading. Reading with a purpose helps active readers focus on understanding and recalling what they read.

501

Changing
with the
Seasons

Are winters cold or mild where you live? Are summers cool or hot? Different places have different temperatures throughout the seasons.

ACTIVE **READING** As you read these two pages, turn the main heading into a question in your mind. Underline sentences that answer the question.

States like Colorado, where the Rocky Mountains are, have cold winters with lots of snow.

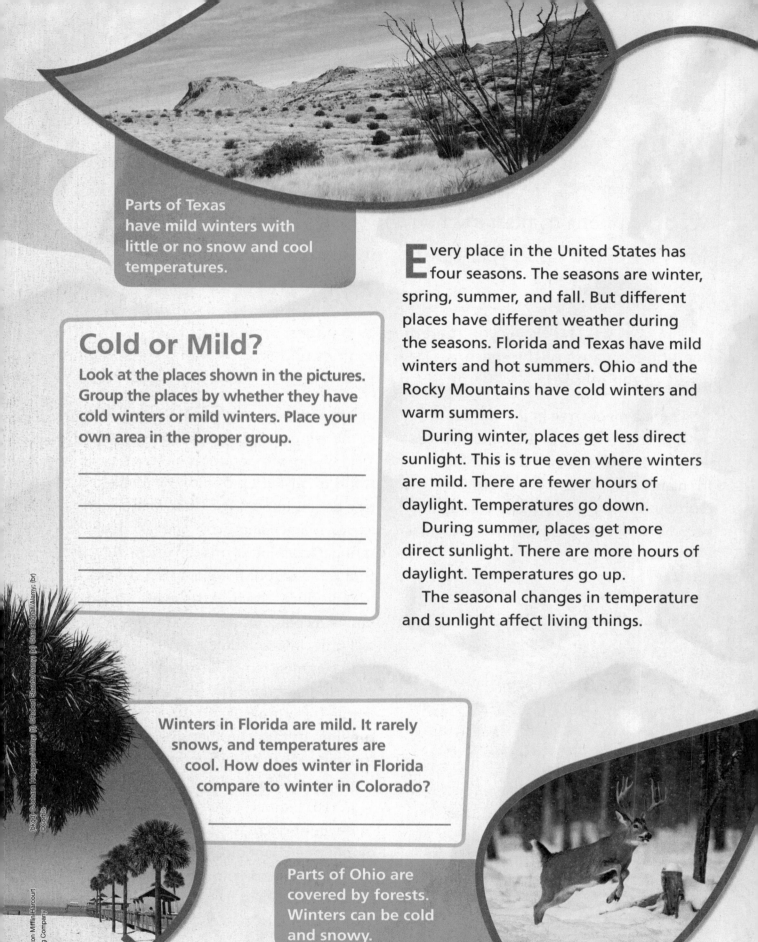

Parts of Texas have mild winters with little or no snow and cool temperatures.

Cold or Mild?

Look at the places shown in the pictures. Group the places by whether they have cold winters or mild winters. Place your own area in the proper group.

_____

_____

_____

_____

_____

Every place in the United States has four seasons. The seasons are winter, spring, summer, and fall. But different places have different weather during the seasons. Florida and Texas have mild winters and hot summers. Ohio and the Rocky Mountains have cold winters and warm summers.

During winter, places get less direct sunlight. This is true even where winters are mild. There are fewer hours of daylight. Temperatures go down.

During summer, places get more direct sunlight. There are more hours of daylight. Temperatures go up.

The seasonal changes in temperature and sunlight affect living things.

Winters in Florida are mild. It rarely snows, and temperatures are cool. How does winter in Florida compare to winter in Colorado?

_____

Parts of Ohio are covered by forests. Winters can be cold and snowy.

Plants and Seasons

What happens to plants when the seasons change?
Are plants the same year-round, or do they change
with the seasons?

Picture a maple tree in the winter. The branches of the tree are bare. The tree is dormant. **Dormancy** is a rest period for plants. The plant does not grow or reproduce when it is dormant. Plants become dormant when temperatures go down. Dormancy helps plants save energy in the winter when there is less sunlight.

In spring, temperatures get warmer. Hours of daylight increase. The maple tree begins to bud. The buds will turn into leaves. Many plants grow and reproduce in spring. Flowering plants can grow fruit. The fruit is the part of the plant that enables it to reproduce. The fruit has seeds. A seed has a tiny plant inside of it. The tiny plant will grow into an adult plant.

In summer, temperatures are warmer still. Hours of daylight are long. The maple tree continues to grow during the summer. Its branches become longer. The tree gets taller. Many plants spend the summer growing.

In fall, temperatures cool down. Hours of daylight decrease. The leaves on the maple tree change color. They become red, orange, and gold. Then they fall to the ground. Many trees lose their leaves during the fall. They also drop their fruits.

Plants such as palm trees and evergreens do not lose their leaves in the fall. But they still might become dormant if temperatures go down. Places with mild winters, like Florida, have many palm trees.

What Happens When?

Fill in the blanks to show the effects of seasons on maple trees.

Cause	Effect
Winter	
Spring	
Summer	
Fall	

Fall

Winter

Spring

Summer

A maple tree changes with the seasons. The changes are caused by differences in temperature and hours of sunlight.

Animals and Seasons

Plants are not the only living things that change with the seasons. Seasons affect animals, too.

ACTIVE **READING** As you read these two pages, find and underline the definition of *hibernation*.

Many animals eat plants. In many places during the winter, there are fewer plants for animals to eat. Some animals get through this time of little food and cold temperatures by entering an inactive state called **hibernation**. The heart barely beats, and body temperature drops to just above freezing. Because its body is barely working, a hibernating animal doesn't use much energy and doesn't need to eat.

Other animals use different ways to cope with seasonal change. Some animals change colors. The fur of the arctic fox turns white during fall and winter. In spring, the fur turns brown again. This helps the fox blend in with its surroundings.

The fur of arctic foxes changes colors with the seasons, so they blend with their surroundings. This makes it easier for them to stay hidden while they hunt.

The ground squirrel hibernates. There is enough fat stored in its body to keep it alive through the winter.

Some animals take a break from cold winter temperatures. They spend the winter in warm places. In spring, they migrate to their summer homes. When animals regularly move as a group from one region to another and back, it's a **migration**. Manatees spend the winter in Florida's warm natural springs. In spring, ocean water temperatures warm up. The manatees migrate north to ocean waters from Louisiana to Virginia.

Many animals reproduce in spring. They spend the summer eating and growing. In fall, some animals are busy storing food. Other animals begin to migrate to their winter homes.

Where Do They Go?

Draw the migration routes of the humpback whale on the map. Use arrows to show the direction of migration.

Manatees spend the winter in warm waters around Florida. They'll even gather in rivers at the openings of water pipes that pump out warm water.

Humpback whales migrate along the Atlantic Coast. They feed in cold waters off Canada during spring and summer. In fall, they head south to warm waters near Puerto Rico.

Winter Foods

Most plants do not grow during the winter when temperatures are cold. So how do places with cold winters get their food during the cold winter months?

ACTIVE READING As you read these pages, put a *P* next to the sentences that describe a problem. Put an *S* next to the sentences that describe a solution.

Picture winter in the Rocky Mountains. Deep snow covers the ground, but you can still walk into a grocery store and buy fruit. Where does the fruit come from?

Often, it comes from places that have mild winters, such as Florida and California.

These states can grow plants year-round. That's one reason why you can have fresh fruit and vegetables in the middle of winter no matter how cold it is outside.

Many plants that we eat can be grown across the country during the summer growing season. Some of these plants are potatoes, green beans, and tomatoes. The foods are harvested at nearby farms. They are taken from the farms to nearby markets. The foods do not travel far. So, it does not cost very much to transport them.

During winter, though, foods cannot be grown locally in most places in the United States. Foods grown in Florida, California, and other warm places are sent across the country. The foods cost more because their prices include transportation costs.

Transportation costs are not the only things that affect food prices. Sometimes places that have mild winters have freezing weather. Plants may be damaged. Fewer plants are harvested and sent across the country. The prices of the plants go up.

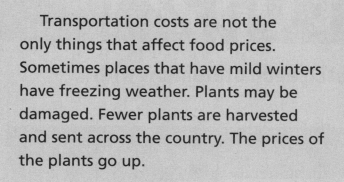

 **DO THE MATH**

Solve Real-World Problems

In the town where Teresa lives, strawberries are grown during the summer. The cost of the locally grown strawberries is $1.00 per pint. During the cold winter, strawberries are brought in by truck from California. The cost of these strawberries is $3.00 per pint. Teresa's family eats 13 pints every month. How much more does Teresa's family spend on strawberries in December than they do in June? Show your work.

_____

_____

Sum It Up »

Read the summary statements. Match each statement with the correct image.

1 Some living things become dormant during winter.

2 Some living things hibernate during winter.

3 Some living things migrate during winter.

Fill in the missing words to tell about changes with the seasons.

During winter, places get less direct 4. _____. This is true even where winters are mild. There are 5. _____ hours of daylight. Temperatures go 6. _____.

During 7. _____, places get more direct sunlight. There are 8. _____ hours of daylight. Temperatures go 9. _____.

Some plants become 10. _____ during the winter so they can save energy. Some animals 11. _____ to save energy. Other animals, such as humpback whales and manatees, 12. _____ to different places.

Brain Check

Name _____

Vocabulary Review

1 Use the clues to fill in the missing letters of the words.

1. _ _ b _ r n _ _ _ _ _ _   an inactive time for some animals

2. _ i _ _ e _   a season with the fewest hours of daylight

3. _ _ r _ a _ _ _ _   a rest time for plants

4. m _ _ a _ _ e   an animal that migrates in Florida's warm waters

5. _ u _ m _ _   a season with the most hours of daylight

6. _ _ g r _ _ i _ _   a movement of animals from place to place

7. s _ u _ r _ _ _   an animal that hibernates

8. _ a _ i _ _ r _ _ _   a state that grows food during winter

Apply Concepts

2 On the lines below, list some fruits that you eat during winter. Tell where the fruits might have been grown.

_____

_____

_____

_____

Apply Concepts

3 The pictures show a maple tree in four different seasons. Label the seasons and tell what happens to the tree during that season.

_____

_____

4 Fill in the concept map showing how the seasons affect animals.

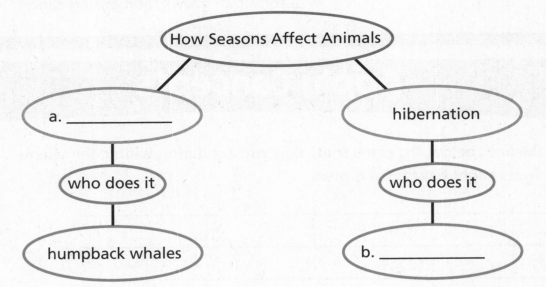

How Seasons Affect Animals

a. _____   hibernation

who does it   who does it

humpback whales   b. _____

5 The map below shows Florida. Draw the migration route of the manatee on the map.

6 In the space below, draw your schoolyard during summer. Then draw your schoolyard during winter. Show how plants change during the seasons.

7 In the chart below, write some changes that happen to hours of sunlight and temperatures during summer and winter.

Changes With Seasons	
Summer	Winter

8 These pictures show the arctic fox during different seasons. Label the seasons.

_____ _____

SC.4.L.17.2 Explain that animals, including humans, cannot make their own food and that when animals eat plants or other animals, the energy stored in the food source is passed to them.

LESSON **2**

ESSENTIAL **QUESTION**

How Do Organisms Obtain and Use Food?

 Engage Your Brain

Find the answer to the following question in this lesson and record it here.

How does this caterpillar get energy?

_____

_____

_____

_____

ACTIVE **READING**

Lesson Vocabulary
List the terms. As you learn about each one, make notes in the Interactive Glossary.

_____ _____

_____ _____

_____ _____

Main Ideas
The main idea of a paragraph is the most important idea. The main idea may be stated in the first sentence, or it may be stated elsewhere. Active readers look for main ideas by asking themselves, What is this paragraph mostly about?

A Bite of Energy

Walking, jumping, playing. Where do you get the energy to move your body?

ACTIVE READING As you read these two pages, find and underline two facts about food.

Living things need water, air, shelter, and food. Plants can make their own food. They get their nutrients from the soil. **Nutrients** are materials used by living things for growth and for other life functions.

Animals cannot make their own food. They get their nutrients from eating food. Food also gives living things energy. **Energy** is the ability to do work.

The food that you eat is broken down into smaller materials in your body. These materials are used by your cells to help you grow, move, think, and talk.

Monkeys get their energy from eating fruits and other foods.

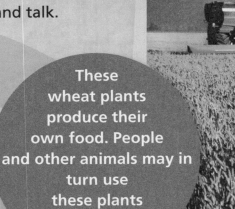

These wheat plants produce their own food. People and other animals may in turn use these plants for food.

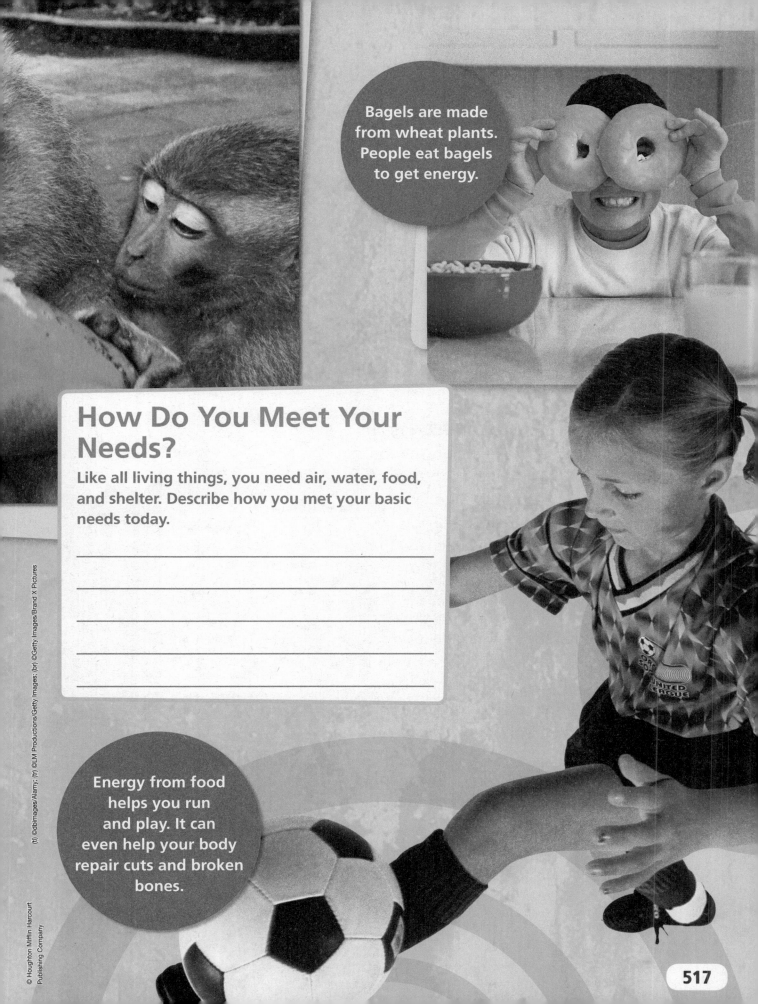

Bagels are made from wheat plants. People eat bagels to get energy.

How Do You Meet Your Needs?

Like all living things, you need air, water, food, and shelter. Describe how you met your basic needs today.

_____

_____

_____

_____

_____

Energy from food helps you run and play. It can even help your body repair cuts and broken bones.

The Food-Makers

Plants don't eat fruits and veggies.
They don't go out for hamburgers.
So how do plants get energy?

ACTIVE **READING** As you read these
two pages, draw a star next to the sentence
you think is most important, and be ready to
explain why.

Most plants are producers. **Producers** are
living things that make their own food.
Producers make their own food through
a process called photosynthesis. During
photosynthesis [foht•oh•SIHN•thuh•sis],
producers use water, carbon dioxide, and the
energy from sunlight to make food. This process
takes place in the leaves of plants. Sunlight
shines on the leaves. Water from the soil is
brought up through the plant to the leaves.
Carbon dioxide is taken in from the air. Cells in
the leaves change these materials into sugars.

During photosynthesis, producers give off
oxygen. You use this oxygen each time you
breathe.

Some of the food made by producers is used
for growth and other life processes. Some of the
food is stored for later use.

sunlight

water

food

oxygen

carbon dioxide

The Ins and Outs of Photosynthesis

Fill in the blanks to show what happens during photosynthesis.
Some of the words are filled in for you.

Sunlight + _____ + _____ yields _____ + Oxygen

The Food-Eaters

Cereal, toast, eggs, bacon, orange juice, milk. Do these foods come from plants or animals?

ACTIVE **READING** As you read these two pages, draw boxes around the names of consumers.

People and other animals are consumers. **Consumers** are living things that eat other living things. Some consumers, such as zebra and elk, eat plants. Other consumers, such as frogs and snakes, eat animals. People eat both plants and animals.

Elk eat the tender green shoots of plants in the spring. They eat grasses in the summer. Elk nibble on shrubs and the buds of trees in fall and winter.

 DO THE **MATH**

Find Percentages

The table shows how much different animals eat every day. It also shows the weight of an adult male animal. Study the table, and then answer the questions.

Animal Facts		
Animal	How much it eats a day	How much it weighs
Giant panda	20 kg	160 kg
Giraffe	25 kg	1,250 kg
Blue whale	7 metric tons	180 metric tons

1. What percentage of its body weight does the panda eat in food every day?

_____

2. What percentage of its body weight does the giraffe eat in food every day?

_____

3. What percentage of its body weight does the blue whale eat in food every day?

_____
_____

4. Which animal eats the highest percentage of its body weight in food every day?

_____

A frog eats insects and other small animals. Some frogs have long tongues for catching bugs. They can catch a bug, and roll their tongues back into their mouths in about 1 second.

A heron eats mostly fish. But it will eat any animal it can swallow, including frogs and snakes.

A snake eats other animals. Some big snakes even have eaten young hippos.

The Clean-Up Crew

The creepy, crawly things on these pages have an important role in ecosystems—they clean things up!

You may already know that vultures are scavengers. So are crabs and worms. Scavengers help clean up ecosystems by eating dead plants and animals. Any remains left by scavengers are consumed by **decomposers**, which are living things that get energy by breaking down wastes and dead plant and animal matter. They break down this matter into simpler substances. Decomposers use some of these substances, and some are returned to the air, soil, or water, where they are available to other living things. That's why decomposers are known as nature's recyclers!

A blue crab is a scavenger. It eats the remains of other organisms. It is not a picky eater—it will also eat living organisms!

What Would It Look Like?

In the space below, draw what an ecosystem might look like if there were no scavengers and decomposers.

Mushrooms help decompose logs and other materials in forests.

Worms live in soil. They eat dead leaves and other plant parts. Their wastes help make the soil richer.

Millipedes can have more than 100 pairs of legs! They eat dead plants.

Sum It Up »

Read the summary statements. Each one is incorrect. Change the part of the summary in blue to make it correct.

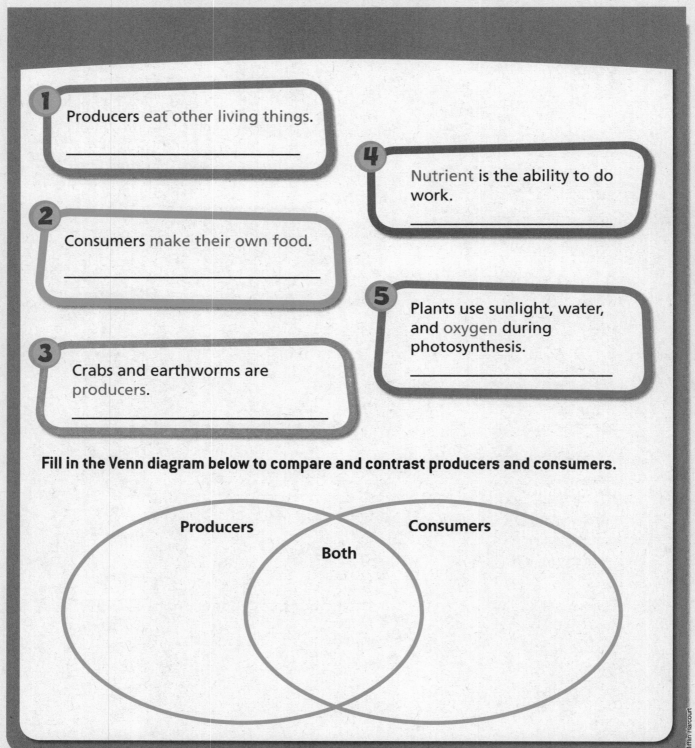

1 Producers eat other living things.

_____

2 Consumers make their own food.

_____

3 Crabs and earthworms are producers.

_____

4 Nutrient is the ability to do work.

_____

5 Plants use sunlight, water, and oxygen during photosynthesis.

_____

Fill in the Venn diagram below to compare and contrast producers and consumers.

Producers   Consumers

Both

Name _____

Vocabulary Review

1. Use the clues to unscramble the words in the box.

1. | tiunsernt | _____ Materials used by living things for growing and other life functions

2. | yxgone | _____ Given off during photosynthesis

3. | mesoncur | _____ Living thing that eats other living things

4. | rcuprdoe | _____ Living thing that makes its own food

5. | cedpsremoo | _____ Consumer that breaks down the remains of plants and animals

6. | tosthhpynssioe | _____ Process of making food using sunlight and other materials

Apply Concepts

2. In the space below, draw two ways that your body uses energy.

3 The pictures show different kinds of living things. Label each living thing as a producer, consumer, or decomposer.

_____ _____ _____

4 Fill in the concept map below about the roles of decomposers in ecosystems.

Decomposers Help Ecosystems

Share what you have learned about food energy with your family. Which foods keep you strong and healthy? With a family member, make a menu for a healthy meal. Help cook the meal for your family.

SC.4.L.17.3 Trace the flow of energy from the Sun as it is transferred along the food chain through the producers to the consumers.

LESSON **3**

ESSENTIAL QUESTION
What Are Food Chains?

 Engage Your Brain

Find the answer to the following question in this lesson and record it here.

Is this frog a predator, or is it prey?

_____

_____

_____

📖 ACTIVE **READING**

Lesson Vocabulary

List the terms. As you learn about each one, make notes in the Interactive Glossary.

_____   _____

_____   _____

_____   _____

Main Ideas

The main idea is the most important idea of a paragraph or section. The main idea may be stated at the beginning, or it may be stated elsewhere. Active readers look for main ideas by asking themselves, What is this paragraph or section mostly about?

Food Chains

Did you know that you are fed by the sun? Find out how!

ACTIVE READING As you read these two pages, circle common, everyday words that have a different meaning in science.

Lettuce is a plant that uses energy from the sun to make its own food. When you eat lettuce, some energy passes from the lettuce to you. You can show this relationship in a food chain. A **food chain** is the transfer of food energy in a sequence of living things. In a diagram of a food chain, arrows show how energy moves. Here is a food chain that shows how energy moves from lettuce to you.

lettuce ⟶ you

The food chain above has only two steps, or links. Food chains can have more than two links. Look at the pictures to see a food chain with five links.

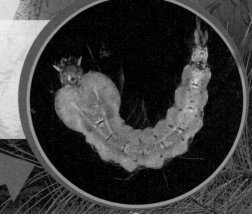

Producers make up the first link. In this pond, tiny algae [AL•jee] are the producers. Mosquito larvae eat the algae. They make up the second link in this food chain.

Make a Food Chain

Choose a food that you ate for breakfast or lunch today. Make a food chain showing how energy from the sun flowed from the food to you.

Minnows are small fish. They eat the mosquito larvae. They make up the third link in this food chain.

Bass are bigger fish. They eat the minnows. They make up the fourth link in this food chain.

People eat the bass. People make up the last link in this food chain.

You Are What You Eat

A zebra and a lion are both consumers. But they eat very different foods. How can you group consumers by what they eat?

ACTIVE READING As you read this page, underline the sentence that identifies one characteristic that is used to classify consumers.

Consumers eat other living things. They can be placed into groups according to the kind of food they eat.

- A consumer that eats only plants is a **herbivore**. A zebra is a herbivore. It eats grasses and other plants.
- A consumer that eats other animals is a **carnivore**. A lion is a carnivore. It eats zebras and other animals.
- A consumer that eats both plants and animals is an **omnivore**. People are omnivores. They eat plants such as tomatoes and animals such as fish.
- A consumer that eats dead plants and animals is a scavenger.

A crocodile is a carnivore. It eats mainly fish. But it will eat big animals, such as hippos, when it can catch them.

A rabbit is a herbivore. It eats leafy plants during spring and summer, and woody plants during fall and winter.

Raccoons are omnivores. They eat fruit, acorns, fish, and mice. They'll eat sweet corn right from your garden!

Vultures are scavengers. They eat dead animals.

What Does It Eat?

Look at the pictures below. The top row shows different kinds of consumers. The bottom row shows the kinds of food they eat. Draw lines to match the consumers to the foods they eat. Some consumers might eat more than one kind of food.

Hunt or Be Hunted

A lion crouches in the tall grass. Nearby, a zebra nibbles on the grass. Who is the hunter? Who will be hunted?

ACTIVE READING As you read these two pages, draw boxes around two words that are key to understanding the main idea.

Consumers are grouped by what they eat. But you can also group consumers by whether they hunt or are hunted.

A *predator* is an animal that hunts other animals. Lions are predators. They often hunt in packs. This helps them catch big animals, like hippos and rhinos. They hunt smaller animals, too.

An animal that is eaten is called *prey*. Deer, elk, and moose are all prey for wolves in the Rocky Mountains.

Some animals can be both predator and prey. A frog might eat insects in a forest. But the frog might be eaten by a snake.

A hawk can see the movement of small animals, like this mouse, from high in the sky.

Lions can run fast for short bursts. Zebras may not run as fast, but they can run for a much longer time.

Sharks feed on many kinds of prey. Fish stay in large groups to make it difficult for predators to hunt individuals.

Who's the Hunter? Who's Hunted?

Fill in the table below. Classify the animals shown on these pages as predators or prey.

Animals	
Predators	Prey

Food Webs

A food chain shows how energy moves from one living thing to another. But living things often eat more than one kind of food. How can you show these different feeding relationships?

ACTIVE **READING** As you read these two pages, draw a line under the main idea.

Lobsters eat clams. But they also eat crabs, sea stars, and mussels. Other animals, like the shark and the octopus, eat the lobster. You can use a model to show all these feeding relationships. A **food web** shows the relationships among different food chains. Food web models use arrows to show who eats what.

These green plankton are producers. They are eaten by clams, small fish, whales, and other organisms.

Desert Food Chain

Use arrows to show how energy moves from one living thing to another in this desert food chain.

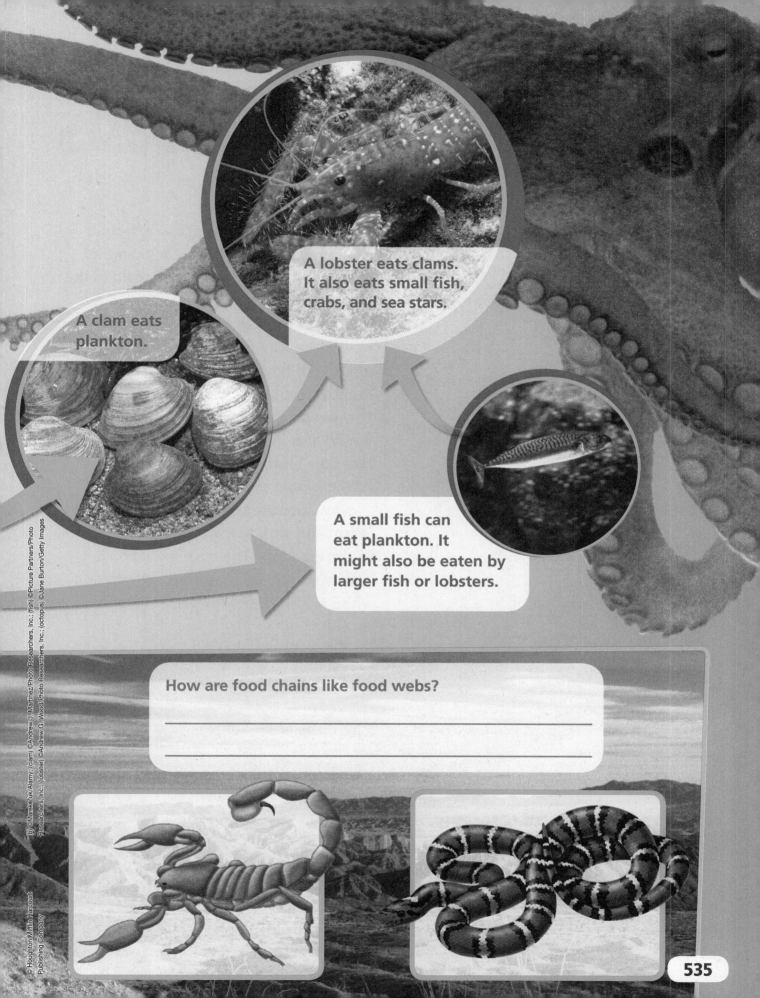

A lobster eats clams. It also eats small fish, crabs, and sea stars.

A clam eats plankton.

A small fish can eat plankton. It might also be eaten by larger fish or lobsters.

How are food chains like food webs?

_____

_____

Changes in Food Webs

Imagine that one animal disappeared. What would happen to the other living things in the food web?

ACTIVE **READING** As you read these two pages, circle clue words that signal a detail such as an example or an added fact.

Changes in food webs can affect all parts of a food web. For example, suppose the weather was very cold in the spring. Only a few plants in a meadow might live through the cold spring. This means that the mice in the meadow would not have enough to eat. Their numbers would go down. The snakes in the meadow eat mice. Their numbers would also go down. The hawks in the meadow hunt snakes and mice. The hawks would be hungry, too.

Now suppose that the spring was warm and wet. Many plants would grow in the meadow. The mice would have plenty to eat. Their numbers would go up. The snakes and hawks would also have plenty to eat, so their numbers would go up, too.

Food webs can be disrupted when one member of a food web goes away. This happened in Yellowstone National Park. During the early 1900s, the gray wolf was hunted in the park. Eventually, no gray wolves were left.

The gray wolf preyed mostly on elk. The number of elk in the park increased after the wolves disappeared. In 1995, scientists returned 14 gray wolves to the park. The number of wolves has since increased. As a result, the number of elk in the park has decreased.

Other changes happened, too. Elk eat trees. Before the wolves were reintroduced, the elk overgrazed the trees in the park. This harmed the trees. Since beavers had fewer trees to build

dams with, the beaver population decreased. After the wolves were reintroduced to the park, both the trees and beavers began to thrive.

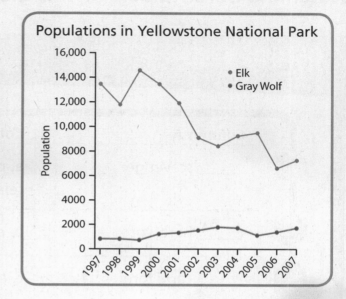

DO THE MATH

Interpret Tables

The table shows the height of trees in Yellowstone National Park before and after the gray wolves returned. Study the table, and then answer the questions.

Kind of tree	Average height before 1995	Average height after 2002
Cottonwood	less than 1m	2 to 3 m
Willow	less than 1m	3 to 4 m

1. Describe the heights of the trees before the gray wolves were brought back to Yellowstone National Park.

_____

2. Describe the heights of the trees after the gray wolves were brought back to Yellowstone National Park.

_____

_____

3. Why do you think the heights of the trees changed?

_____

_____

_____

_____

Sum It Up »

Match the words in Column A to their definitions in Column B.

	Column A	Column B
1	_____ scavenger	a. model that shows all the feeding relationships in an ecosystem
2	_____ herbivore	b. eats other animals
3	_____ carnivore	c. eats only plants
4	_____ omnivore	d. eats dead animals and plants
5	_____ food web	e. eats both plants and animals

The idea web below summarizes the lesson. Complete the web.

Food chains show how energy moves from one living thing to another. The first link in a food chain is always a(n) 6. _____

Herbivores are consumers that 7. _____ .

Omnivores are consumers that 8. _____ .

Carnivores are consumers that 9. _____ .

Scavengers are consumers that 10. _____ .

Name _____

Vocabulary Review

1 **Use the clues to fill in the missing letters of the words.**

1. _ _ _ d _ h a _ _   the transfer of energy from one living thing to another

2. _ m _ _ _ _ _ e   a consumer that eats both plants and animals

3. c _ _ _ _ _ v _ _ _   a consumer that eats other animals

4. _ _ _ y   an animal that is hunted

5. h _ _ _ _ _ o _ _   a consumer that eats only plants

6. _ o _ _ w _ _   shows the relationship among all of the food chains in an ecosystem

7. _ _ _ d _ _ _ _   an animal that hunts

8. _ _ _ _ _ _ _ _ s e r   a consumer that breaks down the remains of plants and animals

Apply Concepts

2 The food chain below is in scrambled order. Put the links of the food chain in the correct order.

wolf $\longrightarrow$ rabbit $\longrightarrow$ grass

_____ $\longrightarrow$ _____ $\longrightarrow$ _____

3 Fill in this graphic organizer about different kinds of consumers.

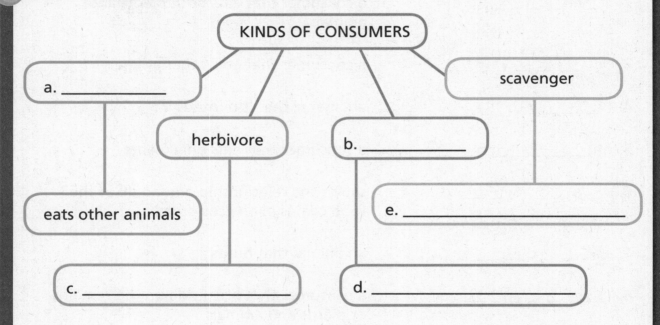

KINDS OF CONSUMERS

a. _____

herbivore

scavenger

b. _____

eats other animals

e. _____

c. _____

d. _____

4 The pictures below show a lion and a zebra. Label the animals as *predator* or *prey*.

_____   _____

5 The picture shows different animals in a pond food web. Use arrows to show who eats what. Remember that arrows should point from the living thing that is being eaten to the living thing that is eating.

6 In the space below, draw an ocean food chain and a forest food chain.

7 The pictures show different kinds of consumers. Label each consumer as a herbivore, carnivore, omnivore, or scavenger.

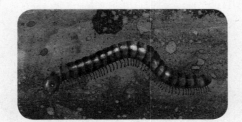

_____

_____

_____

_____

8 The population of a predator in an area has gone up. What do you think will happen to the population of prey in the area? Explain your answer.

_____

_____

_____

_____

_____

_____

Take It Home! Share what you have learned about food chains with your family. With a family member, tell which of the foods you ate for dinner came from plants and which came from animals.

SC.4.L.17.4 Recognize ways plants and animals, including humans, can impact the environment.

LESSON **4**

ESSENTIAL **QUESTION**

How Do Organisms Affect Their Environment?

 Engage Your Brain

Find the answer to the following question in this lesson and record it here.

How can planting a garden on a rooftop help the environment?

_____

_____

_____

_____

ACTIVE **READING**

Lesson Vocabulary

List the terms. As you learn about each one, makes notes in the Interactive Glossary.

_____

_____

_____

Comparisons

Signal words show connections between ideas. Words that signal comparisons, or similarities, include *like*, *same as*, *similar to*, and *resembles*. Active readers remember what they read because they are alert to signal words that identify comparisons.

Role of Plants

Many animals depend on plants for food. But plants are helpful—and harmful— in other ways.

ACTIVE **READING** As you read these two pages, find and underline four examples of the helpful effects of plants.

Living things can change their environment. Recall that the environment is all the living and nonliving things in a place.

Plants have helpful effects on the environment. They are food for many animals. Apples, oranges, tomatoes, peas—these foods all come from plants. Plants also release oxygen as a part of the process of photosynthesis. Most animals need this oxygen to live.

Plants are shelter for many animals. Birds and squirrels nest in trees. Insects live in the bark of trees. Plant roots also help hold soil in place. This is important. If soil is washed away, we cannot grow plants to eat.

People and other animals depend on plants for food.

The roots of these mangrove trees provide shelter for many living things.

Owls use cactus plants for shelter.

Kudzu can grow up to 2 meters in a week.

Plants can harm the environment, too. The oils on some plants can cause an itchy rash. You can get the rash if you touch the leaves or stems of plants such as poison ivy.

Other plants can grow so fast that they become pests. Kudzu is a plant that was brought to the United States to help keep soils from blowing away. Few animals eat kudzu, so it grows very fast. It takes nutrients and space from other plants. It can quickly cover houses and other things.

Compare and Contrast

List some ways that plants are helpful. List some ways that plants are harmful.

_____

_____

_____

_____

_____

Green plants give off oxygen during photosynthesis. People and most other animals use this oxygen for important life functions.

Role of Animals

Just like plants, animals are food for other animals. What other effects do animals have on their environments?

ACTIVE READING As you read these two pages, draw a box around the clue words that signal when things are being compared.

Eggs, hamburgers, cheese, milk—many of the foods that you eat come from animals. Animals are important foods for people and for other animals.

Some animals, such as sheep, goats, and cows, are grazers. If too many goats are in one place, they can eat too many plants. Then, there are not enough plant roots to hold the soil in place, and it blows away.

Bats eat insects. They help keep down the number of biting insects.

Like plants, animals can change their environments. These changes can be helpful or harmful. Animal wastes help the environment. The wastes add nutrients to the soil. Nutrient-rich soils are good for growing plants.

Animals hunt other animals or eat plants. This helps keep the numbers of living things in a place from becoming too large or too small.

Other animals such as bees and butterflies spread pollen from one plant to another. This helps the plants reproduce.

Like plants, animals can be brought into a place, changing its environment. Zebra mussels live in water. They were brought into the Great Lakes by accident. They take food and space from animals that are native to the lakes. As a result, the numbers of native animals have decreased.

What Would Happen?

Lions are predators in Africa. They prey on zebra, gazelles, and other animals. Some of these animals are grazers. Suppose that there were no lions in Africa. What might happen to the populations of other animals? What might happen to the environment?

_____

_____

_____

People Can Be Harmful

Wow! Did you know that what you do each day can affect the environment in different ways?

S imple actions such as riding in a car can have harmful effects on the environment. Buses, cars, and trucks put pollution into the air. **Pollution** is any substance in the environment that can harm living things. Pollution can harm human health.

Pollution also comes from factories and energy stations that burn coal for energy. The pollution can go into the air and into the water. It can harm living things in the water. It can make the water less clean for people and other living things.

People build roads and houses. They cut down trees to make products from wood and to clear space for farms. These actions destroy habitats. As a result, there is less living space for other organisms.

Oil can spill from ships and pollute water. The oil can cover living things. The animals must be cleaned, or they could get very sick.

Cars, trucks, and buses put pollution into the air.

Boats move through rivers and oceans near manatees. Manatees swim slowly and can't always get out of the way when a boat is near. Sometimes they get struck by boats.

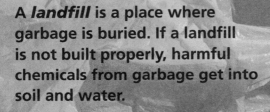

A *landfill* is a place where garbage is buried. If a landfill is not built properly, harmful chemicals from garbage get into soil and water.

⊞ DO THE **MATH**

Interpret a Table

The table below shows how the number of cars in the United States has changed over time. Study the table, and then answer the questions.

1935	1956	2005
27 million	65 million	240 million

1. Between 1935 and 1956, the number of cars increased by how much?

   _____

   _____

2. Between 1956 and 2005, the number of cars increased by how much?

   _____

   _____

3. How might the increase in cars affect the environment?

   _____

   _____

   _____

People Can Be Helpful

You can make a difference and help the environment!

ACTIVE READING As you read these two pages, draw a box around the sentences that give key information about the main idea.

People can help conserve natural resources. **Conservation** means using natural resources wisely.

We can plant new trees to replace trees that are cut down. People can plant gardens on rooftops. Rooftops, streets, and sidewalks take in and give off heat. Planting gardens on rooftops and trees in parks helps keep cities cool. Less air-conditioning is used and energy resources are saved.

People can also recycle, reuse, and reduce. Recycling means making something new from something used. Old soda cans are recycled into new cans.

Planting trees makes new habitats for living things. It also helps keep the soil in place.

People can ride a bike or walk to nearby places. These actions reduce air pollution.

People help clean up animals that have been harmed by oil spills.

Some playgrounds are made from recycled materials, such as rubber tires.

Reusing means using something in a new way. For example, an old T-shirt can be used to wash a car. Reducing means using fewer resources. Turning off lights when no one is in a room conserves energy.

How Can You Use It?

Suppose you have an old T-shirt. In the lines below, list some ways you can reuse the T-shirt. Try to come up with as many uses as possible. Share your list with the class.

_____

_____

_____

_____

Some bags are not thrown away after one use. They are used again and again. Reusing items helps reduce the amount of garbage in landfills.

Sum It Up »

Place the correct letter(s) from the list below the summary under each picture. Some choices might go in more than one box.

Summary:

Plants, animals, and people have both helpful and harmful effects on the environment.

List:

a. provides shelter for other living things

b. causes pollution

c. replants trees

d. provides food

e. eats other living things

f. destroys habitats

g. causes overgrazing

h. makes soil richer with its wastes

i. helps reduce pollution

1

_____

2

_____

3

_____

Complete the graphic organizer below about the helpful and harmful effects of people on the environment.

Effects of People on the Environment

Pollution is a
4. _____ effect.

Conservation is a
5. _____ effect.

An example of pollution is
6. _____.

An example of conservation is
7. _____.

Name _____

Vocabulary Review

1 Use the clues to unscramble the words in the box.

1. lecyrec: to make something from something that is used	
2. moinevntren: the living and nonliving things in a place	
3. ceredu: to use less of something	
4. arevtnoicnos: to use resources wisely	
5. eerus: to use something in a new way	
6. luplotnoi: something that is harmful to living things	

Apply Concepts

2 The chart shows some harmful actions of people on the environment. Next to each harmful action, write a helpful action that people can do to help the environment.

Harmful action	Helpful action
Cut down trees.	
Drive a car.	
Throw away trash.	

3 The pictures show different effects of animals on the environment. Label the effects as helpful, harmful, or both.

_____   _____

_____

4 In the space below, draw a way to reuse an item that you would normally throw away.

Take It Home!

Share what you have learned about conservation with your family. With a family member, take some clean, used items to your local recycling center.

SC.4.L.17.4 Recognize ways plants and animals, including humans, can impact the environment.
SC.4.N.1.2 Compare the observations made by different groups using multiple tools and seek reasons to explain the differences…

INQUIRY
LESSON 5

Name _____

ESSENTIAL QUESTION

How Do People Affect Their Environment?

Materials

apple core
banana peel
plastic spoon
plastic cup
soil
clean, empty soda can
large plastic bin
plastic disposable gloves

EXPLORE

Some materials that people put in landfills are biodegradable. That means that they will break down. Other materials are not biodegradable. How can you tell which materials will break down?

Before You Begin—Preview the Steps

(1) CAUTION: Wear plastic gloves. Fill the bin with soil.

(2) Make a data table in which you write the name and a brief description of each item you will bury. Record the date as well.

(3) Bury each item in the soil. Make sure the items are covered by the soil. Put the plastic bin in a place where it will not be disturbed.

(4) In three days, check the items. Note which items are breaking down and which are not.

(5) Record your observations. Be sure to record the date.

(6) Repeat steps 4 and 5 for three weeks. Record your observations and the date each time.

Set a Purpose

How does this activity show how people affect the environment?

_____

_____

_____

Think About the Procedure

Why do you need to observe the trash for three weeks?

_____

_____

_____

Why do you wear gloves?

_____

_____

_____

Name _____

Record Your Data

In the space below, write or draw your results.

Draw Conclusions

What did the plastic container and soil represent?

_____

_____

What did you observe about the different materials after observing them for three weeks?

_____

_____

Claims • Evidence • Reasoning

1. Interpret your data. Write a claim about what kinds of materials decompose and what kinds do not decompose.

_____

_____

_____

2. Cite evidence that supports your claim and explain why the evidence supports the claim.

_____

_____

_____

3. Compare your results with those of other groups. Did everyone have the same results? If not, what might have made the results differ?

_____

_____

_____

4. Write a claim about how long materials can stay in landfills.

_____

_____

5. Look at the table. How could you display this data in another way? Show your work below.

Object	Time it takes to decompose
Diaper	75 yr
Paper	2-3 months
Milk carton	5 yr
Aluminum can	200-500 yr
Plastic bag	10-20 yr

_____

_____

Meet the Tree-Planting Scientists

Wangari Maathai

Wangari Maathai was born in Kenya. Maathai started an organization that conserves Kenya's forests by planting trees. She recruited Kenyan women to plant native trees throughout the country. In 1977, this organization became known as the Green Belt Movement. The Green Belt Movement has planted more than 40 million trees. Maathai's work inspires other African countries to start community tree plantings.

Seeds from nearby forests are used to grow native trees.

Willie Smits

Willie Smits works to save orangutans in Indonesia. By clearing the forests, people are destroying the orangutan's habitat. The orangutan is endangered. Smits's plan helps both orangutans and people. Smits is growing a rain forest. The new forest gives people food and rainwater for drinking, so they protect it. The sugar palm is one of the trees planted. In 2007, Smits started using sugar palms to make sugar and a biofuel called ethanol. The sugar palms provide income for the community.

Sugar palms are fire-resistant. This protects the forest from fires.

Smits has rescued almost 1,000 orangutan babies. However, his goal is to save them in the wild.

Scientist saves the Day!

Read the story about the Florida scrub jay. Draw the missing pictures to complete the story.

The Problem: Florida scrub jays are endangered. They are found only in parts of Florida with shrubs and other short plants.

Fires kill tall trees that grow in the scrub jay's habitat. But people put out the fires, so the trees survive.

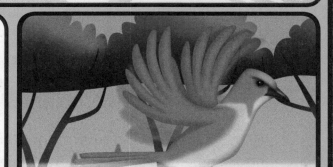

Trees are now growing, so there are fewer shrubs. The scrub jays can't live there.

The Solution: Scientists and firefighters start fires that can be kept under control. These fires kill the tall trees.

Shrubs grow and the scrub jays return.

S.T.E.M.

ENGINEERING & TECHNOLOGY

Underwater Exploration

When you think of underwater exploration, you may think of scuba. The word *scuba* comes from the first letters of the phrase "**s**elf-**c**ontained **u**nderwater **b**reathing **a**pparatus." Scuba divers take everything they need with them; they are not connected to anything on the surface. Follow the timeline to learn how underwater diving equipment has changed over time.

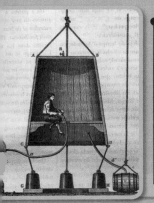

1530s
Guglielmo de Lorena—Diving Bell
Diving bells are airtight containers opened at one end. De Lorena's diving bell rested over a diver's shoulders, allowing the diver to breathe the trapped air and to walk on the ocean floor. Ropes connected the diver to the surface.

1830s
Augustus Siebe—Diving Dress
A metal diving helmet is sealed onto a watertight canvas suit. An air hose and a cable connect the diver to the surface. In this closed-circuit system, used-up air is released into the suit. The diver controls when air is released.

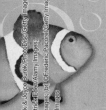

1940s
Jacques Cousteau and Emile Gagnan—Aqua-Lung
This breathing system passes air to a diver from a tank carried on the diver's back. This is an open-circuit system that releases used-up air into the water. Divers can swim without any cables or hoses connecting them to the surface.

CRITICAL **THINKING**

How are the first two types of diving equipment similar?

_____

_____

_____

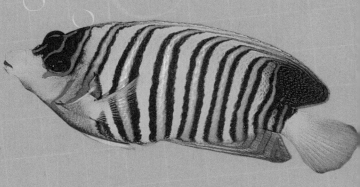

Make Some History

Research another type of diving equipment. Describe how it works and where it should be placed on the timeline.

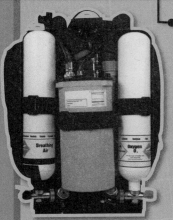

1960s
Rebreather

Rebreathers are closed-circuit systems. A diver breathes through a mouthpiece and used-up air is not released into the water. Instead, it is filtered to remove carbon dioxide and used again. This design feature extends the amount of time a diver can spend underwater.

1980s
ADS

Atmospheric Diving Suits (ADS) were developed for deep diving activities. They use rebreather technology and a hard suit that enable divers to safely dive to great depths. Modern ADS can work in water up to 610 m deep!

_____

_____

_____

Design Your Future

What features do you think the next diving suit should have? What needs would those features meet?

_____

_____

_____

_____

Solve It:

Getting Around a Dam

A dam is a barrier usually built to control the flow of a river and prevent floods. However, some dams are built to generate electricity.

As you might imagine, building a dam affects local ecosystems. Dry land behind a dam is often flooded as water slowly rises, forming a lake. Dams decrease the amount of water and nutrients carried by the river downstream.

Dams make it hard for aquatic organisms to move freely along the river. Salmon, for instance, need to migrate upstream to lay eggs. How could you design a system to allow salmon to get around a dam?

DESIGN PROCESS STEPS

1 Find a Problem
2 Plan & Build
3 Test & Improve
4 Redesign
5 Communicate

What to Do:

1 Do research to learn about dams and how they affect ecosystems.

2 Find out more about salmon behavior.

3 Think of ways to help salmon get around dams. Write three ideas.

4 Choose two ideas. Make a diagram of each design.

5 List the advantages and disadvantages of each design.

Design	Advantages	Disadvantages
1		
2		

6 Compare and contrast these advantages and disadvantages to select the best design to help the salmon get around the dam. Explain your selection.

7 Keep a record of your work in your Science Notebook.

Name _____

Vocabulary Review

Use the terms in the box to complete the sentences.

> conservation
> consumer
> producer

1. The use of less of something to make its supply last longer is called _____.

2. An organism that makes its own food is called a(n) _____.

3. An animal that eats plants or other animals to get energy is called a(n) _____.

Science Concepts

Fill in the letter of the choice that best answers the question.

4. Solid wastes that people throw into the oceans include various paper products. The table below shows how long it takes for these items to decompose in salt water.

Item	Decomposition time
Paper towel	2–4 weeks
Newspaper	6 weeks
Cardboard box	2 months
Waxed milk carton	3 months

Based on the evidence, which would you claim will decompose the fastest?

(A) cardboard box

(B) newspaper

(C) waxed milk carton

(D) paper towel

5. The fish in a stream near Esha's house have been dying. What is the **most likely** cause?

(F) A new bridge has been built across the stream.

(G) The water level in the stream has decreased slightly.

(H) A nearby factory releases warm water into the stream.

(I) The number of insects living near the stream has increased.

6. The manatee is on the threatened species list. What is the **best** way that people can protect the manatee?

(A) Provide food for the manatee.

(B) Avoid areas where manatees live.

(C) Visit manatees in aquarium exhibits.

(D) Keep predators away from manatees.

7. For breakfast, Madison ate a bowl of cereal with milk. For breakfast, a chipmunk ate seeds. How are Madison and the chipmunk alike?

(F) They are both being herbivores.

(G) They are both being carnivores.

(H) They are both getting some energy.

(I) They are both being food producers.

8. Emi is studying animals that live in Florida marshes. She makes the following graphs to show how the number of fish and marsh birds changed in a certain area over time.

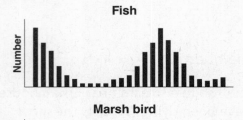

Fish

Marsh bird

What **most likely** happened when the number of fish was highest?

(A) The bird population began to decrease.

(B) The birds moved away for lack of food.

(C) The fish population continued to increase.

(D) The bird population increased because there was more food.

9. Each year, humpback whales travel from Alaska to Hawaii.

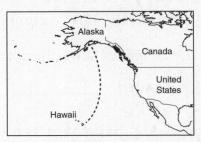

What is the correct word for this process?

(F) migration

(G) adaptation

(H) hibernation

(I) reproduction

10. A farmer in Florida grows tomatoes throughout most of the year. In the winter, the farmer changes his main crop from tomatoes to cabbages. What is the **main** reason for growing cabbages instead of tomatoes in the winter?

(A) Tomatoes require less watering.

(B) Tomatoes grow poorly in winter.

(C) Cabbages require more sunlight.

(D) Cabbages are popular in winter.

11. During the winter, purple finches are often seen in Florida. During the summer, purple finches are rarely seen in Florida. Which statement **best** explains this change?

(F) The birds hibernate during the summer.

(G) The birds raise their young during the winter.

(H) The birds migrate to Florida during the winter.

(I) The birds reproduce in Florida during the summer.

Name _____

12. Winston has plants in his house. He waters them every other day. He leaves them by the window so that they can get sunlight. Why do the plants need sunlight?

Ⓐ to stay dry

Ⓑ to stay warm

Ⓒ to make food

Ⓓ to break down soil

13. The diagram below shows how a compost pile works.

Garden compost pile

The dead plants and food scraps will decay.

Earthworms eat the dead plants and scraps. This helps create rich soil.

Think about what the earthworm does in the compost pile. Which word describes the earthworm?

Ⓕ carnivore

Ⓖ scavenger

Ⓗ predator

Ⓘ producer

14. Carla wants to show how living things get energy. Which sequence is correct?

Ⓐ Sunlight → Consumer → Decomposer → Producer

Ⓑ Sunlight → Consumer → Producer → Decomposer

Ⓒ Sunlight → Decomposer → Producer → Consumer

Ⓓ Sunlight → Producer → Consumer → Decomposer

15. The picture below shows some animals that you can find in grassland food chains.

1   2

3   4

Which is the carnivore?

Ⓕ 1   Ⓗ 3

Ⓖ 2   Ⓘ 4

16. Horses get energy by eating grass and oats. Florida panthers get energy by eating deer and raccoons. Raccoons get energy by eating frogs and fruit. Bobcats get energy by eating lizards and birds. Which is an herbivore?

Ⓐ bobcat   Ⓒ panther

Ⓑ horse   Ⓓ raccoon

17. Each year a maple tree's leaves change from green to orange.

During which season does this change happen?

Ⓕ fall   Ⓗ spring

Ⓖ winter   Ⓘ summer

Apply Inquiry and Review the Big Idea

Write the answers to these questions.

18. This illustration shows a food web.

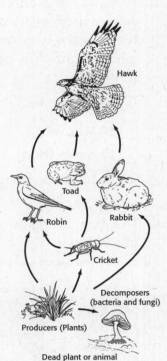

A) Identify the organisms shown in the food web as producers, consumers, or decomposers.

Producers: _____

Consumers: _____

Decomposers: _____

B) Classify the consumers as herbivores, omnivores or carnivores.

Herbivores: _____

Omnivores: _____

Carnivores: _____

C) Make a claim about why all animals depend on producers such as plants. Use an example from the food web to help explain your reasoning.

_____

_____

_____

_____

19. Juan studied this food web and claimed that hawks were the last link in every food chain shown. Vicky pointed to a different organism and claimed that it was the last link. Which organism did Vicky identify? What was her reasoning?

_____

_____

_____

_____

_____

21st Century Skills
Technology and Coding

When you hear the word computer, what comes to mind? You might think of a laptop computer like this one. Despite its small size, this laptop computer can perform many complex tasks. It can help you create documents, organize photos, and stay in touch with your friends and family.

Many other devices contain computer technology, too. Video game consoles, tablets, and cell phones are computers with specialized functions. There are even traffic lights and kitchen appliances that use computer technology!

If you are interested in computer technology and how it works, you might like computer science. Computer science is the study of computer technology.

ACTIVE READING

As you read, underline examples of tools and devices that use computer technology.

Computers at work...

A computer is any device that receives, stores, processes, and outputs data. Today's computers can perform complex calculations very quickly. For this reason, computers are valuable tools in math and science.

However, computers are useful in many other fields, too. Doctors use medical computer technology to diagnose and treat patients. Architects use computers to plan and model buildings. Even artists use computer technology to entertain people in unexpected ways. Here you see someone interacting with a digital art display!

Think of three devices in your home that contain computer technology. List what they are and how they are used here.

_____

_____

_____

Computer scientists study and develop computer technology. For example, they might use their knowledge to improve weather satellites or special effects in movies. Many people enjoy studying and developing computer technology for fun, too. Learning how to create computer-controlled vehicles, video games, or interactive webpages can be rewarding hobbies. And who knows—maybe some day that hobby will become a career!

Computer science, whether for work or play, is a bit like solving a puzzle. Applying knowledge of computers to solve real-world problems requires logical thinking, collaboration, and creative problem solving.

Get with the program

Computers carry out tasks by following instructions, or programs, that people design. Examples of computer programs include web browsers, mobile games, and digital photo editors. Computer programs are sometimes called *software*, *applications*, or *apps*.

Computer programs are not written in human language. They are written in a special programming language, or code, that the computer can interpret. If you learn how to write code, you can create computer programs, too!

Human languages follow certain rules. Programming languages follow rules, too. One difference is that if you make just a small mistake in your code, the computer will not know what you mean. Some errors in code will be caught by the computer. But other errors may cause the program to operate incorrectly or not at all.

```
19
20 # Check if player gets another attempt to play level
22 if player_attempts < 4:
23 print ("Try level again?")
24 else:
25 prinnt ("Game over. Restart?")
26

! Error, line 25: 'prinnt' is not defined.
```

This code contains a mistake. Fortunately, the computer identified where the error occurred and why. Read each line of code, and then see if you can infer what the code does and how to fix the error.

Writing code is just one part of creating a computer program. Planning, sharing, testing, and revising computer programs are important, too. People who write computer programs might ask questions like these. Can you think of other questions to add to this list?

- Who will use this program?

- Why will people want to use it?

- Is the program easy to use?

- Are there ways to improve the program?

Safety First

You should always use computers safely and responsibly. Handle computers and other electronic devices carefully. They can be damaged if dropped. Protect electronic devices from dust, dirt, and moisture. Avoid using a connected computer during thunderstorms.

While building your own electronics projects can be fun, it's important to understand circuits and electrical safety first. Don't try to take apart a computer unless you have permission! Otherwise, you may lose parts or hurt yourself.

It is easy to lose track of time when you're sitting in front of a computer or game console. Balance computer time with other activities, including exercise.

© Houghton Mifflin Harcourt Publishing Company

Talk to your family about rules for Internet use. Do not share private information such as photographs, your phone number, or your address. It is important to treat others with respect when on the web. However, not everyone follows this rule. If someone sends you unwanted contact online, do not reply. Alert a trusted adult.

⊞ DO THE **MATH**

Computer Safety

Complete this table summarizing computer safety tips.

✔ Do...	⊘ Don't...
Take breaks from using the computer to stretch or move around. _____ _____ _____	Drop electronic devices or expose them to dirt or moisture. _____ _____ _____ _____

Careers in Computing

Astrophysics is the study of our universe. But how does someone study enormous and far-away stars, galaxies, and planets? Astrophysicists can use computers to model complex systems in space.

Astrophysics Q & A

Q: What skills are needed in astrophysics?

A: Astrophysics requires an understanding of science, math, engineering, and computer science.

Q: How can computers help astrophysicists conduct research?

A: Astrophysicists use computers to create 3D models, identify data trends, and test theories.

Interactive Glossary

As you learn about each term, add notes, drawings, or sentences in the extra space. This will help you remember what the terms mean. Here are some examples.

fungi [FUHN•jee] **A group of organisms that get nutrients by decomposing other organisms.**

 A mushroom is an example of fungi.

physical change [FIHZ•ih•kuhl CHAYNJ] **Change in the size, shape, or state of matter with no new substance being formed.**

When I cut paper in half, that's a physical change.

Glossary Pronunciation Key

With every glossary term, there is also a phonetic respelling. A phonetic respelling writes the word the way it sounds, which can help you pronounce new or unfamiliar words. Use this key to help you understand the respellings.

Sound	As in	Phonetic Respelling	Sound	As in	Phonetic Respelling
a	bat	(BAT)	oh	over	(OH•ver)
ah	lock	(LAHK)	oo	pool	(POOL)
air	rare	(RAIR)	ow	out	(OWT)
ar	argue	(AR•gyoo)	oy	foil	(FOYL)
aw	law	(LAW)	s	cell	(SEL)
ay	face	(FAYS)		sit	(SIT)
ch	chapel	(CHAP•uhl)	sh	sheep	(SHEEP)
e	test	(TEST)	th	that	(THAT)
	metric	(MEH•trik)		thin	(THIN)
ee	eat	(EET)	u	pull	(PUL)
	feet	(FEET)	uh	medal	(MED•uhl)
	ski	(SKEE)		talent	(TAL•uhnt)
er	paper	(PAY•per)		pencil	(PEN•suhl)
	fern	(FERN)		onion	(UHN•yuhn)
eye	idea	(eye•DEE•uh)		playful	(PLAY•fuhl)
i	bit	(BIT)		dull	(DUHL)
ing	going	(GOH•ing)	y	yes	(YES)
k	card	(KARD)		ripe	(RYP)
	kite	(KYT)	z	bags	(BAGZ)
ngk	bank	(BANGK)	zh	treasure	(TREZH•er)

A

acceleration
[ak•sel•er•AY•shuhn] Any
change in the speed or direction
of an object's motion (p. 418)

axis [AK•sis] The imaginary
line around which Earth rotates
(p. 112)

chemical change [KEM•ih•kuhl
CHAYNJ] A reaction or change
in a substance, produced by
chemical means, that results in
a different substance (p. 299)

chemical energy [KEM•ih•kuhl
EN•er•jee] Energy that can be
released by a chemical reaction
(p. 333)

C

carnivore [KAHR•nuh•vawr] An
animal that eats only other
animals (p. 530)

complete metamorphosis
[kuhm•PLEET
met•uh•MAWR•fuh•sis] A
complex change that most
insects undergo that includes
larva and pupa stages (p. 473)

change of state [CHAYNJ uhv
STAYT] A physical change that
occurs when matter changes
from one state to another, such
as from a liquid to a gas (p. 262)

computer model [kuhm•PYOO•ter
MOD•l] A computer program that
models an event or object (p. 51)

condensation [kahn•duhn•SAY•shuhn] The process by which a gas changes into a liquid (p. 263)

constellation [kahn•stuh•LAY•shuhn] A pattern of stars that form an imaginary picture or design in the sky (p. 116)

conduction [kuhn•DUK•shuhn] The movement of heat between two materials that are touching (p. 376)

consumer [kuhn•SOOM•er] A living thing that can't make its own food and must eat other living things (p. 520)

conductor [kuhn•DUK•ter] Materials that let heat travel through them easily (p. 390)

convection [kuhn•VEK•shuhn] The movement of heat in liquids and gases from a warmer area to a cooler area (p. 377)

conservation [kahn•ser•VAY•shuhn] The preserving and protecting of a resource (p. 550)

D

data [DEY•tuh] Individual facts, statistics, and items of information (p. 35)

© Houghton Mifflin Harcourt Publishing Company

decomposer [dee•kuhm•POHZ•er] A living thing that gets energy by breaking down dead organisms and animal wastes into simpler substances (p. 522)

dormancy [DAWR•muhn•see] In a state of rest or inactivity (p. 504)

density [DEN•suh•tee] The amount of matter in an object compared to the space it takes up (p. 238)

E

electrical energy [ee•LEK•trih•kuhl EN•er•jee] Energy that comes from electric current (p. 333)

deposition [dep•uh•ZISH•uhn] The dropping or settling of eroded materials (p. 166)

electromagnet [ee•lek•troh•MAG•nit] A temporary magnet caused by an electric current (p. 276)

design [dih•ZYN] To conceive something and to prepare the plans and drawings for it to be built (p. 70)

energy [EN•er•jee] The ability to do work and cause changes in matter (p. 327)

engineering [en•juh•NIR•ing] The use of scientific and mathematical principles to develop something practical (p. 69)

food chain [FOOD CHAYN] **A series of organisms that depend on one another for food** (p. 528)

erosion [uh•ROH•zhuhn] **The process of moving sediment from one place to another** (p. 166)

food web [FOOD WEB] **A group of food chains that overlap** (p. 534)

evaporation [ee•vap•uh•RAY•shuhn] **The process by which a liquid changes into a gas** (p. 263)

force [FAWRS] **A push or a pull of any kind** (p. 416)

F

fertilization [fur•tl•ih•ZAY•shuhn] **The joining of an egg and sperm** (p. 444)

G

gas [GAS] The state of matter that does not have a definite shape or volume (p. 258)

germination [jer•muh•NAY•shuhn] The sprouting of a seed (p. 442)

H

heat [HEET] The energy that moves between objects of different temperatures (p. 374)

herbivore [HER•buh•vawr] An animal that eats only plants, or producers (p. 530)

heredity [huh•RED•ih•tee] The process by which traits are passed from parents to offspring (p. 481)

hibernation [hy•ber•NAY•shuhn] A dormant, inactive state in which normal body activities slow (p. 506)

hydroelectric energy [hy•droh•ee•LEK•trik EN•er•jee] Electricity produced using the energy of falling water (p. 356)

hypothesis [hy•PAHTH•uh•sis] A possible explanation or answer to a question; a testable statement (p. 9)

I

igneous rock [IG•nee•uhs RAHK] A type of rock that forms from melted rock that cools and hardens (p. 192)

incomplete metamorphosis [in•kuhm•PLEET met•uh•MAWR•fuh•sis] Developmental change in some insects in which a nymph hatches from an egg and gradually develops into an adult (p. 473)

inference [IN•fer•uhns] An untested conclusion based on your observations (p. 19)

instinct [IN•stinkt] An inherited behavior of an animal that helps it meet its needs (p. 488)

insulator [IN•suh•layt•er] A material that does not let heat move through it easily (p. 392)

investigation [in•ves•tuh•GAY•shuhn] A procedure carried out to gather data about an object or event (p. 7)

K

kinetic energy [kih•NET•ik EN•er•jee] The energy of motion (p. 328)

L

learned behavior [LERND bee•HAYV•yer] A behavior that an animal doesn't begin life with but develops as a result of experience or by observing other animals (p. 486)

liquid [LIK•wid] The state of matter that has a definite volume but no definite shape (p. 258)

mass [MAS] The amount of matter in an object (p. 232)

M

magnet [MAG•nit] An object that attracts iron and a few other (but not all) metals (p. 273)

matter [MAT•er] Anything that has mass and takes up space (p. 232)

magnetic field [mag•NET•ik FEELD] The space around a magnet in which the force of the magnet acts (p. 274)

maturity [muh•TYOOR•ih•tee] The stage at which organisms can reproduce (p. 442)

magnetic pole [mag•NET•ik POHL] The parts of a magnet at which its force is strongest (p. 275)

mechanical energy [muh•KAN•ih•kuhl EN•er•jee] The total potential and kinetic energy of an object (p. 328)

metamorphic rock
[met•uh•MAWR•fik RAHK] **A type of rock that forms when heat or pressure change an existing rock** (p. 196)

model [MOD•l] **A mental or physical representation of a process or object** (p. 49)

microscope [MY•kruh•skohp] **A tool that makes an object look several times bigger than it is** (p. 31)

moon phase [MOON FAYZ] **One of the shapes the moon seems to have as it orbits Earth** (p. 133)

migration [my•GRAY•shuhn] **The movement of animals from one region to another and back** (p. 507)

motion [MOH•shuhn] **A change of position of an object** (p. 411)

mineral [MIN•er•uhl] **A nonliving solid that has a crystal form** (p. 178)

motor [MOH•ter] **A device that uses electricity to make things move** (p. 276)

N

nonrenewable resource
[nahn•rih•NOO•uh•buhl
REE•sawrs] **A resource that,
once used, cannot be replaced
in a reasonable amount of time**
(p. 214)

nutrients [NOO•tree•uhnts] **The
parts of the soil that help plants
grow and stay healthy** (p. 516)

nymph [NIMF] **An immature form
of an insect that undergoes
incomplete metamorphosis**
(p. 473)

O

observation
[ahb•zuhr•VAY•shuhn]
**Information that you gather with
your senses** (p. 7)

omnivore [AHM•nih•vawr] **An
animal that eats both plants
and other animals** (p. 530)

orbit [AWR•bit] **The path of one
object in space around another
object** (p. 114)

P

pan balance [PAN BAL•uhns] **A
tool that measures mass** (p. 32)

photosynthesis
[foht•oh•SIHN•thuh•sis] **The
process that plants use to make
sugar** (p. 518)

© Houghton Mifflin Harcourt
Publishing Company

physical change [FIZ•ih•kuhl CHAYNJ] **A change in matter from one form to another that doesn't result in a different substance** (p. 297)

position [puh•ZISH•uhn] **The location of an object in relation to a nearby object or place** (p. 411)

physical property [FIZ•ih•kuhl PRAHP•er•tee] **Anything that you can observe about an object by using one or more of your senses** (p. 232)

potential energy [poh•TEN•shuhl EN•er•jee] **Energy that an object has because of its position or its condition** (p. 328)

pollination [pol•uh•NEY•shuhn] **The transfer of pollen from the male structures to the female structures of seed plants** (p. 446)

producer [pruh•DOOS•er] **A living thing, such as a plant, that can make its own food** (p. 518)

pollution [puh•LOO•shuhn] **Waste products that damage an ecosystem** (p. 548)

prototype [PROH•tuh•typ] **The original or model on which something is based** (p. 71)

R

radiation [ray•dee••AY•shuhn]
The movement of heat without
matter to carry it (p. 379)

rotate [ROH•tayt] To spin on an
axis (p. 112)

renewable resource
[rih•NOO•uh•buhl REE•sawrs]
A resource that can be replaced
within a reasonable amount of
time (p. 213)

S

science [SY•uhns] The study of
the natural world (p. 5)

resource [REE•sawrs] Any
material that can be used to
satisfy a need (p. 212)

scientist [SY•uhn•tist] A person
who asks questions about the
natural world (p. 5)

rock [RAHK] A solid substance
made up of one or more minerals
(p. 192)

sediment [SED•uh•ment] **Very small pieces of rock, sand, and silt carried by water** (p. 167)

space probe [SPEYS PROHB] **An unmanned spacecraft designed to explore the solar system and transmit data back to Earth** (p. 142)

sedimentary rock [sed•uh•MEN•tuh•ree RAHK] **A type of rock that forms when layers of sediment are pressed together** (p. 194)

speed [SPEED] **The measure of an object's change in position during a certain amount of time** (p. 414)

solar energy [SOH•ler EN•er•jee] **The power of the sun** (p. 360)

spring scale [SPRING SKAYL] **A tool that measures forces, such as weight** (p. 32)

solid [SAHL•id] **The state of matter that has a definite shape and a definite volume** (p. 258)

states of matter [STAYTS uhv MAT•er] **The physical forms (such as solid, liquid, and gas) that matter can exist in** (p. 258)

T

technology [tek•NOL•uh•jee] Any designed system, product, or process used to solve problems (p. 87)

telescope [TEL•uh•skohp] A device people use to observe distant objects with their eyes (p. 141)

three-dimensional model [THREE-di•MEN•shuh•nuhl MOD•l] A model that has the dimension of depth as well as width and height (p. 51)

tool [TOOL] Anything used to help people shape, build, or produce things to meet their needs (p. 86)

two-dimensional model [TOO-di•MEN•shuh•nuhl MOD•l] A model that has the dimensions of width and height only (p. 49)

velocity [vuh•LAHS•uh•tee] The speed of an object in a particular direction (p. 414)

volume [VAHL•yoom] The amount of space that matter takes up (p. 236)

weathering [WETH•er•ing] The breaking down of rocks on Earth's surface into smaller pieces (p. 165)

wind energy [WIND EN•er•jee] The energy of moving air, which can be used to generate electricity (p. 358)

Index

A

Abruña, Héctor, 315
acceleration, 418–419, 429
aerogel
    as insulator, 403–404
    use of, 404
air guns, 45
airplanes, 93
algae, 528
amphibians, frog, 520–521
Analyze and Extend, 41,
    42, 57, 81, 99, 125, 187,
    247, 253, 285, 311, 345,
    351, 385, 399, 425,
    457, 555
animal behaviorists,
    493–494
animal reproduction,
    466–475
    care of young, 468–469
    eggs, 468
    fertilization, 467
    humans, 470–471
    metamorphosis,
        472–473
animals. *See also*
    amphibians; birds;
    carnivores; consumers;
    decomposers; fish;
    herbivores; insects;
    mammals; omnivores;
    plants; producers;
    reptiles
    consumers, 520,
        524–526
    crocodile, 530
    decomposers, 522,
        525–526

dolphin, 499
effect on the
    environment,
    546–547, 552
endangered, 474
energy, 516–517
as food eater, 520–521
hibernating, 506,
    510–512
hunting, 547
instincts of, 488–489
learned behaviors of,
    486–487, 490
life cycles of, 466–467
lion, 532–533
lizard, 11
migration, 507,
    510–511
nutrients, 516, 523–524
panther, 439
pollination and,
    446–447
rabbit, 530
raccoon, 531
role of, 546–547
and seasons, 504–505,
    512
sea turtle, 1, 474–475
seed distribution and,
    448–449
shelter for, 544
wastes, 547
whale, 23
wolf, 537
zebra, 532–533
anthers, 444–445
Apollo, 142
aspirin, 252
astrolabe, 141

astronauts, 148
    Aldrin, Buzz, 143
    Armstrong, Neil, 130, 142
    technology used by,
        148–149
astronomers, 140–141, 151
    ancient, 140–141
    Galileo, 141
astrophysics, 123–124,
    576
Atlas V Rocket, 147
attract, 273, 278,
    280–181, 283
axis, 112, 119
Aztec calendar, 135

B

bar graph, 35
Benerito, Ruth Rogan, 315
Big Dipper, stars of, 116
birds
    chicken, 482
    eggs, 468
    geese, 489
    heron, 520–521
    life cycles of, 466–467
    vulture, 531
body armor, 317–318

C

calendars, 134–135
Careers in computing,
    576
Careers in Science
    animal behaviorist,
        493–494
    astronaut, 142–144, 148

astrophysicist, 123–124, 576

   conservation biologist, 1

   medical chemist, 251

   soil scientist, 223–224

   sports biomechanist, 429–430

carnivores, 530

Cause and Effect, 111–112, 163, 271, 276, 280, 362, 389

Celsius scale, 33, 375

centimeter (cm), 33

change of state, 262

chemical changes, 298–309

   decay, 300, 302, 307

   fireworks, 303

   at home, 302–303

   in making pizza, 304–305

   rotting, 299

   in rubber, 299

   rust, 298–299, 307

   smoke, 299, 302, 307

   tarnish, 303

   vs. physical change, 300, 306

chemical energy, 333, 335, 363–364.
See also **energy**

chemical weathering, 165

Chinese Zodiac calendar, 134

chrysalis, 472

claims, evidence, reasoning, 44, 60, 84, 102, 128, 190, 250, 256, 288, 314, 348, 354, 388, 402, 428, 460, 558

classifying, 22

clean energy source, 358

clue words, 140, 546

code, 572–573

coding, 569

color, 234

communicating, 19, 36–37

Compare and Contrast, 211, 257, 523, 545

comparing, 19, 543

compass, 278, 284

complete metamorphosis, 472–473

computer, 569–576

   safety, 574–575

computer models, 51

computer programming, 572–573

computer science, 569–576

computer technology, 569–576

condensation, 263

conductors, 390–391

cones, 444–445

conservation, 213, 221, 550, 553

   fossil fuels, 215, 221

conservation biologist, 1

constellation, 116, 118–119

   Orion, 116, 121

   position change, 116–117

   Ursa Major, 116

consumers, 520, 523–525, 530–533.
See also **decomposers; producers**

   and producers, 523

contrast, 214

convection, 377

convection currents, 377

craters, 131

Culpepper, Martin, 45–46

cycads, 445

data, 35

   real time, 52

   recording and displaying, 23 34–35

   using, 36–37

data bases, 37

Daytona Beach, Florida, 323

decomposers, 521, 524–524

   blue crab, 522

   millipede, 522

   mushroom, 522

   roles in ecosystems, 525

   worm, 522

Delta, Nile, 167

density, 238–239

deposition, 166, 173

   landform, 176

   rocks, 166, 173, 176

   sand, 161, 168

   sediment, 172

desert food chains, 534–535

designed systems, 90–91

design process, 70–75

   planning, 72–73

   prototypes, 71–72

   spacecraft, 153–154

steps in, 71
testing and
  redesigning, 74–75
Diebold, John, 45–46
displacement, 237
diving equipment,
  561–562
dormancy, 504, 511
Do the Math!
  calculate speed, 415
  compare numbers, 23
  estimate fractions and
    percentages, 133
  equivalent fractions,
    305
  find percentages, 520
  graph the data, 277
  interpret a graph, 215
  interpret a table, 93,
    549
  interpret tables, 537
  make measurements, 33
  measure angles, 170
  measure the volume of
    objects, 237
  solve a problem, 469
  solve a two–step
    problem, 147
  solve real–world
    problems, 330, 361,
    395, 509
  use and represent
    numbers, 112
  use a number line, 485
  use fractions, 50
  use temperature
    scales, 375
  work with fractions, 447
Draw Conclusions, 21, 36,
  37, 101
dry ice, 374

earth
  axis of, 112, 119
  day and night
    formation, 112, 118
  draw conclusions, 128
  geographic pole, 278
  hemispheres, 114
  moon and, 130–131
  movement in space,
    127–128
  Northern hemisphere,
    114–115
  orbit, 114, 119
  record data, 127
  revolve, 118–119
  rotation, 112–113, 119
  seasons, 118–119
  Southern hemisphere,
    114–115
ecosystems,
  consumers in, 530–533
  food chains in, 528–529
  food webs in, 534–537
  pond, 528–529
  predators and prey in,
    523–533
  producers in, 528
  roles of decomposers,
    525
  scavengers, 521
eggs, 444, 468
egg cells, 482
electrical energy, 333.
  See also **electricity;**
  energy
  change, 364
electricity, 276, 280,
  330, 333. *See also*
  energy

from dam, 356
hydrogen and oxygen,
  361
motor, 276, 281
from nonrenewable
  resources, 215
piezoelectricity,
  341–342
wind turbine, 358
electromagnet, 276–277,
  208–281. *See also*
  magnets
  kinds of, 279
electronics, 94–95,
  569–576
  safety, 574–575
endangered species,
  474–475
energy, 326–335. *See*
  also **electricity; heat**
  for animals, 516
  change of form, 334,
    335
  chemical, 333, 335,
    363–364
  electrical, 333, 335
  from food, 516–517
  gasoline, 363
  hydroelectric, 356
  kinds of, 328–329
  kinetic, 328–329,
    362–364
  light, 330, 362, 364
  mechanical, 328–329,
    335 363
  potential, 328–329,
    362, 364–365
  renewable, 360–361
  solar, 360
  sound, 330–331, 362,
    364

sources of, 326–327
turbine, 356
water, 356–357
wind, 358–359
windmills, 358
engineering, 68–69. *See also* **design process**
Engineering and Technology. *See also* **STEM (Science, Technology, Engineering, and Mathematics)**
body armor, 317–318
code, 572–573
coding, 569
gyroscopes, 431–432
piezoelectricity, 341–342
refrigeration, 269–270
space exploration, 153–154
underwater exploration, 561–562
water irrigation, 461–462
evaporation, 263
evidence, 12–13
environment, 553
effect of animals, 546–547, 552, 554
effect of people, 534, 548–552
effect of plants, 544–545, 552, 554
keeping in clean, 218–219
planting trees, 550
pollution, 218, 221, 223, 548–551, 553

erosion
causes of, 166
landform, 176
rocks, 166, 173
experiments, 8, 20

Fahrenheit scale, 33, 375
fall, 501, 504. *See also* **seasons**
Artic fox in, 514
maple tree and, 505, 512
fertilization, 444, 467
fish
bass, 529
minnow, 529
shark, 533
Fleming, Alexander, 252
Florida
Daytona Beach, 323
dolphin, 499
International Space Station, 109
Kennedy Space Center, Cape Canaveral, 146–147
limestone, 217
Miami,
art deco building, 293
fair, 407
panther, 439–440
phosphate, 216
resources in, 216–217
and seasons, 503–504
sand dunes, 161–162
silica, 216
soil, 217
flowering plants, 504
flowers, 444–445, 484

food, 363
as energy, 516–517
transportation costs of, 509
in winter, 508–509, 511
food chains, 528–529
food maker, plant, 518–519
food webs, 534–537
forces, 416–418, 429–530
fossil fuels, 214, 221, 360
conservation, 215, 221
oil, 214
use of, 214
frame of reference, 413
freezing, 262
friction, 416–417
fuel cells, 361

Galileo, 141, 151
gases, 258, 261
gasoline, 363
Gemini 7 Space Capsule, 143
genes, 482–485, 491–491
genetic engineering, 483
germination, 442
gimbals, 431
glacier, 169, 173
erosion of rocks, 169
ice of, 124
glow sticks, 335
gram (g), 32
graphs, bar, 35
gravity, 175, 416
cause on rocks, 170
gyroscopes, 431–432

H

Hamdan, Halimaton, 403–404

hand lenses, 31

hardness, 234

heat, 371, 374–379
  conduction and convection, 376–377
  conductors, 390–391
  insulators, 392–393
  radiation, 379
  temperature measurement, 375

heat proofing, 394–395

herbivores, 530

heredity, 480–481, 490–491

hibernation, 491, 506, 510–511

home insulation, 394–395

Howard, Ayanna, 103–104

Hubble Space Telescope, 144–145, 151

humans
  in food chains, 529
  stages of development, 470–471
  traits of, 480

hydroelectric energy, 356. *See also* **energy**

hydrogen fuel cell bus, 361

hypothesis, 9, 21, 286, 312, 346, 386, 400, 426

 I

ice, 169, 175, 260

identification guides, 11

incomplete metamorphosis, 473

inferences, 18–19

inquiry skills
  analyze and extend, 41, 57, 81, 99, 125, 187, 247, 253, 285, 311, 345, 351, 385, 399, 425, 457, 555
  claims, evidence, reasoning, 44, 60, 84, 102, 128, 190, 250, 256, 288, 314, 348, 354, 388, 402, 428, 460, 558
  contrast, 214
  draw conclusions, 347
  record data, 43, 83, 101, 127, 249, 255, 287, 313, 347, 353, 387, 427
  record your observation, 59
  set a purpose, 42, 43, 58, 59, 82, 83, 100, 101, 126, 188, 248, 249, 254, 255, 286, 312, 313, 346, 351, 386, 387, 400, 401, 426, 427, 458, 556
  state your hypothesis, 286, 312, 346, 386, 387, 400, 401, 426, 427
  think about the procedure, 42, 43, 58, 59, 82, 83, 100, 101, 126, 188, 248, 249, 254, 255, 286, 312, 313, 346, 351, 386, 387, 400, 401, 426, 427, 458, 556

insects
  butterfly, 472
  caterpillar, 472
  grasshopper, 473
  metamorphosis of, 472–473
  mosquito, 528

instincts, 488, 490
  of animals, 488–489
  vs. learned behaviors, 488

insulators, 392–393. *See also* **conductors**
  aerogel, 403–404

international space station, 109, 144

investigations, 7–11, 21

irrigation, 91, 461–462

 J

Jenner, Edward, 252

 K

Kennedy Space Center, Cape Canaveral, 146–147
  atlas V, rocket, 147

kinetic energy, 328–329, 362–364. *See also* **energy**
  change, 356

Kobrick, Michael, 123

 L

land form, 167, 172–173 175
  deposition, 176
  erosion, 176

land slides, 170

larva, 472–473

learning behaviors, 486–487, 490–492

of animals, 486–487, 490

of chimpanzees, 487

vs. instincts, 488

life cycles

animals, 466–467

plants, 442–443

light energy, 330, 362, 364. *See also* **energy**

lightning, 330

like poles, 275, 280

limestone, 215

Florida, 217

liquids, 258, 260

living things. *See also* **Animals; Plants**

consumers, 520

composers, 521

dormancy, 510

energy for, 500

hibernation, 510

kinds of, 525

migration, 510

producers, 518

lunar calendars, 134–135

Ma, Lena Qiying, 223

Maathai, Wangari, 559

magnetic field, 274, 279, 281

magnetic force, 276

magnetic planet, 278

magnetic pole, 275

like poles, 275, 280

N poll, 275, 278, 280–281, 283

S poll, 275, 278, 280–281, 283

unlike polls, 275, 280, 283

magnetic resonance imaging (MRI), 279

magnifying box, 31

magnetism, 273

magnets

attract, 273, 278, 280–281, 287–288

barriers, 272

compass, 278, 284

distance, 273

draw conclusions, 288

pull, 272–273

record data, 287

repel, 275, 278, 280–281, 283

using, 279

Main Idea and Details, 27, 231, 295–296, 325, 355–356, 409, 479, 482, 484, 490, 550

Main Ideas, 3, 85, 527

mammals

arctic fox, 506, 514

bat, 547

calf, 488

chimpanzee, 487

cow, 546

elk, 520

goat, 546

ground squirrel, 506, 511

humpback whale, 507

manatee, 507, 511, 513, 549

monkey, 516

sheep, 546

whale, 479

zebra, 547

manatee, 507, 511, 513, 549

mangrove trees, roots of, 544

Mars, 10

mass, 232–233

Mathematical Skills

classify and order, 22

measure, 22

record and display data, 23

use numbers, 22

use time and space relationships, 23

matter, 232–241. *See also* **physical properties of matter**

chemical changes of, 298–309

magnetic, 273

mass and, 232–233

physical changes of, 296–298, 300–301, 304, 306–310

physical properties of, 232–239

sorting, 240–241

states of, 258–263

maturity, 442

measuring, 22

mass, 323–233

temperature, 375

tools for, 32–33

volume, 236–237

mechanical energy, 328–329, 335, 363. *See also* **energy**

medical chemist, 251

medical discoveries

aspirin, 252

penicillin, 252

polio, 252
small pox, 252
melting, 262
mental models, 49
metals
aluminum, 215
arsenic, 223
metamorphosis, 472–473
meteorologists, 52
meter (m), 33
Miami, Florida
The Fair, 406
microscopes, 31
migration, 507, 510–511
humpback whales, 507
manatee, 513
millimeter (mm), 33
minerals. *See also* **rocks**
as nonrenewable resources, 215
phosphate, 216
models, 48–53
molting, 473
moon, 130–133
Apollo, 142
humans on, 142–143
maria, 131
moon phases, 132–133
motion, 410–419
acceleration and force, 416–419
position and, 411–413
speed and velocity, 414–415
motor, 276, 281

Native Americans, 48
natural resources, 460

Niebla, Elvia, 223
Nile, river delta, 167
newton, 32
nonrenewable resources, 214–216, 221
aluminum, 215
electricity from, 215
fossil fuels, 214, 221, 360
limestone, 215
minerals, 215
rocks, 215
soil, 215
Northern Hemisphere, 214–215
earths tilt in, 121
spring in, 118
winter in, 118
North Pole, 115, 275, 278, 280–281, 283–284
number relationships, 22
nutrients, 516, 523–524
nymph, 473

observations, 7, 18–19
oceans, 45
underwater exploration, 561–562
ocean waves, 171
odor, 235
offspring, 481, 491
oil as fossil fuels, 214
omnivores, 530–531
orbit, 114
ordering, 22
Orion, 116, 121
oxygen in
photosynthesis, 518, 524–525, 544–545

pan balance, 32, 232–233
patents, 75
penicillin, 252
People in Science
Abruña, Héctor, 315
Benerito, Ruth Rogan, 315
Culpepper, Martin, 45–46
Diebold, John, 45–46
Hamdan, Halimaton, 403–404
Howard, Ayanna, 103–104
Kobrick, Michael, 123
Ma, Lena Qiying, 223
Maathai, Wangari, 559
Niebla, Elvia, 223
Smits, Willie, 559
Tyson, Neil deGrasse, 123
pesticides, 93
petals, 444–445, 481
ph soil, 224
phases of moon, 132–133
photosynthesis, 519
oxygen in, 518, 524, 544–545
physical changes, 296–298, 300–302, 306–309
of clay, 297
in making pizza, 304–305
of paper, 296–297
vs. chemical changes, 300, 306

physical properties,
232–241
density, 238–239
sorting and , 240–241
volume, 236–237
**physical properties of
matter,** 296–297, 306
magnetism, 273, 280
piezoelectricity, 341–342
pistils, 444–445
pitch, 330
plants. *See also* **animals**
dormant, 504, 510
effect on environment,
544–545, 552, 554
energy for, 518
evergreens, 504
as food maker, 518–519
fruit, 504
hydrangea, 484
kudzu, 545
make food, 362
mangrove tree, 544
maple tree, 504–505,
512
need of oxygen,
544–545
palm trees, 504
photosynthesis,
518–519, 524, 544
producers, 518, 523–525
reproduce, 547
role of, 544–545
roots, 544
and seasons, 504–505
snapdragon, 481
planets. *See also* **earth**
Mars, 10
plankton, 534–535
plant reproduction,
444–451

fertilization, 444
flowers and cones,
444–445
pollination and,
446–447
seeds and, 448–449
spores and, 450–451
plants,
cones, 444–445
ferns, 450–451
flowers, 444–445
life cycles of, 442–443
lima bean, 443
pollination and,
446–447
radish, 442
stems, 445
polio, 252
pollen, 442, 444, 446–447
pollination, 446–447
pollution, 218, 221, 223,
548 553
air, 548, 550
arsenic, 223
garbage, 549
landfill, 549
oil spills, 548, 551
water, 548
pond food chains, 528–529
position, 411–413
potential energy,
328–329, 362,
364–365. *See also*
energy
predators, 532–533
lion, 547
predicting, 20
prey, 532–533
gazelle, 547
population of, 547
zebra, 547

producers, 518, 523–525,
528
and consumers, 523
prototypes, 71–72
pull, 272–273. *See also*
gravity
pupa, 472–473
pyramids, 140

R

radiation, 379
radio waves, 335
railroad system, 91
Reading Skills
cause and effect,
111–112, 163, 271,
276, 280, 362, 389
clue words, 140, 546
compare and contrast,
211, 257, 523, 545
contrast, 214
draw conclusions, 128,
288, 354,
main idea and details,
27, 116, 231, 295,
296, 325, 355, 356,
409, 479, 482, 484,
490, 515, 550
main ideas, 3, 85, 527
sequence, 129, 465
signal words, 47, 67,
139, 373, 441, 459,
543
using headings, 501
visual aids, 17
real–time data, 52
Record Data, 23, 34–35,
43, 83, 101, 127, 287,
249, 255, 313, 353,
387, 427

Record Your Observations, 59
recycle, 550–553
    resources, 219, 221
reducing, 551, 553
reference points, 411, 413
refrigeration, 267–268
renewable energy, 360–361
renewable resources, 213, 217, 221. *See also* **nonrenewable resources**
    sunlight, 213
    water, 358
    wind, 358
repel, 275, 278, 280–281, 283. *See also* **attract**
reproduce, 547
reptiles, 468
    snake, 520–521
research, 28–29
reservoir, 356
resources, 212, 221
    conservation, 213, 221
    in Florida, 216–217
    nonrenewable, 214–215
    recycle, 219, 221
    renewable, 213
    use of, 222
reusing, 551, 553
revolve, 118–119
Rocket, Soyuz, 109
rocks,
    break down, 164–165
    deposition, 166, 173, 176
    effect of water, 167, 171
    erosion, 166, 173, 176
    glaciers and, 169
    and gravity, 165, 170
    and movement, 166–172
    sediment, 167, 173
    weathering, 165–166, 173–174
Rocky Mountains, 502, 508
rotate, 112–113, 119
rotting, 299
rust, 298–299, 307

S

safety
    body armor, 317–318
    electronics, 574–575
    technology, 89
Sahara Desert, 168
Salk, Jonas, 252
sand dunes, 161–162
satellites, 130
scale models, 51
scavengers, 521, 523, 530–531
science, 5–13. *See also* **Inquiry Skills**
    data, 23, 34–37
    evidence, 12–13
    experiments and variables, 8, 20
    hypotheses, 9, 21
    investigations, 7–11, 21
    models, 48–53
    observations, 7, 18–19
    research, 28–29
    scientific methods, 9
    skills, 18–23
    tools, 30–33
scientists, 1, 5
seasons, 114–115, 119
    changing, 502–503, 512, 514
    in different places, 114
    fall, 501, 504
    and plants, 504–505
    spring, 504
    summer, 503–504, 510–511
    winter, 502–504, 507–509, 511
sediment, 167, 173
    deposition, 172
senses, 232–233
sequence, 129, 465
Set a Purpose, 42, 43, 58, 59, 82, 83, 100, 101, 126, 188, 248, 249, 254, 255, 286, 312, 313, 346, 351, 386, 387, 400, 401, 426, 427, 458, 556
shape, 235
signal words, 47, 67, 139, 373, 441, 459, 543
silica in Florida, 216
size, 234
sky patterns, 116–122
Smits, Willie, 559
software, 572
soil, 215
    crops, 224
    in Florida, 217
    as nonrenewable resources, 215
    pH, 224
soil scientist, 223–224
solar calendars, 134–135
solar cell, 360
solar energy. *See also* **energy**
    calculators, 360
solar system,
    early model, 141
    model of, 50
solids, 258, 360

sound,
draw conclusions, 354
loud, 354
record data, 353
vibration, 365
sound energy, 330.
See also **energy**
production of, 365
Southern Hemisphere,
114–115. *See also*
Northern Hemisphere
South Pole, 275, 278,
280–281, 283–284
Soyuz Rocket, 109
space
Florida's role in,
146–147
technology in, 144–145
space age, 146
space cooling system, 149
space exploration,
153–154
space probes, 142, 151
Viking I, 144
space shuttle, 144
space spin–offs, 148–149,
151
speed, 414, 429
sperm, 444
sperm cells, 482
spiders, 489–490
spores, 450–451
sports biomechanist,
429–430
spring, 504, 507. *See also*
seasons
artic fox in, 506, 514
effects on maple trees,
505
manatee in, 507
maple tree in, 512

spring scale, 32–33.
See also **science tools**
sputnik, 142, 151
stamens, 444–445
states of matter,
258–263
star pattern, 116
stars
of Big Dipper, 116
State Your Hypothesis,
387, 401, 427
STEM (Science,
Technology,
Engineering and
Mathematics)
See also **Engineering**
and Technology
Baby, It's Cold Inside:
refrigeration,
267–270
How It Works:
Gyroscopes,
431–434
How It Works:
Piezoelectricity,
341–344
How It Works: Water
Irrigation
System, 461–464
Space Exploration,
153–156
Tools that Rock, 209–210
Underwater Exploration,
561–564
What's It Made Of: Body
Armor, 317–320
stems, 445
summer, 503–504,
510–511. *See also*
Seasons
artic fox in, 506, 514

effects of maple trees,
505
maple tree in, 512
sunlight, 362, 510

tape measure, 33
tarnish, 303
taste, 234
technology, 86–95
code, 572–573
coding, 569
designed systems,
90–91
electronics, 94–95
light bulbs, 92–93
problems with, 92–93,
94–95
process, 89
products of, 88–89
smartphone, 87
tools, 86–87
video games, 88
telescopes, 30, 141–142.
See also **science tools**
Hubble Space, 144–145,
151
measuring, 33, 375
texture, 235
thermometers, 33, 375
thermos, 393
Think About the
Procedure, 43, 59, 83,
101, 249, 255, 313, 387,
401, 427
three–dimensional map,
Earth, 123–124
three–dimensional
models, 51. *See also*
models

time and space relationships, 22–23
tools, 30–33, 65, 86–97
trade–offs, 153–154
traits, 481–482, 490–491
  control of, 482–483, 490
  environment affecting, 484–485, 492
  of humans, 480
trees,
  cone–bearing, 445
turbine, 356
  wind, 358
21st Century Skills: Technology and Coding, 569–576
two–dimensional models, 49
Tyson, Neil deGrasse, 123

underwater exploration, 561–562
unlike poles, 275, 280, 283. *See also* **like poles**
Ursa Major, 116
using headings, 501

variables, 8, 20
velocity, 414

vibrations, 330
video games, 88
Viking I, 144
visual aids, 17
volcano
  satellite photo of, 124
volume, 236–237.
  See also **Physical properties of matter**
vultures
  scavangers, 521

water, 175
  condensation and evaporation, 263
  effect on rocks, 171
  energy usage, 356–357
  freezing and melting, 262
  pollination and, 447
  reservoir, 356
  states of, 260–263
water irrigation system, 91, 461–462
water mills, 357
water vapor, 261
weather,
  models, 52–53
  reporters, 53
weathering, 173

  chemical, 165
  living things on, 165
  rocks, 165–166, 173
Why It Matters, 52–53, 94–95, 134–135, 148–149, 218–219, 240–241, 278, 304–305, 360–361, 394–395, 474–475, 482–485, 508–509, 536–537
wind, 175
  energy, 358–359
  pollination and, 446–447
  sand deposition, 161–162, 168
windmills, 358, 360
wind turbine, 358
winter, 511
  arctic fox in, 506, 514
  in different regions, 502–503
  effects on maple trees, 504–505 512
  foods, 508–509
  manatee in, 507

Yellowstone National Park, 537